Marriage, for Equals

The Successful Joint (Ad)Ventures of Well-Educated Couples

Shauna Howarth Springer, Ph.D.

© 2012 Shauna Howarth Springer
All Rights Reserved.

No part of this publication may be reproduced, stored in a retrieval system, or transmitted, in any form or by any means, electronic, mechanical, photocopying, recording, or otherwise, without the written permission of the author.

First published by Dog Ear Publishing
4010 W. 86th Street, Ste H
Indianapolis, IN 46268
www.dogearpublishing.net

ISBN: 978-1-4575-0906-3

This book is printed on acid-free paper.

Printed in the United States of America

Marriage, for Equals: The Successful Joint (Ad)Ventures of Well-Educated Couples shows...

- The chilling manipulations of "love story" reality shows that trap people into falling in love with people who are not likely to sustain a healthy marriage with anyone

- Why the 50% divorce rate may have nothing at all to do with your own chances of sustaining a healthy marriage; your chances may be much higher, or lower, than 50% depending on a numbers of factors that will be described

- How the snorting of crack cocaine is the most apt comparison to the state of falling in love and the implications of this reality for the process of selecting a spouse

- How "catch-a-mate" books have set up a boom and bust phenomenon in the marriage market

- Why anyone who would help you find "the One" or your "soul mate" or who would assist you in sealing the deal within a short time frame is giving you very foolish advice

- Why Christian couples are especially prone to poor decision-making in their choice of a spouse

- Why you should get into some meaty fights before you even consider marrying someone

- And finally, why the best marriages are happening now, despite "chicken little" proclamations about the escalating divorce rate

To Utaka, who has shown me that a marriage of equals is not an empty ideal.

Acknowledgements

First, I want to express my sincere gratitude to the women who participated in the Lifestyle Poll project. Thank you for taking the time to share your truth and your insights about how to create an uncommonly good marriage.

I would also like to thank Maree (Woollard) McGuane who dedicated weeks of her life to help me launch the Lifestyle Poll – a true act of friendship and love.

I gratefully acknowledge Maya Payne Smart for her input in the early stages of the writing process, for her encouragement, organizational assistance, and for her clever and incisive title suggestions for some of the chapters herein.

Several friends and colleagues responded to requests for help along the way, offering encouragement, insights, and helpful suggestions on early drafts. I especially want to thank Kristi Steh, Lisa (Castaneda) Murphy, Caroline (Chuang) Merchel, Kate Sweeny, Carmen O'Shea (Kourtidis), Sharon (Wing) Gibson, Michelle Cove, Tal Ben-Shahar, and Tyler Hargan.

I have benefited greatly from the mentorship of Dr. Benjamin Karney, whose fascinating research and keen intelligence have had a significant influence on my thinking.

I also want to thank my very supportive parents, Don and Kathy Howarth. I specifically thank my father for giving me the right push at the right moment on this project. I selected the picture at the end of the book with you in mind, Dad. I am also grateful to my mom and my sister, Aimee, for spending some of their vacation time searching for typos and giving this book a final read before publication.

I have been richly blessed by the unconditional love of Marty and Michiko Springer. Thanks Ma and Pa for your unflagging support, for helping pack up our house (twice!) and for making the trek across country with me when the timing was right to make the move back to California. When people say that they have struggles in their relationships with their in-laws, I'm sure they are telling the truth, but I just cannot identify.

I am very grateful for the photographic talents of Brian and Valerie Howarth, whose work is featured on the cover of this book. Related to this, I want to especially thank my friends Julie and Ryan Lucas, the lovely cover model couple, for being such good sports on the snapping cold morning of our photo shoot.

I also want to acknowledge a number of people who have engaged in surprising acts of kindness and generosity at different times in my life with no expectation of any return. I think of this group of people whenever I encounter pockets of human unkindness and have held onto this list in the privacy of my own mind, until now. These people are…

1. Peggy Vaughan
2. Todd Maki
3. Jeanne Moberly
4. Susie Phillips
5. Marcos DeStephano
6. David Mischoulon
7. Peggy (Margaret) Clark
8. Dale Hicks
9. Karen and Wayne Halladay
10. Dorothy Davenport and Larry and Karen McDougal

Finally, I want to thank my husband, Utaka Springer. I am so grateful to have a husband with such strength of character, intelligence and kindness.

Contents

Introduction 1

Chapter 1: Bridge to Nowhere 7

Chapter 2: The Cocaine-Rush Phase 23

Chapter 3: The Man or Woman in the Mirror 35

Chapter 4: Selecting a Partner for the Conversation of a Lifetime 60

Chapter 5: Profile of a More Perfect Union 96

Chapter 6: The Testing Phase: Confronting the Usual Suspects in a Marriage of Equals 139

Chapter 7: Tested romanticism 193

Appendix: Further Information about the Lifestyle Poll 208

Table: Demographic characteristics of the Lifestyle Poll sample 210

Further Recommended Reading 211

Notes 214

Sentimentalists, purists, and some
preachers advocate marital absolutes—
stability, a clear hierarchy for
decision, a predictable union,
 unflawed as a blank page. No wonder
it ends up flat. A true wedding's
grounded in paradox, answers the pull
of the particular, grapples a score
of rugged issues. Like horned toads
in Eden, incongruities add surprise
in a complacent landscape.

Excerpt of the poem entitled "Spice" from *Polishing the Petoskey Stone*, Regent College Publishing, Vancouver, BC. Copyright 2003.

Used by permission of the author, Luci Shaw

Introduction

During my senior year at Harvard University, my parents' marriage dissolved, and I met the love of my life. That year in my life was an emotional bender like I have never experienced before – soaring hopes for my own future clashed with deep fears about the viability of lifelong relationships. All things being equal, I'm not sure whether it is more difficult to grow up with separated parents or to have your understanding of the world as you knew it completely rocked much later in life. But, my parents' separation was definitely one of the most painful things I had encountered up until that point in my life. Ultimately, the combination of this pain and my enduring hope in the possibility of lasting love fueled a relentless drive to understand why marriages succeed or fail.

Why do half of marriages fail? Is there a way to reliably create an uncommonly good marriage? Being academically inclined, I initially sought the answers to these questions in graduate school. I pursued a doctoral degree in Counseling Psychology with a specialty in relationship therapy. I have accumulated thousands of hours of experience counseling distressed couples and have obtained training in several pre-marital education programs. I have worked as a clinical psychologist in academic teaching hospitals, college counseling centers, and a successful private practice. Currently, I am working at a Veterans hospital, helping men and women, individuals and couples alike, to navigate a wide variety of relationship problems and create some truly exceptional marriages.

While gaining this specific clinical expertise, I benefited greatly from the mentorship of a nationally renowned marital researcher, Dr. Benjamin Karney. During graduate school, I was heavily involved in conducting his research on the processes through which initially satisfying marriages either remain satisfying or deteriorate over time. His central study, the Florida Project on Newlywed Marriage and Adult Development (FPN-MAD), followed approximately 200 newlyweds over the first four years of their marriages. I interviewed a large number of these couples at various stages of their marriages. To gain even more perspective on my chosen topic, I also wrote a 200-page dissertation summarizing the results of more than 300 articles on how various stressors affect marriage (133 of which I statistically meta-analyzed).

Even after all this, I had many lingering questions. The "disconnect" for me was that many of the existing ideals for marriage fell short of helping me understand how to create the kind of marriage that my husband and I envisioned – that is, a marriage of equals. Most traditional models of marriage are based on some separation of roles and a hierarchy of power in which one spouse – usually the husband – holds a position of "headship" and leadership in the relationship. In contrast to this, my husband and I both have very strong professional goals and have sought to create an equal partnership, which would be both a meeting of the minds and a joint adventure.

So, a few years after completing my doctoral degree, I set out to profile the marriages of a set of women who might also be inclined to create a less traditional type of partnership: many of the women I met during my undergraduate years at Harvard. I assembled more than 200 questions and recruited participants primarily through unofficial networks of Harvard graduates. Word of the project spread organically, mostly through word of mouth and invitations between friends. Even though I could not afford to pay my research participants, my goal was to see if I could get 500 respondents within a year. In fewer than eight months, more than 1200 women voluntarily completed the poll.

In the Lifestyle Poll, I posed many questions about the nature of love and marriage, such as:

- What has been your biggest personal betrayal and how has this shaped the person you are today?

- To what extent do you agree with the statement, "A person can't help falling in love if they meet the right person, even if they meet that person when he or she is already married to someone else."

- Because of the high divorce rate, some have adapted their marital vows to reflect the reality that love often does not last. How do you feel about the alternative wedding vow: "As long as we both shall *love*" as opposed to "As long as we both shall *live*"?

- What do you feel are the three biggest threats to your marriage?

- When disagreements arise, how are they usually resolved (the response choices given were: you giving in, your husband giving in, you both agree to disagree, and you both negotiate until you find a compromise)

- In your marriage, how do you handle attractions to other people?

- Several participants have acknowledged having ambivalent feelings about having children – can you identify with this? How do you feel about having children?

The insights I gathered from the Lifestyle Poll participants illustrate the inner workings of marriages that do not necessarily make for good TV, but who represent a highly intelligent and accomplished group of individuals who have overwhelming created very successful marriages. While Lifestyle Poll respondents admit to many of the same struggles that we all encounter in long-term relationships, they also offer solid wisdom and deep insight into the inner workings of a marriage of equals.

Ultimately, after fifteen years of intensive study and reflection, I'm left with the conclusion that *what people often think is love, is not love at all.* I'm not writing this to be a marital doomsayer, a global pessimist, or a connubial killjoy. I write this with the best of intentions and I ask your permission to speak bluntly.

Along these lines, I'll admit that my driving goal is to completely explode the model of courtship that I perceive to be heavily embedded in our cultural conversation, so that fewer people end up as casualties of marriages built on top of landmines. I am not targeting any particular person, of course, but rather a set of traps that too commonly ensnare us when we attach to other people. Although I am not asking for your blind trust—and I certainly concede that my own insights are imperfectly developed and in process—I aim to speak with boldness and complete candor, making no efforts to temper my insights on the predictable devastation that I see in many love relationships.

I offer this blunt and uncompromisingly honest approach for the benefit of…

- Those who are seeking lifelong partnerships
- Those who are navigating the early phases of an exciting new relationship

- Those who are already committed to long-term relationships who want to improve their relationships, identify areas for further growth, and develop a deeper understanding of the struggles that most married couples face throughout the lifespan of a marriage

As the title of this book suggests, the model of marriage I favor is what I call a marriage of equals, a concept that I will fully explain in Chapter 5. A marriage of equals does not mean that chore sharing is divided exactly down the middle on a daily basis or that roles are permanently interchangeable. The essential core of a marriage of equals is one in which roles are not pre-defined and in which power is shared throughout the course of the life you create together. It is a marriage in which each person is equally valued and equally respected, where there is significant flexibility and crossover in roles, and one in which both partners feel that they are getting the deal of a lifetime to be with the partner they have. Such a marriage comes with costs. This kind of relationship requires you to develop certain character traits before even considering that you are ready for marriage. It is also a relationship that requires ongoing negotiation and intentional cultivation of the individual and shared growth of both partners. It requires sacrifice, compromise, and the ability to handle your own emotions with skill. To me, and to many others who are working toward this ideal, the costs are well worth the result—a love that ripens like a fine wine over the years of your union.

To describe this model of a marriage of equals and to provide you with clear guidance on how to create and sustain an exceptional marriage, I will cover the following terrain in chapters to come:

In Chapter 1, I lay the groundwork for my argument about what it really takes to create and sustain an exceptional marriage. I do this by constructing an intentional contrast with a dangerously stupid model for how to find love that will last a lifetime. There are many cultural and media-based examples of poor models for launching and maintaining healthy relationships, but I will focus on one that is regularly transmitted to an audience of more than 10 million viewers – ABC's *The Bachelor/The Bachelorette* franchise. The result is a lighthearted, yet deliberately disturbing, case study of the ways in which we overlook the coercive power of a dizzying array of psychological factors that compel feelings of false love.

The remainder of this book is divided according to my three-phase model of successful love relationships. This three-phase model is: 1) All love relationships kick off with a "cocaine-rush" phase, 2) some relationships survive and thrive through a prolonged "testing" phase, and 3) highly successful relationships ultimately achieve a state of what I refer to as "tested romanticism."

Chapters 2, 3, and 4 are associated with the initial cocaine-rush phase of romantic relationships. Chapter 2 will expand your understanding of the three-stage course of a healthy relationship by closely examining the process of falling in love. This chapter will help you to see the difference between false love and real, sustainable love, with frequent application to real-life situations and scenarios. Chapter 3 is a frank discussion of the importance of reflecting on what you have to offer to the kind of partner you hope to find. Related to this idea, I will also present an argument about why it is important that you develop certain character qualities before considering yourself ready for marriage. Chapter 4 reveals strategies and models to help you discern the character and potentials of possible life partners.

Chapters 5 and 6 are associated with the testing phase of love relationships. Chapter 5 fully describes the concept of a marriage of equals. To do this, I draw heavily from the results of the Lifestyle Poll, sharing the perspectives of a remarkable group of women. I also draw on my own insights, relevant clinical examples, high-quality social psychology studies, and my dissertation research, which examined the effects of different types of stress on marriage in a collective group of more than 164,000 married individuals.

Chapter 6 offers a fresh take on a number of the usual suspects in the destruction of a good marriage—chore sharing, sexual problems, co-parenting, and financial stress, to name a few—examining these problem areas from the vantage point of a marriage of equals. I use data and examples from the Lifestyle Poll to illustrate particular areas of challenge and to provide creative solutions to these difficult, though common, problems.

Chapter 7 focuses on the tested romanticism phase of highly satisfying long-term relationships. This chapter closely examines the final chapter of an exceptional marriage and describes what you have to look forward to if you've successfully created a marriage of equals.

Finally, this book comes with a warning: reading this book will probably challenge your notions of romance and may permanently redefine your understanding of love. As in the movie *The Matrix*, you have the option of taking the "blue pill" or the "red pill." If you want the truth, you risk exposing yourself to a reality you may not like, but, in doing so, you have a better chance of making your life authentic and informed, and, consequently, you then have a much better shot at putting yourself among the successful half of marriages.

Chapter 1

Bridge to Nowhere

Consider the following casting call for a new TV show:

"Apply now for an opportunity to be manipulated into feeling that you love a total stranger with a 96% chance that you will be rejected and humiliated in front of 11 million people."

If you saw such a casting call, would you sign up? Would you want to watch the story of those who answered this casting call? Unthinkable, right? Yet, year after year, people are moving like moths to a flame to this scenario, allowing ABC to create an unshakeable dynasty of its shows *"The Bachelor"* and *"The Bachelorette."* These shows have an average weekly audience of 10 million viewers. In 2009, ABC's *The Bachelor* ranked behind only *Grey's Anatomy* and *Desperate Housewives* among ABC's most-watched series among young women. As of February 28, 2011, *The Bachelor* moved into first for ABC in the 9 p.m. hour with 11.9 million viewers. Even among those with a college education, these shows gain an audience and in some cases, viewers form betting pools that are similar to fantasy football leagues about which contestant(s) will make it to the end. The show is so popular that Nintendo has even produced a Wii game based on the series. The problem is that these shows regularly transmit a dangerously stupid model for how to form a lasting love relationship.

Alarmingly, in real life, many people follow similar lines of behavior when falling in love and legally binding themselves to each other. The 50% divorce rate has long signaled the difficulty of identifying and nurturing the kind of love that lasts a lifetime. A study of extremes is often revealing; specifically, an analysis of the manipulations of *The Bachelor* demonstrates what we must be aware of if we want to avoid heartbreak in the real world. To lay the groundwork for the principles of healthy and successful love relationships, this chapter pulls back the curtain on the strategies employed in the show that compel unhealthy bonding to ultimately fabricate a false sense of love.

As a psychologist with specific expertise in the principles of what attracts us to potential spouses, I find the apparent intentionality of the show's emotional manipulations to be chilling. Even more chilling, however, is the possibility that viewers would find these stories romantic or would aspire to the type of "love" portrayed on these shows. Pointed examination of the manipulations of shows like *"The Bachelor"* reveals how a number of unseen and under-appreciated biological forces and environmental cues compel poor decision-making in real-world relationships. Whether the show intends to manipulate people in these ways is known only to a small group of producers and ABC insiders. Nonetheless, let's imagine that a panel of psychologists with very poor ethical standards had been hired to advise ABC's producers in the methods for engineering love. If there were such a panel, here is what they would advise:

First, the hired panel of experts would make sure to select a cast with unusually good looks. To achieve this aim, they would probably circulate pictures of potential contestants among the employees of ABC television and might even post the faces of the show's applicants on one of those very classy "rate-my-face" programs you can find online. They would be aware that individuals in the very top tier of physical attractiveness would likely feel increased pressure to conform to sex-role stereotypes of the active male and passive female[1] which is helpful because it wouldn't do to have multiple aggressors in a throng of 25 women. (For the sake of added drama, however, they might include a couple of "firecrackers." The panel would know that such women probably signed on in the hope of securing 5 minutes of fame, but it would create a lot of exciting drama to have a few very narcissistic, egotistical women in the group to collide with some of the other contestants.)

Of course, this slippery panel of experts would privately be aware that possessing extremely good looks puts people at risk for some unfortunate psychological challenges. For example, the most beautiful people are often the most insecure of all. Like a person who is flush with material wealth, the possessors of great beauty often struggle with questions about why people seek them out and what people are *really* after when they form relationships with them. They often ask themselves whether their friends are *true* friends or whether they are attaching themselves—by way of an entourage—because of their obvious physical beauty. ABC's consultants would also be aware of research demonstrating that physical beauty does not often result in good self-confidence.[2] I've often thought about this finding because it seems counterintuitive. Specifically, a strong line of research shows that physical beauty paves a smooth path in life—beautiful people are given opportunities that others don't have, and are let off the hook more easily when they behave badly ("don't hate me because I'm beautiful").[3] It's hard to say this any better than Julian Fellowes does in his novel *Snobs*:

> "Of the four great gifts that the fairies may or may not bring to the christening—Brains, Birth, Beauty, and Money—it is Beauty that makes locked doors spring open at a touch. Whether it is for a job interview, a place at a dining table, a brilliant promotion or a lift on the motorway, everyone, regardless of their sex or sexual proclivity, would always rather deal with a good-looking face. And no one is more aware of this than the Beauties themselves. They have a power that they simultaneously respect and take for granted."[4]

Great beauty is a form of social capital, yet when one considers that others respond to it as such, one realizes that great beauty may put people at higher risk of failing to develop strong character in some cases. No doubt, some people are truly beautiful inside and out. For others, however, if rewards in life come fairly easily, the hard work of managing disappointment and coping with one's own emotions may be somewhat stunted. The most beautiful among us are more likely to have a "spoiled child" element in their personalities—that is, an expectation that their wishes will be granted with little opposition, resulting in an acute coping crisis (an adult tantrum) when their desires are not met. But, no matter—the bottom line for our TV consultants would be that in the initial phase of any new relationship, beauty enhances the appeal of a love match. So, a cast of unusually good-looking people they must find. This is *especially* important for the central character of the drama, the bachelor himself.

Let's say that the hired experts, based on these attractiveness traits, have located a chiseled specimen of a man who is so hyper-masculine that he bears a remarkable resemblance to Disney's cartoon rendition of Brom Bones in *The Legend of Sleepy Hollow*. They would then conceal his identity from the female contestants, leaking only brief, one-dimensional phrases designed to heighten his desirability in the eyes of the women. For example, they might suggest that producers mention the words "Harvard graduate" or "doctor" or "pro football player," or any similar phrases that identify other stock characters in the uber-masculine array. The shallower the bachelor's character, the better—the producers will need their chosen stud to be capable of making statements like "I've got the ring and I'm about to propose to someone tomorrow, but I'm so confused right now about who that will be." The consultants would also specify that any details about his background or character should be largely concealed, allowing the female contestants to speculate themselves into a froth of excitement about a man they really know nothing about at all. Instead of allowing contestants to know anything of substance about the bachelor's true character, the producers would instead emphasize his raw masculinity. If he is well built, then the plans for the show should include multiple opportunities for him to strip off his shirt and flex his muscles. If he is athletic, they should suit him up like Bear Grylls from the TV show *Man vs. Wild* and have him lead the ladies through some hair-raising adventures that cast him in the role of the supreme protector.

Throughout the duration of the show, the consultants would make sure that things stay fairly superficial. With this goal in mind, their solution of separating the contestants from the bachelor would pack a double punch. It not only prevents contestants from seeing the bachelor when he is not "on," but also ensures that the powerful principle of scarcity will be tapped to full effect. That is, when our options are scarce, what is available becomes more attractive. The power of the scarcity principle is illustrated in many real life scenarios, ranging from the extended confinement of Anne Frank during the holocaust to a night at the local college bar. If you have read the diary of Anne Frank, you may remember that she fantasizes about an attractive boy named Peter Schiff, whom she met before her confinement, calling him "the ideal boy: tall, good looking and slender, with a serious, quiet and intelligent face."[5] When she and her family go into hiding, she carries with her an enduring love for Peter Schiff, saying, "Nothing has changed…on the contrary, as I've grown older and more mature, my love has grown along with me."[6] At the same time, she is actually confined with another Peter, Peter van Daan. Initially, Anne's description of Peter van Daan is much less approving: She informs her diary that he is a "shy, awkward boy whose company won't amount to much"[7] and later she repeats, "[Peter van Daan] is hypersensitive and lazy…he's an absolute hypochondriac."[8]

Yet, the powerful effect of the context ultimately blends the two Peters into a single romantic object. In this climate of generally heightened arousal (i.e. the ever-present fear of being discovered and summarily executed), with no other viable romantic options, the "seclusion goggles" have their way with Anne, and she begins to blur the perceptive line between the original object of attraction and the only non-married male in her pitifully shrunken world. She writes, "Peter Schiff and Peter van Daan have melted into one Peter, who's good and kind and whom I long for desperately."[9] We see that the conversion of her affection is complete when she says, "Oh, Peter and Petel [sic], they're one and the same… [the others] don't understand us… They have no idea of what draws us together!"[10] (After reflecting on the power of seclusion and on the context of Anne's confinement, we just may have some idea of what draws Anne to Peter van Daan so compellingly.)

It doesn't take years of seclusion to effect this transformation of affection—even a short period of time in a highly charged context will lead to the same result. Any Christian teenager who has ever been on a short-term mission trip to a foreign land is familiar with this phenomenon—I have often heard it referred to as having "mission goggles." The essence of having "mission goggles" is that at the start of a mission trip, even if your first thought is, "Too bad there aren't any cute boys on this trip," when you are swept off to a foreign land where you are forced to rely on others in a number of uncomfortable situations, inevitably, by the end of the trip, one of the boys ends up looking like Hugh Jackman. The same thing happens at science camps and band camps across the country every summer – hundreds of scrawny boys get magically transformed into Hugh Jackman.

In fact, the influence of limited romantic options is even tapped in the course of one night out in a college bar. Some creative researchers, "vigilant in the honky tonk as well as in the laboratory,"[11] aimed to test the Country and Western hypothesis that "all the girls get prettier at closing time." They found good support for this theory—perceived attractiveness of members of the opposite sex increased around closing time at the bars.[12] This result was repeated in 2010 by a group of Australian researchers, and the finding held even when researchers polled participants who had not been drinking alcohol.[13] So, what some have called "the beer goggle effect" is not actually about beer—it's about the same principle that salespeople use routinely to increase the purchasing drive of potential consumers ("We have one more left in the warehouse…someone else expressed interest in this house earlier today, so we'd better submit the highest offer you can afford as soon as possible...Call now—the remarkable 'thneed'[14] is available only while supplies last..."). This is why the shrunken-world element is so important in *The Bachelor*—it effectively reduces the range of choices to one man, which increases the appetitive (and competitive) drives of the contestants.

Furthermore, making the bachelor's intrusions into the bachelorette pad unpredictable, and on his terms, builds the false reality that he is a very powerful man of the world who keeps others waiting on his schedule and whims. In fact, the hired consultants would urge the producers to temporarily imbue their created hero with all sorts of superpowers—the power to afford dates at the most glamorous locations, the power to shut down the Hollywood Bowl for a private concert, the power to summon the best musicians to remote locations to stimulate some intimate dancing, access to all manner of superior transport, whether this be private jets, helicopters, or the perfect pair of elephants for traveling through a lush rain forest. The bachelor will transport various women on a globe-trotting journey through a number of exotic locales to give their respective love stories the luster of an epic romance. All the while, it will never occur to the contestants that they are really dating ABC, who is the provider of the lifestyle with which they are falling in love. As one male contestant remarked in the May 30, 2011, *Bachelorette* episode, "I feel like a million bucks....My heart is soaring higher than the fountains [in the Bellagio Hotel]...this is the kind of date that you marry this person" (*sic*). This is what psychologists would call "displacement." In a miasma of such fantasy, rarely will a typical contestant say "you know, he is not really my type" or "I'm actually not that attracted to him." Sure, the producers edit what is on screen, and certainly, contestants have fame-seeking motives as well as love-connection ones, but if people were feeling this type of thing, they would probably leave the show more often than they do or would signal in some other way their relative disinterest, perhaps by occasionally making themselves slightly less physically available to the bachelor's romantic overtures. Think about it—how many times has a contestant on the show turned her face away at the approach of a bachelor's wet mouth, even in cases when she has seen him making out with someone else not 30 seconds previously?

Quartering the female contestants together in a shared house and preventing them access to this mysterious stud also prompts the women to do the work of advertising the bachelor's purported charms to each other. Providing the women with a steady flow of alcohol and little else to do for several weeks, the producers can count on a high level of emotional contagion between the contestants, which results in something like a collectively brainwashed state of mind. The constant cross-pollination of each other's minds with fantastical statements such as, "He's so sweet!" "He's such a good man!" and "Isn't he wonderful?!" will result in each woman's detachment from her independent thinking ability and any meaningful evaluation of whether the bachelor is actually a desirable partner. Ultimately, this process will be much more effective than any brainwashing campaign that our psychological consultants could promote themselves because the source of the messages about the bachelor's desirability is multiple and seemingly *unorchestrated*.

If even one other suitor were on the show, it would diminish the scarcity principle. If the show were not *"The Bachelor"* but *"The Bachelors"*, surely some of the women might find themselves evaluating the situation differently and thinking about the degree of fit between their own personalities and each of the suitors (although, even then, after a few weeks, each of the bachelors are bound to start looking like Hugh Jackman to each of the women). With only one bachelor present, it is comical to hear women with very different personalities say things like "He's perfect for me…it's almost as if we were meant to be together." These types of statements are frequently confessed during the filming and are always stated in the absence of any *real* information about who this man is. Of course, the viewers are looking at the bachelor from an outside perspective and are much more likely to say things like "I wouldn't marry a guy like that." In the context of the show, however, contestants appear to lose their critical-thinking abilities. In addition to the scarcity and seclusion effects, we try to make meaning out of the strong emotions we are experiencing. We engage in meaning-making to better understand our feelings, but the meanings we make in certain situations can be comically off-center. Consider the artist who gets high on LSD and then creates pieces of art that seem to compellingly whisper the ultimate mystical meaning of life, only to later notice (in a more sober state) that her art actually resembles a 5-year-old child's finger painting.

Related to this meaning-making process is the concept of "emotional reasoning," which means that we take our feelings as evidence of absolute truths. For example, in the context of falling in love, we might think, *"Because my heart goes pitter patter and I feel swoony in a way I never have before, it must be because I've found* 'the One.'" Contestants often look back on their time on the show and make comments like "I thought what we had was so unique and special, but in watching how he was with the other women, I can see now that what we had wasn't as special as I thought it was." The fabric of any potential new relationship between the final contestant and the bachelor will be predictably shredded during the screening of the show as, week after week, the finalist is confronted with the harsh reality that what she had with her now-fiancé wasn't really that unique. And, to return to an earlier point, I wonder, how exactly does one make peace with many a bachelor's pre-proposal statement, "I'm so confused...I don't know who I'm going to propose to tomorrow." To my way of thinking, there's no good way out of such a statement. If the bachelor says, "You know, I didn't really mean it, babe, the producers made me say that," then wouldn't one have equally big concerns about his weakness of character?

To really manipulate the bonding process, the hired experts would orchestrate exposures to some of the women's existing fears (which the experts would intentionally assess during the casting interviews), whether this involves deep sea diving, race car driving, or helicopter travel. The woman of the day would then be faced with intense pressure to conform to the expectations of the bachelor (and of the TV-viewing audience) to confront a fear that she otherwise would have avoided by any means possible. By engaging in this fear-confronting behavior with the "steady" presence and frequently voiced reassurances of the strapping stud by her side, each woman will confuse the feeling of triumph after confronting a long-held fear with something that begins to feel like love. This same principle of bonding is what requires strong ethical principles in the practice of providing psychotherapy. Specifically, a strong bond is formed when one walks through a valley of fear with another, so an ethical therapist must be aware of this and maintain professional behavior to avoid taking advantage of a patient's vulnerability. Conveniently, the bachelor is *not* a professional and is *not* held to these inconvenient ethical standards, so he will be able to move right into the hearts of these women after their fear experiences have been manufactured and "jointly" overcome. In the context of such hair-raising scenarios like swimming with sharks or rappelling off the side of a skyscraper with a handsome man constantly assuring them that they are safe with him, the women are likely to mistake temporary physical safety for *emotional* safety, which is a vastly different concept. As a result, after conquering a fear, the contestants will predictably begin to share a number of highly personal experiences with the bachelor (and 10 million anonymous viewers).

Furthermore, these ethically impaired experts would also know that misattributions of love will bloom in a context of general arousal paired with the presence of an attractive suitor. Thanks to a group of researchers from the University of Texas, Austin,[15] we now know that when you put people on a roller coaster and then ask them to rate the attractiveness of members of the opposite sex, they will rate them as more attractive than if you had asked them to do so after knitting a scarf. This finding has been repeated in other hair-raising scenarios such as on high, swinging bridges. Researchers call this "excitation transfer theory." It basically means that when you get aroused by anything, whether it be bungee jumping, roller coastering, or even jogging on a treadmill, your heart rate goes up, and, in the presence of an attractive person, you are likely to misattribute your general level of excitement to excitement caused by the attractive person's presence. This is why the helicopter would be such a common form of transport for the show—it would ensure that each female contestant experiences a shot of adrenaline while feeling "carried away by" a man who is smashed against her side in the womb-like berth of the flying craft. In fact, excitation transfer theory goes a long way to explain the theme we might label as "love collisions of former rivals" throughout big-screen history. For example, picture Princess Leia and Han Solo snapping at each other one minute and then suddenly embracing each other passionately the next. The seeming paradox between the states of fighting viciously one moment and clasping each other in an amorous embrace a moment later may be partly explained by the triggering of adrenaline and increased heart rate paired with the presence of an attractive person—in other words, excitation transfer theory.

Another move to further heighten the feeling of "falling in love" would be to "dose out" the interactions with the chosen stud in a way that promotes an addictive pattern. From the isolated bachelor pad, selective invitations to various female contestants would be sent at random intervals. This would simulate the effect of the one-armed bandit—otherwise known as a casino slot machine—in both cases, the payoff is uncertain and the timing of the payoff is unknown. When there is the payoff of access to the bachelor, the thrill will be heightened by its very unpredictability. At the same time, this heightens the power difference between the bachelor (who is really a proxy for ABC) and the clutch of women who live in waiting for the favor of his attention. The intoxicating alternation between the state of being prevented access to the bachelor and the state of being thrust into dates that involve both close physical proximity and situations that masquerade as emotionally intimate ones will heighten the addictive power of the contestants' connections. As an additional measure, naturally, the psychological consultants would recommend supplying a steady stream of brain-altering substances, by hosting a continuously open bar on every date and at every event, whether it is a brunch date (mimosas, anyone?), an afternoon outing (glass of wine, anyone?) or the everyday pool party (margaritas, anyone?).

Lots of additional strategies might be suggested by the show's consultants to further reduce the power of the female contestants. In addition to controlled information about the bachelor, and limited access to him, the sheer number of contestants accepted on the show is sure to send a solid message that each woman is just one among many. If two contestants have the same first name, there would be a natural opportunity to engineer a "date for three" with two women of the same name (like those "double your pleasure with double-mint gum" commercials in the 1980s). This will further establish that no one is special enough to deserve the elusive bachelor's full attention in any consistent way. The inclusion of "group dates" will also brilliantly advance this agenda. On these group dates, with the pressure to compete and vie for the bachelor's attention, the women are sure to act in unnatural ways—desperately playing up and magnifying their most superficial charms to get some attention. Truthful communication will be minimal because women in such a competitive state will feel that they cannot afford to tell the truth when everyone else is working so furiously to get noticed during this very limited "face time" with the bachelor. The women's competitiveness will ensure that they maintain a very low standard for their behavior. Producers would be instructed to hatch a number of scenarios that underscore the women's sexual interchangeability and powerlessness, such as filming a mock movie in which multiple contestants have passionate kissing scenes with the bachelor while the others stand by passively witnessing these saliva swapping escapades. A variation on this theme might be a date on which some of the women are photographed for a *Sports Illustrated* swimsuit issue, including an element of sexual brinkmanship to pressure them to take their tops off while the bachelor enjoys the view of "his women" objectifying themselves in this way.

It would also be wise for the producers to establish a clear policy that the bachelor must conceal his feelings of special attachment to any of the women he is getting to know. He will, however, be coached to encourage the women to "not hold anything back" lest he dump them before they have revealed that they are madly in love with him. Using the tried-and-true "live with no regrets" line or the directive "you have to trust me," he will engage in a relentless campaign to get them to openly state their undying love for him and their willingness to seal the deal if he nods in their direction, while he hides behind the show's "policy" about not making any admissions of his feelings in return. Each time a woman hears herself say that she is "in love" with the bachelor, she will advance the state of her own brainwashing, progressing from obsessive thoughts like, "He's the perfect guy" to a conclusion like, "He's my soul mate…It's a miracle that it took a TV show to bring us together." The ensuing rejections, when they come each week, will therefore be all the more devastating. The women will not only feel rejected but will also feel completely humiliated because they have been making grandiose statements about how they have found their soul mate, only to be dumped unexpectedly a few days later ("If you did not get a rose, take a minute, say your goodbyes.") If the bachelor acts like a cad in handling these women's hearts and someone calls him out on this during the "Women Tell All" episode, his best defense is to pull out the tried-and-true omnibus excuse for bad behavior: "I'm not perfect, I'm only human, and I'm just trying to do the best I can."

The piece de résistance is the invitation during the final weeks of filming for the finalists to join the bachelor in the "fantasy suite." For the first time in the season, it is advantageous for the show's host to come out from behind the curtain to issue the invitation to stay as a couple in the fantasy suite. This effectively adds a layer of protection to the bachelor's character—making it appear as though he is not the cad who is propositioning two different women about a week before he plans to propose to one of the them, and completely devastate the other. Although not a perfect parallel, the fantasy-suite scenario is akin in some ways to a sexualized version of what psychologists refer to as the prisoner's dilemma, with a powerful pull in the direction of sleeping with the bachelor. In the prisoner's dilemma, two prisoners who robbed a bank together are both caught and placed in separate isolation cells. Naturally, both care much more about their own personal freedom than about the welfare of their accomplice. A clever prosecutor might make the following offer to each: "You may choose to confess or remain silent. If you confess and your accomplice remains silent, I will drop all charges against you and use your testimony to ensure that your accomplice does serious time. Likewise, if your accomplice confesses while you remain silent, your accomplice will go free while you do the time. If you both confess, I get two convictions, but I'll see to it that you both get early parole. If you both remain silent, I'll have to settle for token sentences on firearms possession charges. If you wish to confess, you must leave a note with the jailer before my return tomorrow morning." Each prisoner is then left to judge in isolation whether it is better to sell their partner out or to maintain silence and trust that their partner will do so as well.

When the fantasy-suite idea is presented at the end of each woman's individual date, each contestant is likely to overlook consideration of whether it is a wise idea to be sexually intimate with this man (whom she doesn't really know at all) and reflect instead on how her "chances of finding love" may be derailed by anything less than offering herself to him sexually. If neither woman accepts the offer, then no one has the advantage of a burst of oxytocin, a bonding hormone that is released at the moment of orgasm. If one accepts and one does not, then, predictable of a shallow thinking process, the bachelor will typically begin to question the "readiness for commitment" of the one who does not make herself sexually available to him. Ultimately, each woman has probably been mind-tripping about whether the other finalist had a night of passion with the bachelor the previous night (or will have the following night), and, in such a perpetual position of powerlessness, she is likely to tap the full arsenal of her mate-capturing powers by accepting the offer to "stay as a couple."

Finally—the most morally twisted part of their strategy—the hired consultants would use their psychological assessment skills to identify people with specific psychological needs that compel reckless attachments to doomed relationships. That is, the hired experts will either identify contestants who believe that they "need" to be married to have a full and meaningful life, or will find people marked by some formative trauma from which they have not healed. On season 13 (in 2009), the poor, confused Jason Mesnick, who proposed to one of two finalists (Melissa Rycroft) only to change his mind and propose to the other (Molly Malaney) after the airing of the show, was an ideal bachelor from this perspective. After being dumped on the previous season of *The Bachelorette* (in 2008) by a woman named DeAnna Pappas, he said, "God, I want to fall in love...I've had a huge hole in my heart for years." So, if, during the screening interviews, a potential contestant says the words, "I am looking for someone to complete me" or identifies the movie *Jerry McGuire* as his or her favorite love story, the unethical expert consultants will give a hearty thumbs-up to the producers. The feeling that one "needs to be completed" may or may not be driven by the experience of an early life trauma, and if there is an appropriate trauma in a potential contestant's history, all the better. The psychological consultants know that when there is trauma, there is unfinished business, a raw emotional edge that people will try to repair through engaging in an emotionally corrective experience. When someone has been repeatedly abused or traumatized from a young age, others who remind them of the abuser feel "the most like home" to them. Those who have been abused often feel compelled to re-enact elements of their trauma experience with the hope of getting a different outcome. For example, without the benefit of insight, a woman whose father was an explosively angry alcoholic will feel pulled toward the same type of person and will attempt to rescue and rehabilitate him into her very own Prince Charming. This principle goes a long way to explain frequently repeated variations of statements made by many a patient in therapy: "I always go for the bad boys…and I always end up getting hurt."

Furthermore, when people have had their boundaries violated in the formative stages of their lives, they often struggle with respecting their own and others' boundaries. Those with a history of trauma emit subtle (and sometimes obvious) behaviors that chum the waters for the psychopathic sharks in the dating pool. This is an unfortunate law of nature, much the same as the fact that jailed criminals who are asked to view videotapes of various potential victims walking down the street will tend to select the same women to victimize.[16] We might even say that until trauma is addressed and a person has made significant progress in healing any existing psychological wounds, that person's "atomic" structure destabilizes and they are much more likely to bond with others whose "atomic" structure mirrors their lack of wholeness. Although anthropologist Dr. Helen Fisher was not specifically referring to this atomic model of dysfunctional attraction, a statement she made on a recent Discovery Channel program comes to mind: "If you know something of Mother Nature's plan, you can speed up the process so you can collide with someone else faster."[17] This is exactly what a group of morally challenged experts would encourage ABC's producers to arrange for the show's contestants.

In the ultimate abuse of their power as healers, the psychological experts might take turns offering their professional services in the back of the post-rejection hearse…I mean limousine. Their soothing tones of voice and professionally worded, open-ended questions would provide the guise of safety. But really, is there anything less safe than revealing your raw, pain-driven thoughts and feelings to an invisible audience of 10 million viewers across the country?

So, there you have it—the essential elements of the hired experts' nefarious plot to systematically set people up using a number of scientific principles to forge what feels like bonds of love, only to emotionally disembowel people on national TV. My purpose in engaging in this exercise (that is, projecting the hypothetical thought patterns of a panel of unethical psychological consultants) is not to challenge the show's ability to entertain us. People will still watch it, in the same way one person is driven to say, "Whew, what a bad smell…here…smell this," and the other person is driven to obligingly lower his or her nose to the foul-smelling object. Rather, my purpose is to dispel any illusion that what is manufactured on *The Bachelor* is anything like "love," by laying bare the show's manipulative elements. The cards are stacked so that almost anyone on the show would experience the feeling of falling in love.

The show is ultimately very successful in achieving its goal, which does not appear to be the creation of lasting love relationships, but the facilitation of endlessly entertaining scenarios generated by colliding chemically-altered people together. The psychological and emotional fallout of these collisions does not seem to be a serious concern to the network, or a reason to scale back the show's manipulations. I once thought that the show would fade away after its initial launch in 2002 because I lost my own taste for watching it after the first few seasons, but when I tuned back in to the two most recent cycles of the show (in 2011), it soon became apparent that the show's producers have become increasingly unrestrained in advancing their agenda. In fact, I was disturbed to witness three additional manipulative elements in the script of the show. The first is the increased tendency for the host to plant foolish ideas that seem to be (more often than not) swallowed whole by the bachelor or bachelorette. For instance, in the 2011 seasons of *The Bachelor* and *The Bachelorette*, one of the "stock" lines issued by host Chris Harrison in the very first show of the season, after the bachelor and bachelorette have just laid eyes on their respective pools of contestants, is "Do you think your future wife (or husband) is in that room?" Essentially, the thrust of this statement is that after just clapping eyes on a set of attractive strangers, one *ought* to be mentally projecting toward a decision that will be legally and emotionally binding for the rest of one's life (even when two people divorce, continuing legal and emotional ties often have a significant effect on both partners for the rest of their lives). This emotionally manipulative statement, a form of psychological priming, is paired with an effort to convince the bachelor or bachelorette that the path to true love requires one to "trust one's feelings."

Both of the 2011 cycle lead contestants (Bradley Womack and Ashley Hebert) swallowed this faulty logic entirely, both uttering versions of the statement, "Last time I was on the show, I held back from trusting my feelings. This time, I don't want to have any regrets, because life is too short, so I'm going to put myself out there and trust what I feel no matter what." During the second episode of the season, Ashley Hebert, a contestant with a significant family history of alcoholism who characterizes herself as a "storybook-romance kind of girl" says, "After this week of dating, I can say that I think my husband is standing in this room," and announces just prior to the second rose ceremony, "I feel strongly that this is working and that my husband is in this room." (Of course, it soon became clear that her judgment was dangerously impaired, as she had fallen head over heels for a sadistic man who appeared devoid of a conscience).

The second unfortunate new development in more recent seasons is the staging of narcissistic fantasies that quickly become subsumed into the "love story." It's as though the contestants have been selected by the Make-A-Wish Foundation for the fulfillment of whatever grandiose fantasies they may have, usually something on the theme of performing for thousands of people or having dinner in the middle of the Bellagio fountain, which "no one has ever done before." As the 2011 season's bachelorette, Ashley Hebert said, "I live in a fairytale…I'm going to be dancing in front of two thousand people…I seriously got the chills." From this admission, it is but a hop, skip, and a jump for someone to feel, 'This *must* be love, because I feel *so amazing* when I'm with [insert whoever happens to be on the narcissistically stimulating date]."

The third disturbing new development is what I would call "the trauma pitch." That is, there seems to be an unchecked expectation that contestants reveal their deepest traumas during their first one-on-one conversations with the bachelor or bachelorette. As a professional counselor, I find it very disturbing to watch contestants open up about alcoholic parents, brain hemorrhages, deaths of their beloved first spouses, and other traumas of similar depth to another person they have just met (and an anonymous viewing audience of 10 million people). Due to limited and unpredictable access to the bachelor or bachelorette, there is intense pressure to "make a pitch"—that is, to form a sound bite about how one's deepest trauma has taught them some valuable life lesson, usually some variant of one of these three or four themes…

> "The experience of [insert horrible trauma that the bachelor/bachelorette and audience have no right to know] has taught

me to...."never take life for granted/make the most out of every day/tell the people I care about that I love them more often/make the most out of the chances I'm given."

On the basis of this trauma pitch, a person's character is weighed and judged (by the bachelor/bachelorette and the huge, anonymous viewing audience). What a terrible model for the development of trust and appropriate timing of self-disclosures in an intimate relationship!

For the show's producers, there is no apparent downside to all of the emotional suffering they are creating. After all, the shrapnel of a disastrous "love" collision from this season's show may become next season's star, in a "rebound" relationship scenario that endlessly repeats itself. Can there be anything more emotionally dangerous, and less romantic, than a show that predictably fails to result in sustainable love matches? The only thing that actually appears real in the show is the emotional devastation and gut-wrenching pain of the heartbroken and emotionally-damaged contestants. Is it any surprise that Mike Fleiss, the real-life producer of *The Bachelor* and *The Bachelorette* also produced two re-makes of *The Texas Chainsaw Massacre*? Given the intense manipulation of contestants and the unpredictable emotional carnage that ensues, the show has elements of a horror flick.

This is not to say that true love does not exist. Love can and does work, but what is widely portrayed by the media is not love, but rather examples of unsustainable collisions. It's easy for us to be fooled because we tend to believe the cultural lore (promoted so widely in the media) that explosively positive feelings are the mark of true love. In reality, such feelings suggest three possibilities, only one of which is true love (alternatively, you could end up heart-broken or trapped in the nightmare of an abusive relationship). To continue in this vein, the next chapter focuses on what I call the cocaine-rush phase of romantic relationships, and sheds further light on how things can go terribly wrong before a relationship even leaves the gate.

Chapter 2

The Cocaine-Rush Phase

The simplest way to conceptualize the life course of a long-term relationship is to think in terms of three phases; that is, all love relationships kick off with a cocaine-rush phase, some relationships survive and even thrive through a prolonged testing phase, and highly successful relationships may achieve a state of what I refer to as tested romanticism. The cocaine-rush phase is an initial period of intense, highly pleasurable bonding based on the mutual fantasy that you and the other person are ideally matched and perfectly suited for each other. After the cocaine-rush phase of the relationship simmers down (typically after a period ranging from six months to two years, accounting for some special circumstances*), the relationship transitions into what I refer to as the testing phase. The testing phase can also be wonderful, but not in the same breathlessly excited way as the cocaine-rush phase of the relationship. In successful relationships, the testing phase is followed by what I refer to as tested romanticism, a phase of love associated in several research studies with the highest levels of reported marital satisfaction. The present chapter focuses on the cocaine-rush phase of the relationship, further describing the essence of it and many of the potential fake-outs and traps within the initial bonding process.

I would not be the first person to draw a comparison between the state of falling in love and the state of feeling high on drugs. The concept of new love as addiction appears with frequency in many aspects of popular culture. If a bit pessimistic, selected excerpts of the song "A New Way to

---

*For example, long-distance relationships, relationships with a lengthy internet-based beginning, or relationships that are formed in emotionally supercharged environments. In most of these cases, it may be wise to wait longer than two years before committing to marriage.

Fly" performed by Garth Brooks certainly demonstrate a healthy level of insight of how this can play out in love relationships:

> Like birds on a high line/They line up at night time at the bar/They all once were lovebirds/Now bluebirds are all that they are/They landed in hell/The minute they fell from love's sky/And now they hope in the wine/That they'll find a new way to fly.../They've all crashed and burned/But they can leave it behind/If they could just find/A new way to fly/...By the end of the night/They'll be high as a kite once again...[18]

A less insightful, and certainly less dark and foreboding, version of this notion surfaces in the song "Hooked on a Feeling" written by Mark James and performed by B.J. Thomas:

> I'm... hooked on a feelin'/High on believin'/That you're in love with me/Lips as sweet as candy/The taste stays on my mind/Girl, you keep me thirsty/For another cup of wine/..I got it bad for you, girl/But I don't need a cure/I'll just stay addicted/and hope I can endure! [19]

Despite the existence of many cultural (and lyrical) analogies between love and addictive drugs, the degree to which this effect drives poor decision-making in relationships suggests that this concept may yet be underestimated and underappreciated. Though I'm not the first writer to compare falling into love to becoming addicted to a mind-altering drug, I'd like to launch this chapter by emphasizing my view that the most fitting comparison drug is crack cocaine. That is, there are *striking* similarities between the brain state of a person falling in love and that of a person who has just snorted crack cocaine. We're not talking about the slightly buzzed feeling you might get from drinking a glass or two of wine, but rather about the high-octane euphoria associated with freebasing crack cocaine. Falling in love is the best high you can get without breaking any laws. Dr. Helen Fisher, the anthropologist and relationship researcher I referenced in the previous chapter, conducted a series of illuminating studies on the brain chemistry of love. Specifically, she found that the same brain chemicals (that is, massive amounts of dopamine and norepinephrine[20]) are in play, and many of the same brain pathways and structures are active when we are falling in love and enjoying a cocaine-high. Consider the specific euphoric effects of snorting crack cocaine. In the short run, according to the website cocaine.org, *snorting cocaine* leads to enhanced mood, heightened sexual interest, a feeling of increased self-confidence, greater conversational prowess and intensified consciousness... "It offers the most wonderful state of consciousness, and the most intense sense of being alive [that] the user will ever enjoy."[21] I wonder...if we replace the words "snorting cocaine" with the words "falling in love," does the sentence still make sense? *Falling in love* leads to 'enhanced mood, heightened sexual interest, a feeling of increased self-confidence, greater conversational prowess and intensified consciousness...It offers the most wonderful state of consciousness, and the most intense sense of being alive that the user will ever enjoy.' Yes, I'd say that fits, wouldn't you?

A further common marker of both falling in love and snorting cocaine is a clear stimulatory effect. Users of cocaine feel that the drug sharpens their focus and allows them to achieve an almost superhuman state of electrifying purpose. Making this connection between the two states of being may provide insight into some of the commonly reported experiences associated with falling in love. For example, the similarity between the two states may explain why new love prompts us to float and flit between our daily activities with a certain glow, bursting with vitality and charged with energy, all while whistling a cheerful tune. The stimulatory effect may also help explain how we are able to stay up night after night for weeks on end, staring into each other's eyes and whispering words of adoration to each other despite having full days of work or school. Later in a relationship, romance continues to be possible and even deepens in many ways in healthy relationships; however, our behavior in later stages tends to be governed more by the laws of normal reality. When the initial stimulatory effect of new love wears off, we are much more likely to tell our partners that we love them and that we wish them a good night's rest lest we invite massive headaches and foggy thinking at work the next day.

I previously mentioned that the same chemicals are at play, and many of the same brain structures and pathways are activated when a person falls in love or snorts cocaine. In addition to the typical crack cocaine pleasure pathways, there is also a notable similarity between the glistening state of new love and the clinically debilitating condition we refer to as obsessive-compulsive disorder (OCD). I spent my residency year offering intensive treatments to individuals with incapacitating forms of OCD. While immersed in clinical work with this population, I learned that one of the brain structures that is particularly active when we are falling in love, two tiny lima bean-shaped structures called the caudate nuclei, are also highly active for individuals who suffer from OCD.[22] That is, the caudate nuclei are hard at work when our brains are processing repeated circular patterns of obsessive thought, which happens in the case of both the debilitating condition we call OCD and during the thrilling process of falling in love. Of course, in another sense, these conditions are at polar ends of a spectrum. In the case of OCD, an individual experiences a highly distressing repeated thought or disturbing image (an obsession) and he or she behaves in ways that are typically designed to fend off or avoid what is feared (the associated compulsive behavior). The intrusive thoughts or images associated with OCD are dreadful and the most natural response to them is avoidance. On the "falling in love" end of the spectrum, the obsessive thoughts are supremely pleasurable. These obsessions are not unwanted mental intrusions, like pop-ups on the computer screens of our minds, but are activated by us in a highly motivated fashion. Instead of avoiding these images and thoughts, we actively generate these very welcome images and emotionally rush into them, finding that they are paired with mini-brain bursts that suffuse us with a sense of well-being and supreme happiness.

In this scenario, our relationship with an exciting new partner is akin to a blank movie script. When we fall in love with someone, we cast them as the perfect leading man or woman, fleshing out the script with all manner of fantasies about who they are. As researchers from the University of Waterloo put it, "people immersed in the experience of romantic love often appear to bend reality to the will of their hopes and desires."[23] Having cast our perfect romantic lead, we start to believe that if our love story were made into a movie, it would be one of the greatest romances to light up the silver screen (if you've ever been in love, haven't you thought, "Our story would make a great movie script"?). *In fact, this untested idealization of the other person is the essence of the cocaine-rush phase of a relationship.* In the early days of relationships, when we each have little real information about each other, we are particularly prone to this type of obsessive identification.[24] In a highly motivated way, we obsess about our new love partners and continuously make compelling cases for how they are absolutely perfect (recall the *Bachelor* contestants' tendency to say things like "Isn't he wonderful?! He's the perfect guy!").

In people with narcissistic tendencies, the even greater delight is that the other person generates a reciprocal fantasy about who we are. *Folie à deux*, which translates from the French as "a madness shared by two," is a psychiatric syndrome in which symptoms of a delusional belief are transmitted from one individual to another. A high level of emotional contagion is typical in cases of such shared psychosis. Further, this syndrome is ripe to occur when the involved individuals are in constant proximity to each other, while being socially or physically isolated from other people. When people fall in love, an invisible cocoon of delight seems to drop down around them. Within this bubble of perfection, new lovers will endlessly reflect each other's desirability, creating a delightful *folie à deux* of mutual flawlessness. The proportion of what is known compared to what is unknown about each other is huge during early courtship, and what is perceived to be known is usually quite distorted, to add further challenge to perceiving truths. Your new partner, flush with love-induced "cocaine", will perceive you to be a much better person than you really are in some ways (and you'll perceive your partner, and yourself, this way as well). New lovers will often say things like, "I like who I am when I am with her," and, to my ear, the translation of this statement is something like, "I am really enjoying my partner's false projection that I am perfect, and, come to think of it, when I am with her, I actually do feel rather perfect."

Perhaps the most insidious offspring of the *folie à deux* fantasy is the mental creation of the other as your soul mate. To my mind, the idea of finding one's "soul mate" has about as much basis in truth as the idea that each of us has a doppelganger (an "evil twin") and that if we somehow chance to meet up, a bloody duel will surely ensue because one of us must die. The idea of a soul mate comes from the ancient tale of Aristophanes, a comic playwright and contemporary of Plato. He told a story of some two-headed hermaphroditic giants who were cleaved apart by a jealous Zeus, fated thereafter to forever seek their other halves. If you can look past the unromantic image of two-headed giants lumbering around on legs, I suppose there is some romantic appeal to the idea of the one-in-a-million quality of one's supposed soul mate. The concept of finding a soul mate is riddled with logical errors, however, the biggest of which is the idea that our personalities are fixed and unchanging over the course of life (a close second would be the statistical improbability that teenagers in towns with tiny populations across America seem to keep meeting their soul mates in their very own high schools). In other words, the soul mate idea implies that we are the way we are (with a number of fixed attributes and personality factors) and that there is one other person who is a perfect match for us due to their collection of complementary attributes and personal qualities. The goal in finding one's soul mate is to identify this person, and the assumption is that once this person has been correctly identified, it will be smooth sailing because the two halves have become reunited. In this way, the soul mate script is fundamentally a happily-ever-after script. This script surely has a place in fairy tales, but not in real life.

In the book *Crucial Conversations*, author and philosopher May Sarton depicts the character of a wife who has outgrown her husband. This discontented wife says, "One of the things I've been wondering...is whether all marriages don't have the seeds of dissolution in them. Can people be expected to keep on growing at the same rate?"[25] How, then, do we reconcile the idea of soul mates or of finding "the One" with the frequently uttered statement "we've grown apart over the years"? The wide use of this explanation for the dissolution of marriage demonstrates that the soul mate notion overlooks a critical truth—that we are not static but are instead in a continual process of growth and change. Of course, the speed of change depends on a number of factors: on the positive side, things like adaptability and openness to positive influence, and on the negative side, things like weakness of character and areas of unhealthy rigidity. In addition, life circumstances can sometimes compel significant changes in personal philosophies and approaches to life. Significant traumas can completely uproot a previously established sense of trust in others and will often change someone's personality greatly. More than half of the women who responded to the Lifestyle Poll (a total of 633 women) reported that they've experienced an event that has made them a "much less trusting person than they used to be." For example, here are three illustrative responses to the open-ended question "What has been your biggest personal betrayal and how has this shaped the person you are today?"

> I have been repeatedly broken up with by boyfriends I really liked (and thought had long-term potential). This has made me insecure about my worthiness of being loved (i.e. what is wrong with me that this keeps happening?) I think it makes me make the same mistakes over and over out of desperation.

> My father left my mother and me and pretty much his entire family over 10 years ago. I'm still not sure the extent of things he was involved in to cause him to do that...to me it was very much out of character. But it made me believe that you can NEVER really know someone...only what they want you to see. I think I tend to look for negative outcomes in my relationships with men and I'm not very trusting at all...I don't give a lot of people the benefit of the doubt.

I had a bad relationship with someone who dated/courted me (even though he had a long-distance girlfriend at the time). But, in public, he kept our relationship secret. He then unexpectedly cut off all ties with me with no explanation (but I later found he was dating someone else and their relationship was very public). I wondered whether he was ashamed of me and I wondered why I let myself be deluded by his charm. Now, I am much more cautious about people. I tend to distrust men's friendliness towards me and I try to avoid men who are too friendly, too outgoing (basically men who remind me of this person).

In addition to the effects of traumas, adoption of a new belief system or withdrawal from previously held beliefs is also associated with sweeping and often permanent changes in personality. Thus, we can never count on the notion of having met our soul mates to keep us together through all the changes that life brings; to do so would be to build our marriages on a foundation of shifting sand.

Furthermore, when we buy into the concept that our spouses are our soul mates, the inevitable transition from the cocaine-rush phase to the testing phase becomes much more threatening to the security of our bond. That is, if we are convinced that we have met "the One", whenever we discover that this person is not what we first imagined, our sense of disillusionment with them will be much greater and our hopes for the future of the relationship will be squashed. A belief in destiny is part of a larger set of romantic beliefs[26] that incorporates such tenets as:

a)   Love finds a way to conquer all.
b)   For each person there is one and only one romantic match.
c)   The beloved will meet one's highest ideals.
d)   Love can strike at first sight.
e)   We should follow our hearts rather than our minds when choosing a partner.

In fact, as I was writing this, I took a quick chocolate break and opened up a "Dove Promise" to read the message, "Always follow your heart – it's never wrong" contributed by a woman named Amanda from Deltona, FL. It's hard these days to even eat a bon-bon without being bombarded with these kinds of foolish statements. Since advertising has reached the level of bon-bon bombardment, I'd like to suggest a new product line, called

"Dove Truths." A sample message might be, "Don't just follow your heart. It might be right, but it's more likely to lead you down a foolish path." Such a message would certainly make up for the empty calories, but I suppose it's not as fun as the sugar-coated fantasies many of us tend to indulge in.

Contrast this model with the alternative philosophy that successful relationships are intentionally and actively created by conquering obstacles and growing together over time (what researchers refer to as the growth model). If our beliefs align with the growth model, when we transition from initial fantasies to something more like real life, our expectations are set to give us room to live into the testing phase without facing the troublesome thought, "I thought he/she was my soul mate, but after that fight, I guess I was wrong. I'd better keep looking because I haven't found IT yet." In fact, this is exactly what researcher Raymond Knee found. As he explains, "Belief in destiny was associated with disengaging from the relationship and restraining oneself from maintenance attempts in response to a negative relationship event, whereas belief in growth was associated with endorsement of relationship-maintenance strategies."[27] So, in common parlance, people who believed that they had met their soul mates and who then encountered some information that contradicted their illusions of their partners' total perfection felt disillusioned, gave up the fight, and started detaching. Another damaging element of the destiny belief, as Knee points out, is the tendency to make global dispositional inferences for undesirable behavior. That is, if we were to believe that each of us is the way we are, with a number of fixed traits, then when the initial thrill of falling in love subsides, and our new partner behaves like a complete turd one morning, we would tend to conclude that they behaved that way because that is who they *really* are rather than because other things in their life have been stressing them out lately.

Another unfortunate offshoot of the soul mate concept is the pop culture logic that true love "completes us." It seems to me that elements of the Shel Silverstein story "The Missing Piece"[28] have somehow become deeply integrated into our cultural scripts. "The Missing Piece" is a story about a nearly round circle (let's call him "Millstone" for short) who rolls around searching for the perfectly sized pie-shaped wedge (which I will hereafter refer to as "Wedgie") to complete him. Consider how the following adaption of brief, selected portions of "The Missing Piece" reflects the prevailing cultural love script (apologies to the descendants of Mr. Silverstein for taking some liberties with his charming story):

Once there was a woman who felt she was incomplete, that something was missing. She felt like she had a huge hole in her heart. She wanted to feel whole, with nothing missing, so she went around and around, looking for a man to complete her, because in her incomplete state, her life was not very satisfying.

She had a lot of flings, one-night stands with strangers, and short-lived love affairs but did not find "the One." Some were too big and some were too small. Some were too square and some, too pointy. So she kept responding to their "winks" on her e-dating service and continued searching for "the One" at all the local bars and nightclubs.

Then one day she found someone who felt like her soul mate. She was happy. Now she could feel completed, with nothing missing.

This is the narrative that underlies almost every Hollywood romance in the last several decades. It is also the same fallacy that drives shows like ABC's *The Bachelor* and *The Bachelorette*. The interesting thing is that the full read of Shel Silverstein's story doesn't actually have anything to do with being happier once one finds the "missing piece." In the story, as Millstone is searching for various Wedgies, he rolls along slowly, admiring flowers, chatting with butterflies, and enjoying the warmth of the sun. When Millstone finds a suitably sized Wedgie, he explodes with happiness then lapses again into his baseline state of chronic dissatisfaction. With the perfectly sized Wedgie in place, the pace of his life has sped up and he now rolls too fast to smell the flowers or chat with the butterflies (I wonder if the "flowers" and "butterflies" represent the garden of sexual and romantic opportunities formerly available to Millstone?). Disappointed with what he feels he is missing, he takes action, abandoning Wedgie by the side of the road and moving on as he was before, somehow incomplete.

If we were actually doing a studied analysis of Silverstein's story, the lesson would be quite the opposite of the prevailing cultural love script. The real moral might be about living in a state of acceptable incompleteness, or perhaps about living in a self-reliant way, free from the ties that bind. Or the moral might be that the cost of a long-term relationship is the loss of all other meaningful relationships, or that the thrill of the hunt is better than the experience of creating lifelong love. (As an aside, even as a child, I always felt bad for little Wedgie, who was picked up by this big bully of a Millstone, temporarily stuffed into him, and then summarily dumped on the side of the road.) At any rate, I'm not entirely sure that Shel Silverstein was intending to make any philosophical statements about the nature of intimate relationships, but if he were, then the picture he paints is of two dichotomies – either consumptive love that costs one too much to sustain, or slightly discontented, somehow deficient self-reliance. A marriage of equals is neither of these but is instead a third possibility that offers both sustained love and a sense of freedom (more on this in Chapter 5).

Ultimately, the explosion of pleasurable chemicals released during the cocaine-rush phase of new love relationships leads to some monstrously short-sighted decision making in the cocaine- rush stage of relationships. New lovers often interpret the supercharged emotions they feel as evidence of having found true love. As I mentioned in Chapter 1, psychologists refer to this as emotional reasoning, which means using one's feelings in place of actual evidence of a truth. Without significant quality-control checks in place, this is a dangerous path to take because the feeling of falling in love predictably follows one of three scenarios, two of which entail a dead end at best and an abusive nightmare at worst. When you find yourself saying (or even privately thinking) things like "We just met, but it feels like we've known each other forever" or "I think I just met my soul mate," inevitably, the truth is one of three things:

1) To start out on a hopeful foot, it could be that the relationship is the real deal, the kind of love that is invigorating, freeing, and sustainable for the rest of your life.

2) Alternatively, the case may be that you and your new love are enjoying the *folie à deux* that you are soul mates who are destined to be together (which turns out to be a heartbreaking mirage).

3) Or, unfortunately, what you are feeling may in fact be the echoes of former trauma in your life (which often morphs into the living nightmare of an abusive relationship).

To be fair, because #1 is a possibility, it's not that you are absolutely wrong if you feel these things and interpret them as real, sustainable love—it's just that *you can't possibly know* during the cocaine-rush phase of a relationship whether the feelings are real. Author Stanton Peele puts it well in saying, "love is an ideal vehicle for addiction because it can so exclusively claim a person's consciousness."[29] In such a state of mind, devoid of any real information about who the other person *really* is, we can make some shocking decisions that throw the rest of our lives into unnecessary and avoidable turmoil.

Shift gears away from love relationships for a minute and imagine that you are moving from the East Coast to the West Coast and your realtor tells you that your dream house has just come on the market. She informs you that the house has all the features you've been seeking—enough bedrooms and bathrooms and the type of particular architectural style you favor. Naturally, you might begin to ask about the history and condition of the house. Imagine that your realtor said, "Well, I don't know, there might be some problems, but there's no time to do a home inspection. Someone else expressed interest in this house earlier today, so we'd better submit the highest binding offer you can afford and do it today." What would you do? If the contract were completely binding with no built-in escape clause (which, thankfully, isn't generally true when you buy a home, of course), would you commit all of your savings to this deal? Would you take this particular leap, sight unseen, without any knowledge of serious potential problems in the foundation of the house, legal complications you might get saddled with, extensive infestation of termites, or expensive structural issues that need to be addressed? Yet, these stakes are puny in comparison to your acceptance of a legal bond with another person in which you bind your finances, your hopes, and dreams to theirs while exclusively committing your emotional and sexual fidelity to them for the rest of your life!

When it comes to marriage, sealing the deal quickly establishes a very shaky foundation for success. To put it very bluntly, this sends a strong message that you don't really value yourself very much. That you would give yourself away to another so quickly, and without much thought, is like discounting goods to sell them fast. Do you want to communicate this message ever, to anyone, for any reason? (Along similar lines, if you are dating someone who is pressuring you to marry them within a short time frame—generally anything less than two years—this is the time to be especially careful.) Further, if you are willing to lightly enter such a bond, are you willing to just as lightly disengage when your partner's presence doesn't thrill you in the intense way it did during the very first part of your relationship? If you believe that your feelings are the ultimate guidepost to reality, how vulnerable will your marriage be when someone other than your spouse makes you feel the same tingly way in the future? If the flush of cocaine is the primary agent that binds you to each other, what will happen when you both crash?

Maybe, then, the best kind of life is one of successive new loves with no marriage at all? After all, divorce could be instantly eliminated if marriage were banned. Because the cocaine-rush of new love feels so universally amazing, why don't we all just make a lifestyle of repeatedly falling in love? Here is the fundamental problem with this idea: You don't get endless chances for your relationship(s) to absolutely blow your mind. The law of diminishing returns certainly applies in the realm of love relationships. The reason we never forget our first love is that this was the first time our brains were swimming with all of the chemicals that produce the lover's high. In our first love relationship, the faint brush of our partner's hand on our own was enough to initiate a deep cascade of pleasure. Over time, and in our subsequent relationships, the first touch of a partner's hand generally has diminished power to produce the same explosion of feeling. Likewise, over time, we don't get quite the same zap to our brains when someone haltingly whispers, "I think I love you." And if we play out this theme into multiple marriages, it becomes almost farcical. Picture a bride and groom, both on their fourth marriage, saying to each other, "I'll never leave you…I promise we'll always be together, until death do us part." As an objective observer of this scene, wouldn't you be asking yourself, "Really? How can they stand on these promises when there is so much evidence that just the opposite is likely to occur?"

Related to this, one particularly disturbing research finding is that too many trips to the altar seem to be associated with an earlier death. Researchers at the London School of Hygiene and Tropical Medicine discovered that people who had been married at least three times were 34% more likely to die at any given time after the age of 50 than those who had limited themselves to just one union.[30] If the diminishing returns of new love affairs is not a compelling enough reason to rethink the starter-marriage strategy, perhaps the idea of an earlier death might motivate us to identify healthy partners and create lifelong love. Globally, there are two elements to achieving lifelong love. The first is to work to become the kind of person who can attract and sustain real love, and the second is to accurately identify someone who is equally capable. The next chapter focuses on how you can ready yourself for real love.

Chapter 3

The Man or Woman in the Mirror

If it is true that you are what you eat, then the parallel relationship metaphor is that you'll get what you are. It's well aligned with a consumerist culture to ask variations of the question, "As I shop for a spouse, what qualities does he or she need to have to attract and hold my interest?" There is certainly value in reflecting on the qualities you desire in a potential spouse and in being discriminating as you navigate the dating market. However, the equally important, but less frequently asked question is, "What do I have to offer to the type of person I'd like to attract and build a lifelong relationship with?" The marriage market isn't comprised of long shopping aisles through which you can roam freely, laying claim to exactly what you want. The mate you would pick must pick you back. Any effort to learn how to pick a wonderful partner without first considering whether or not that partner would be likely to pick you is missing half the picture. In fact, you may need to intentionally develop certain character traits before you are even potentially capable of attracting a high-quality spouse.

During the cocaine-rush phase of a relationship, it may be true that opposites attract, that what feels exotic becomes erotic in the eye of the beholder. Most often, though, when opposites try to sustain long-term love relationships, they come to hate the very differences in their partners that first attracted them. For instance, a man who was initially attracted by his partner's "social butterfly" qualities is later irritated that she wants to constantly drag him out to social gatherings. His partner, who once told her friends that she "likes having him all to herself" is later frustrated that he prefers to stay home when she wants to go out and begins to resent the loss of her former social life. A large body of research has demonstrated that, with few exceptions, successful couples tend to "match" each other on levels of attractiveness, personality, moral values, spiritual beliefs, and cognitive complexity.[31]

Matching tendencies have been described in various ways by researchers and clinicians. Some refer to "the rule of mental health in relationships," which means that people usually end up paired with others at the same level of mental health. Others focus on dimensions of compatibility that they feel are critical, such as spiritual beliefs, lifestyle preferences, and financial philosophies. Dr. Helen Fisher, who offers her services to match.com, sorts mate seekers into four "types" of people: explorers (who are risk-taking, curious, creative, impulsive, optimistic, and energetic), builders (who are cautious, calm, traditional, community-oriented, persistent, and loyal), directors (who are analytical, decisive, tough-minded, debate-oriented, and potentially aggressive), and negotiators (who are broad-minded, imaginative, compassionate, intuitive, verbal, nurturing, altruistic, and idealistic).[32] Fisher was quoted in a recent CNN article as stating, "Once you know who you are, you'll know why you're attracted to certain people and you'll also see who might make for a good match (not to mention, who you might want to offer that rain check)."[33] As mentioned previously, on the Discovery Channel program "The Science of Sex Appeal," she pointed out that "if you know something of Mother Nature's plan, you can speed up the process so you can collide with someone else faster."[34] There is truth to these statements, and Fisher's work on the bio-chemistry of falling in love is truly illuminating, but the goal of helping people "collide faster" could not be further from my own goal. Instead of applying an understanding of some levels of compatibility to assist people in bonding more quickly, I am suggesting that people *slow down* and focus on character qualities that are much deeper than these sorts of personality typologies. What follows is a description of the core factors that I feel are important to attend to in order to set yourself up for a marriage of equals, split into three global areas of self management, relationship management, and life management.

Critical Self Management Factors

Heal Old Wounds

Imagine that your car breaks down in a remote spot known to be close to a Federal prison. Your cell phone isn't picking up a signal, so you are thrust on the mercy of a passing driver. In this scenario, would it be wiser to solicit help from another driver yourself or to sit in the car and wait for someone to notice your state of need and offer to help? It would generally be wiser to take an active role in picking the target of your request for help. If you decide to actively request help, you would certainly attempt to screen for certain factors that might indicate that a particular person would be relatively safe to hail—for example, a man or woman who appears to be riding with his or her young children. Even if you picked at random, without looking for indicators of potentially safe helpers, you would be statistically less likely to pick a sociopath relative to the likelihood that a sociopath might pick you when he or she witnesses your obvious state of vulnerability. As threat expert Gavin De Becker explains, "the possibility that you'll inadvertently select a predatory criminal for whom you are the right victim type is very remote."[35] In other words, if you were to wait passively in your car for someone to help you, you would most likely attract one of two types of people—either good Samaritans or opportunistic sociopaths drawn to your state of need.

For individuals with unresolved traumas, the mate-selection process often carries a double risk. That is, unhealed wounds of past trauma in your life lead to a higher likelihood that unsafe people will pick you, and if you actively pick a partner, it is much more likely that you will end up with an unsafe person. For this reason, it is vitally important that you consider whether you've suffered any previous traumas that may have "broken your picker," as one of my patients put it. A useful definition of trauma is an experience or set of experiences that has destroyed former assumptions that you are safe or that other people can generally be trusted. Further, as I've mentioned already, if you have experienced a trauma, it is often true that you will unintentionally emit certain signals and behaviors that chum the water for the psychopathic sharks in the dating pool. You may have a difficult time recognizing these sharks when they present themselves as suitors because somehow they "feel like home" if you have experienced certain types of past traumas. There is also an unfortunate tendency to select partners with whom you will restage similar traumas (e.g., the son of a verbally abusive mother will often end up with a verbally abusive wife), presumably with the hope of getting a different outcome. In relationships, as in politics, if you ignore your history, you will tend to repeat it, so if you have not addressed and achieved healing from your trauma experience(s), doing so in a safe relationship with a treating professional is recommended as a first priority.

Review Your Motivations

In terms of motivations for marriage, thus far I've been focusing mostly on delusional thinking processes caused by fantasies we create during the cocaine-rush phase of relationships. For example, within the context of a short courtship, two delusional reasons for getting married are "because it feels like I've known them forever, even though we just met" and "because our love story would make a great movie." There are a number of other equally bad reasons to take the plunge. These generally fall into three categories—anxiety, inadequacy, and self-centered pragmatics. If you are contemplating marriage or are "on the hunt" for a spouse, I'd advise you to get honest with yourself and plumb the depths of your motivations. Do your motivations stem from any of the following thoughts?

I want to get married...

- because all of my friends are doing it.
- because I don't know if I'll get another chance if I take a pass on this one.
- because I want to feel secure.
- because I don't want to deal with the dating world anymore.

These motivations are fear based. Anxiety is driving the bus when we fear that we will be left behind, when we accept the premise that a full and interesting life without a spouse is less successful than a partnered life, or when we believe that marriage will give us a sense of security that we cannot experience without a partner. In a way, the person who marries for these reasons is looking to his or her partner to function as a different type of drug—not cocaine, but some type of sedative in this case. The supposed stability and security of the marital bond is sought as an antidote to the tumultuousness of "life on the outside." When one looks to one's partner to be any type of drug instead of a living, breathing human being with an agenda of his or her own, the result is often a short-lived bond.

A second category of unwise motivation is marrying because of feelings of inadequacy, typified by any of the following thoughts:

I want to get married...

- because the person I'm dating loves me and that makes me feel special and lovable.
- because marriage will show everyone that I'm an adult.
- because marriage will demonstrate that someone wants me.
- because this will bring my life into better focus.
- because I'm lonely.

If your motivations fall within this category, please read closely the section of this chapter entitled "Examine your Self-Worth."

Finally, a third category of misguided motivation is shallow pragmatics, which boils down to thoughts such as these:

I want to get married…

- because we've dated awhile and this is the next logical step to take.
- because I want to register for nice things and create a Pottery Barn nest for myself.
- because I will not get stationed with this hottie I'm dating unless I marry him/her (for those in the military).

As someone who hears the stories that people don't tell in polite society, I continue to be surprised at the frequency of motivations like these. Ultimately, motivations in any of these categories are likely to result in what author Pamela Paul has referred to as a "starter marriage."

Get Clear on Your Core Values

Taking the time to define your values is another way to protect yourself from destructive relationships. Once you know what you stand for, you're much less likely to settle for relationships that don't allow you to live out your values. Several helpful values-clarification tools are freely available in the public domain. Below is one example of a tool for this type of self-reflection that I found on the internet.

Personal Values Clarification Worksheet[36]

The following is a list of personal values many people consider to be important to their lives. Consider each value carefully, adding more if you like, then rate each one on its degree of importance to you at this time in your life. Use the scale below:

1: Not at all important to me
2: Not very important to me
3: Moderately important to me

4: Very important to me
5: Essential to me

___ Justice: The quality of being impartial or fair; righteousness; conformity to truth, fact, or reason; to treat others fairly or with equality.
___ Altruism: Regard for or devotion to the interests of others.

___ Recognition: Being made to feel significant and important; being given special notice or attention.

___ Pleasure: The agreeable emotion that accompanies the possession or expectation of what is good or greatly desired; stress satisfaction or gratification rather than visible happiness.

___ Wisdom: Ability to discern inner qualities and relationships; insight; good sense; judgment.

___ Honesty: Straightforwardness of conduct; integrity; uprightness of character or action.

___ Achievement: Accomplishment; attainment of a desired end or aim; a result brought about by resolve and persistence.

___ Autonomy: The ability to be a self-determining individual; personal freedom.

___ Wealth: Abundance of valuable material possessions or resources; affluence.

___ Security: Always having enough money to pay the bills and afford basic creature comforts.

___ Power: Possession of control, authority, or influence over others.

___ Morality: The belief in and keeping of ethical standards.

___ Love: Affection based on admiration or benevolence; warm attachment, enthusiasm, or devotion; unselfish devotion that freely accepts another and seeks that other's good.

___ Aesthetics: The appreciation and enjoyment of beauty for beauty's sake.

___ Health: The condition of being sound in body; freedom from physical disease or pain; the general condition of the body; well-being.

___ Skill: The ability to use one's knowledge effectively and readily in execution of performance; having technical expertise.

___ Emotional Well-Being: Freedom from overwhelming anxieties and barriers to effective functioning; peace of mind; inner security; self respect.

___ Knowledge: The seeking of truth, information, or principles for the satisfaction of curiosity, for use, or for the power of knowing.

___ Spirituality: A focus upon matters of the soul; communion with, obedience to, or activity in behalf of a higher being.

___ Loyalty: Maintaining allegiance to a person, group, institution, or political entity.

___ Family: Maintaining strong relationships with spouse or partner, children, and family of origin; commitment to the well-being of family members.

___ Friendship: Experiencing a deep sense of trust with another that results in emotional intimacy and easy companionship.

___ Creativity: The ability to be original or imaginative, to go beyond existing paradigms; the power to create, express, or produce something new.

Make it a point to find a way to honor your 4s and 5s in your personal and professional life. Repeat this exercise every few years.

Prioritize Ongoing Personal Growth

If you find yourself attracted to the notion of doing this type of self-reflection regularly, you may already possess another critical trait, what I would call personal growth orientation. As I've mentioned previously, even if you feel that you have met your soul mate, you will both change over time. How you change is in large part up to you. Will you make efforts to shape your own character and live more fully into your deepest values, or will you allow yourself to be influenced by unhealthy people and foolish thinking?

I would argue that *the desire to become a better person and a better partner may be the most desirable asset anyone can bring to a marriage.* Of course, starting out as the "perfect" partner is neither possible nor desirable. In fact, strong perfectionist traits do not usually lead to healthy relationships. Rather than experiencing a full and healthy range of emotions, a perfectionist often vacillates between two primary emotions—dread and relief. Perfectionists spend most of their time dreading the next potential failure, and successes are met with a feeling of temporary relief, rather than with a feeling of satisfaction in having done a thing well. Self-esteem does not build from feelings of relief, or the temporary reprieve of having succeeded at something. Failures hit especially hard for perfectionists and may lead to long bouts of depression and withdrawal in some individuals. The roller-coasting pattern of dread and relief endlessly repeats itself in the life of a non-recovered perfectionist, and spouses and children are often the unhappy passengers of this not-so-thrilling ride. Further, perfectionist individuals are often hypersensitive to perceived rejection or possible evidence of failure, and there is a fundamental rigidity in the relentless stance of bracing for failure. Unfortunately, when an individual is caught up in the bondage of perfectionist strivings, that person is likely to be less interested in developing a healthy, mutually satisfying marriage and more interested in chasing the elusive rabbit in his or her own head.

A marriage of equals requires a partnership between two people with strong personal growth orientations who are therefore open to influencing each other continuously to become perfect for, and irreplaceable to, each other. The way to achieve one-in-a-million status is not to arrive as the perfect matches for each other but to become this over time. The key is how you will shape each other in the marriage over time. If you develop a personal growth orientation before you go on the marriage market, you are much more likely to attract someone with the potential and desire to work at becoming the perfect partner for you (as opposed to the perfect human being).

Examine Your Self-Worth

Ensure that your self-worth is healthy before you go on the marriage market. I have suggested that people who believe that they need to be married to have a full and meaningful life are at higher risk for developing unhealthy relationships. Author Stanton Peele asserted that "when a person goes to another with the aim of filling a void in himself, the relationship quickly becomes the center of his life....when a constant exposure to something is necessary to make life more bearable, an addiction has been brought about, however romantic the trappings."[37] Chronically low self-esteem and the feeling of needing to be completed are often closely linked. People with higher self-esteem are typically less likely to form relationships out of a sense of need and are more likely to do so because they desire to enlarge their already-satisfying life experiences even further. Self-esteem is a media buzzword, but what does it mean, exactly? "Esteem" is a favorable opinion or judgment. To esteem something is to set a value on something, to appraise something as worthy. I've often felt that the concept of self-esteem is a vague notion that is not as easy to define as the parallel concept of self-worth. Self-worth is, by definition, the result of your own determination of what you are worth. It is by nature a self-reflective conclusion. People often get into a lot of trouble when they give others the power to determine their sense of self-worth, endlessly seeking confirmation of their worth in the eyes of others, when it was never really others' place to determine their self-worth in the first place.

I would go further to assert that self-worth is a function of the alignment between what you say you value and what you actually do with your time, energy, and physical resources. An entire sub-genre of self-help books encourages readers to raise their self-esteem through repeating self-affirmations. It's hard to describe how ridiculous I find these types of assertions. For example, the bestselling book *The Rules: Time Tested Secrets for Capturing the Heart of Mr. Right* encourages readers to "build up their souls with positive slogans like I'm a beautiful woman. I am enough."[38] A few pages later, the authors tell women, "You are not an empty vessel waiting for him to fill you up, support you, or give you a life."[39] (Is this because their readers are already filled up with Stuart

Smalley-esque mantras?). Self-worth isn't something you can instill by brainwashing yourself to believe that you "are somebody" or by listening to taped self-affirmations as these kinds of books would have you believe. The creation of self-worth is an active, energy-consuming endeavor that involves narrowing the distance between what you say are your deepest values and what you actually do with the life you've been given. If you say that you value your spiritual beliefs, are you living in alignment with them? If you say you value fairness and compassion, are you regularly engaging in behaviors that allow you to live out these values? Conversely, how does engaging in private acts of meanness like gossiping or back-stabbing affect your self-worth? If you say that you value intellectual curiosity, how does spending hours in front of the TV every day affect your sense of self-worth? If you say you value adventure and "making the most of life," how is your self-worth affected by the bondage of crippling fears?

When you have identified the ways in which you are living out of alignment with your deepest values and you have narrowed that gap, your self-worth will rise correspondingly. Strong self-worth is not only an antidote to desperation; it allows you to feel secure enough to live into a personal growth orientation. Secure people, with good self-worth, are able to invite feedback and are more open to positive change. They have a strong sense of their own values, but they are flexible in considering how they may be off the mark at times. Self-worth and the ability to seek and accept corrective feedback are so closely associated that one way to assess your current level of self-worth is to ask yourself whether you are able to say the following types of things *regularly, sincerely, and with ease*:

> "I'm sorry."
> "I really messed up."
> "You're right; I'm wrong."
> "Am I missing anything? Can you see anything I can't see?"
> "I don't know. What do you think?"

Manage your Own Emotions

When I lived in Florida, a botanical garden that housed a family of alligators was only a couple of miles from our house. The bull gator (a barrel-chested 16-foot-long alpha male named "Mojo") was a major attraction of the garden. One day, I took my mom to visit the garden and we had a close encounter with Mojo. He was lying stretched out in the sun, not four feet from the walking path. There was no fence or gate to separate us. I might have imagined it, but from this distance, I felt that I could smell his scent—a slightly sweet brackish odor with a tinge of what I might describe as drying clay. When we informed the caretakers of the garden that a prehistoric-looking beast was lying four feet from the walking path, we were told, "Oh, that's Mojo. We've had him for over ten years. He's lazy…he wouldn't hurt a fly." Unfortunately, Mojo did not continue to fit this description. Two weeks after our visit to the gardens, I noticed an animal-attack feature in the local paper. Apparently, the main caretaker was pulling some long swamp grasses and didn't realize that Mojo was resting under the water at his feet. In the blink of an eye, Mojo surged out of the swamp and ripped off the caretaker's arm. In doing this, Mojo had literally bitten (off) the hand that fed him. The caretaker, much to his credit, was very philosophical about this attack—he was saddened that Mojo had to be put down and talked about how Mojo, no doubt surprised at the unexpected incursion into his territory, had acted out of instinct.[40]

I was studying human emotions at the time, and Mojo's attack prompted me to reflect on how humans sometimes turn into alligators in the blink of an eye, lashing out at their partners with verbally and physically assaultive behavior. I remembered back to high school biology, when I learned that humans essentially have an alligator brain encapsulated in our brain stems. In fact, this is why the human brain stem is sometimes referred to as the "reptilian brain." Anatomically, this part of our brain bears a striking resemblance to that of an alligator's. From this part of our brain, the most primitive instincts emerge, and we surge to protect and defend ourselves in a state of anger. Humans, however, also have a part of the brain that alligators do not have—everything that sits on top of the brain stem. An area of our non-alligator brain that plays a strong role in our executive functions, the frontal lobe, is of particular interest in controlling emotional impulsivity. If you were to free-associate on the word "executive," what would come to mind? Perhaps you might reflect that an executive is typically someone with power and authority. Executives of companies plan and strategize, and make decisions based on what is best for the long-term health of their organizations (well, at least they used to before the current age of unsurpassed corporate greed). The executive part of the brain allows us to make decisions based on our values and what is also good for others we love, rather than solely on self-interest. In humans, the executive center of the brain is generally meant to be in control.

The pairing of this close encounter with Mojo and my understanding of emotional processes inspired me to come up with an illustration of how blind rage operates. The following is _not_ a strictly scientific description of what happens when we lose our emotional control, but it has been of great functional value to several patients of mine who have struggled to get better control of their explosive anger. Imagine that when you get triggered by someone or something, your reptilian brain is the first to react, and it sends out a wave of powerful chemicals that put you in attack mode. This wave of chemicals, released from the lower rear side of your brain, pushes closed a solid iron gate between the more primitive part of your brain and the higher-level executive region in the frontal lobe. When the gate is closed, you cannot access the executive part of your brain. You lose control of yourself and begin to get tunnel vision. Your vision may become blurry with anger, and the surging of adrenaline heats your face. You "see red," and the decisions you make in this state mirror the decisions Mojo himself would be making, along the theme of "annihilate the threat NOW!" Logical thought disappears for the time being. Access to your deepest values is blocked and you lose the ability to protect the people you love from your own rage. If you were to wait 10 to 15 minutes, the wave that pushed the gate closed would begin to recede and the gate would begin to open again. Your tunnel vision would expand back to normal range. You would once again have access to your highest levels of thought and best decision-making abilities. In other words, you would begin to think of _strategic options_ for responding to the situation. One of the most critical things in preparing yourself for a healthy marriage is to recognize that you should not respond to your partner when your executive functioning ("control center") has been hijacked by your reptilian brain. This means that you need to be skilled in recognizing that this process is occurring and you need to be able to say things like this:

"I'm getting too angry for my own good."
"I need to take a break. Let's come back to this later."
"Mojo just staged a takeover—let me get this under control before we continue."

In some ways, waiting until your reptilian brain recedes echoes the process of waiting at least a couple years until the cocaine-rush phase has passed so you can make mindful decisions about the potential of your relationship. The common theme in both is to author your life with your best brain. Several helpful resources provide support for getting control of your anger; some of my favorites are listed in the appendix.

Assert Your Needs Respectfully and Maintain Good Boundaries

If I asked you to explain the difference between being aggressive, being passive, and being assertive, could you do it? Let's see if we can derive some helpful distinctions from an example of each of these types of behaviors. Imagine that you are in the midst of a long and stressful week and your partner tells you that she has committed you both to attend the birthday party of one of her friends on Friday night. Here are three possible ways you could respond:

1) "This Friday night, really? You've already RVSP-ed for us? I guess it's too late and I'll have to go, but as I've told you many times before, I really wish you'd check with me first before committing me to social plans."

2) "Crap! That's about the last thing I want to be doing after the week I've had—I don't even like your friend that much! You'll just have to un-RSVP, because we're not going!"

3) "This Friday night? I know that she is one of your best friends. If you had asked if I could go before the week started, and if I knew it was important to you that we both go, I might have been able to shuffle some of my other commitments, but this week has been a wild and woolly one and I'm going to be exhausted on Friday, so I won't be able to go with you. If you want to go without me, of course that would be fine and I'd love to meet up with you for a movie later on if you'd like, once I've had a chance to unwind."

The second response, which is the aggressive example, would obviously be inconsistent with the goal of maintaining a respectful, loving relationship, so there's no need to expand on why this is *not* a good way to respond. Essentially, response 2 bears the clear markings of an alligator brain hijacking—if Mojo could talk, this is what he might say to his wife. On the other end of the spectrum, it might seem that the kindest way to go is response 1. This response appears gentle and accommodating. If this type of passive response is a pattern, however, in the long run, the most likely result would be the growth of a perpetually resentful attitude. In the short run, being assertive almost always takes more energy than being passive, but in the long run, less energy is drained off by chronic resentment.

There are a number of people whom others view as "great givers" whom I would not classify as givers at all. If your giving is based on a lack of boundaries and you give because you can't say no, then what you are doing is not really giving—it's a compulsive behavior. What you do does not come from a position of love or generosity but stems instead from a sense of fear or a feeling of obligation (*"I can't say no...they won't understand...it will hurt their feelings"*). The profile of a passive person is a person who feels resentful but does things for others anyway, who approaches a good portion of the things he or she does with a feeling of dread or irritation (often covered up by a veneer of selfless generosity), and who begins to use avoidance and social withdrawal as a way of getting out of having to say no. Passivity as a lifestyle makes us feel undefended and at the whim of everyone else's agendas. To be a "lover," you must not engage in acts of love compulsively. You must feel free to say yes and equally free to say no in accordance with your values and priorities. This doesn't mean that you always do what is best for you. Some books on assertiveness suggest that being assertive is not only the best, but also the only, healthy response to all situations. I do not believe this to be true. There are times, even in a healthy relationship, to be passive and times when an aggressive approach may be warranted. In a good relationship, you will often take a hit out of love and may choose, in this scenario, to attend the birthday party of your partner's friend after an exhausting week. The point I'm making, however, is that when you do this, it should be a choice you are making, not the result of your inability to take a different path.

A way to understand the difference between aggressive and assertive approaches is that aggressive responses favor your rights more than the rights of others and assertive responses value your own and others' rights equally. In being assertive, you would honestly state your thoughts and feelings and boldly tell someone else what you want while also accounting for the fact that the other person has an equal right to pursue what he or she wants. The picture of two people who use the assertive style as a pattern in their marriage is one that involves continuous negotiation and compromise. As you may have noticed, response 3 from the previous set of examples is the longest and most thoughtfully-worded of the three options. It seems as though the responder is in full possession of his best brain and has considered how to respond in a loving, yet assertive, way.

Although it's relatively easy to be passive or aggressive, it requires energy and thought to practice assertiveness, especially if you are learning to do so for the first time. Assertiveness is a skill, however, and like any skill, it can become quite automatic over time, as it becomes in a marriage of equals. There are a number of good resources for learning how to become more assertive. Two of my favorites are Cloud and Townsend's *Boundaries*[41] series and the chapter titled "Assertiveness Training" in the book *The Relaxation and Stress Reduction Workbook*[42] by Davis, Eshelman, and McKay. In "Assertiveness Training," the authors cover a number of mistaken traditional assumptions such as "It's not nice to put people off. If questioned, give an answer" and a corresponding list of legitimate rights, such as "You have a right to choose not to respond to a situation."[43] Their chapter on assertiveness training also provides a number of scenarios to help you distinguish between passive, aggressive, and assertive responses and offers a helpful script and some key principles in the practice of being assertive. See the appendix for further information about these resources.

Critical Relationship Management Qualities to Develop

Create and Maintain Equal, Respect-filled Relationships

If you are hoping to create a marriage of equals, you need to be able to create and sustain other types of equal relationships. There are a few hallmarks of equal relationships. In equal relationships, power and control give way to mutual respect. There is no sense that one person is always in the "one down" role. Energy between the two people in the relationship flows freely, and over time, those in the relationship are renewed by it in equal proportion. If this describes the kind of life partnership you want, then it makes sense to ask yourself honestly how well you've been able to maintain this kind of relationship in the past. Have your past romantic relationships been characterized by mutual respect and equal sharing of energy? If you have never been involved in a romantic relationship, how do your friendships feel? Have you been able to sustain mutually satisfying relationships with members of your family, some collection of friends, and some of your past or current co-workers? Do you give as much as you receive, or are you under-benefited or over-benefited in your relationships? What have been your driving motivations in close relationships in the past? Have your past relationships been based in insecurity, emotional immaturity, or self-serving motives? Have you paired up with others mainly because you like the way they make you feel about yourself (or because it feels good to be picked)? This kind of love is ultimately selfish and unsustainable. The other person becomes an object, rather than an equal who is worthy of your respect, less a partner than a living embodiment of a drug, a provider of biologically thrilling experiences that you snort up for your own gratification. As I've pointed out previously, when the well dries up and the cocaine high of falling in love stops flowing, you will predictably become disillusioned, begin to detach, and start saying things like "I'm just not in love with you anymore." A marriage of equals cannot be based on motives like this.

Protect your Relationship(s) at the Global Level

For more than a decade, several marital researchers engaged in a lengthy debate that boils down to two opposing viewpoints (paraphrased from the literature):

Do spouses want to be loved as the people they are, with their warts and all?

OR

Do spouses want to be idealized somewhat in their partners' eyes, to be thought to be a little better than they really are?

When I was in graduate school, my colleague Dr. Lisa Neff published some research that suggests that the entire raging debate was grounded in a false dichotomy. Neff and Karney concluded that people want both—we want to be accurately known by our partners at the level of specific behaviors, but we also want to be slightly idealized at the level of global perceptions.[44] That is, we want our partners to be privately aware of our little flaws, and, at the same time, we want to be thought of as a good person and a highly desirable mate. Actually, in a curious way, this parallels the self-worth perceptions of healthy individuals. That is, people with healthy self-esteem perceive themselves to have a balance of specific strengths and weaknesses, and ultimately believe that, overall, they are good and worthy human beings. Narcissistic individuals and depressed individuals struggle with myopia (in other words, a kind of short-sightedness or blindness) of self-perception. The narcissist is blinded to her own weaknesses and believes herself to be better than everyone else at most everything. The depressed person, on the other end of the spectrum, is blind to his strengths and sees himself as less capable and worthwhile than most people in most areas. So, both within ourselves, and in our relationships with others, accurate perception of specific character qualities paired with a generally positive global perception is most beneficial and healthy.

The concept of a marriage existing on, not one, but two levels, evokes applications of several insights about how to protect our close relationships. It seems to me that a healthy relationship can tolerate plenty of change and mutual correction at the level of specific behaviors *if* both

$$G$$

$$s \quad\quad s$$

$$s \quad\quad s \quad\quad s$$

$$s \quad\quad s \quad\quad s$$

$$s \quad s \quad s \quad s \quad s \quad s \quad s \quad s \quad s$$

partners protect each other well on the level of global attributions. Consider the diagram below:

In this diagram, *G* represents the global level of perception, and the region populated by several small *s*'s represents the level of specific behaviors. The variety of specific behaviors may be desirable or undesirable. The global level of perception may also be desirable or undesirable (that is, whether or not your partner views you as a good person overall, despite your flaws). An accumulation of *s* characteristics can and will change *G*, and this is the norm in the development of most new love relationships. At first, on the level of *G*, the other is initially seen to be utterly perfect, the ultimate pinnacle of all human potential. As negative traits and flaws (*s*'s) begin to show up, however, *G* gets recalibrated in a downward fashion (in real life, there are few figures like Jane Austen's William Darcy of *Sense and Sensibility*, who appear less attractive at first but become tremendously appealing as time passes). When enough time has elapsed (i.e., after the end of the cocaine-rush phase), partners should be able to make an informed decision about whether the flaws of the other person are flaws they can learn to flex with or whether there are any deal-breakers in the mix.

Ideally, when there is enough data to support a positive global level of perception (*G*), *G* would achieve a relatively stable set point on a couple's wedding day. Of course, *G* cannot really be reliably set until enough time has passed to allow for accurate evaluation of *G*, and this reality is not lost on either partner, no matter how love struck each may be. When couples court for a relatively brief amount of time before getting married, *G* is still being worked out. Because *G* is in a state of some flux, ample evidence exists in their communication that *G* is not perceived to be set at a positive, generally fixed level. This shows up most often in the heat of conflict, when both begin to engage in predictable patterns of defensiveness and counterattacking behavior. With no *G* set point, each partner is vulnerable to the interpretation that the other's criticisms demonstrate a negative perception of them at the level of *G*. This sets off a primitive panic[45] because a shaky *G* is a shaky basis for continuing the relationship—after all, why would any of us continue in a relationship with someone whom we've concluded is not really a good person? Threatened in this way, we instinctively throw our weight into defending ourselves and simultaneously miss the opportunity to become better partners by listening to what our partners are telling us we need to work on. As a result, we often get stuck in one of a few predictable negative conflict cycles, which progressively weakens our attachment bond.

When you fail to protect your relationship at the level of *G*, you may be committing crimes of commission and crimes of omission (or both). "Crimes of commission" involve things like making statements that condemn your partner's character or threaten the very foundations of your commitment. Some of the fastest ways to set off a primitive panic at the level of *G* are to say things like this:

"You *always* [insert any undesirable behavior]."
"You're such a loser [or another term that indicates broad-sweeping character assassination]."
"I can't take it anymore! I'm done with you!"
"What's the point—why don't we just get a divorce?"
"I don't have the same feelings for you anymore."

Have you ever wondered how children and their parents or two siblings can say the most awful things to each other, often without putting their relationships in real jeopardy, when newlyweds cannot do the same? The difference is that family-of-origin relationships offer a powerful form of protection against a shaky global level of perception (G)—the existence of shared genes and direct kinship that will never change, no matter what. In contrast, one's husband or wife doesn't start out as family but must become family over time. Thus, in the context of a newly forming marriage, these kinds of statements hack away at the foundations of the relationship and destroy feelings of emotional safety.

In Chapter 1, I mentioned the concept of emotional safety as being distinct from physical safety. When I ask patients if they have a good working definition of emotional safety, it is often hard for them to generate a response, but when I ask patients if they can describe what the *opposite* of emotional safety looks like, the responses flow freely. Below are some of the most common responses to the question about what a lack of emotional safety looks like:

> When you feel like your partner doesn't respect or like you very much.
> When you feel like your partner will assume the worst about you.
> When you feel like your partner is looking for ways that you will screw up or let them down.
> When your partner is rude or detached (in the latter case, signaling possible rejection).

Military men and women understand well the overlap between the concept of emotional safety and "having each other's back." When you make statements that set off a primitive panic at the level of G, you are essentially defecting from the stance of having your partner's back. If you want to get your relationship on better footing, the first step is to stop the bleeding by taking statements like these out of your options for responding.

As I think of it, "crimes of omission" involve both failing to proactively protect your relationship at the level of G and failing to perceive and address the primitive panic you may unintentionally trigger in your partner (for example, in the latter case, by failing to ask things like "Did your mood just shift?" "Did I do something that was hurtful to you just now?"). Although it is especially important during conflict situations, reinforcing that G has reached a positive set point is a smart move at any time. Such reinforcement involves frequently letting your partner know that you love them, showing them with your behavior that you respect them, and holding their worth high when you speak of them to other people.

As I mentioned just previously, protecting the relationship at the level of global perceptions (*G*) becomes especially important during times of conflict or when making requests of your partner. Let's say that you want to ask your partner to check in with you before spending a large sum of money in order to prevent your joint account from going into overdraft. Here is one example of how you could make this request in a way that attends to *G*:

> "We are becoming a wonderful team in so many ways. I really like where things have been going in the area of our finances generally. I trust you and I know that you would never intentionally cause me to feel stress. Our checking account went into overdraft again this morning when you bought that new lawnmower, and I need you to know that this really stressed me out. When I get an overdraft notice from the bank, I can almost feel the ulcers coming on. Can we figure out some way to make sure that we're working together to prevent this from happening in the future?"

Now, is there any healthy spouse on earth who would not be inclined to work with you if you made the request in this way? Again, as in the case of being assertive, this takes more work up front, but the payoff is well worth the effort—your partner will feel loved and respected, and you will be able to work through conflicts without getting stuck in needlessly destructive cycles of attack and counterattack.

A further way to protect your relationship at the level of *G* is to make healthy attributions on an ongoing basis. By healthy attribution, I mean an interpretation of an experience, thought, or feeling that is balanced and reasonable. For example, the central thrust of Chapter 2 might be read as an encouragement to develop the following healthy attribution: "The cocaine-rush of this new relationship may feel lovely, but it doesn't mean this is love." Attributions continue to be critical to the success of relationships in later stages of love. The debate about whether we want to be truly known for who we are, or slightly idealized despite our apparent flaws, has augmented an already-rich literature on the process of making attributions in relationships. Two specific concepts are central to the study of attributions. The "fundamental attribution error"[46] refers to the tendency to unfairly attribute negative behaviors to someone else's internal, fixed personality traits, while underestimating the power of situations to influence their behavior. This fundamental attribution error is thought to be especially common when we know very little about the person we are evaluating. One classic example is that when someone cuts us off in traffic, instead of thinking, *They must have had a stressful day and probably didn't see me;* we go into Mojo mode and think, *What a turd!* A second concept is referred to as the "self-serving bias." While we may not give others the benefit of the doubt, when it comes to our own behaviors, we engage in opposite thinking.[47] When we act like turds (come on, admit it, we all do sometimes), our natural instinct is to quickly reassure ourselves that we acted that way because we were having a stressful day. We also tend to let others know, as many a reality TV star has done, that we "weren't acting like ourselves" in that moment and "we're not *really* like that if you were to *really* know who we are." And, on the flip side, when we land our dream jobs, although we might say it to others, we don't often think, *Well, there were many good candidates and I was just in the right place at the right time.* We tend to think instead: *I got the job because I was clearly the best candidate and the interviewers were clever enough to pick up on this fact.*

The interesting thing about these two attribution processes to me is how they interact with the first two stages of love relationships as I've defined them. During the cocaine-rush phase of the relationship, we know very little about the other person, so, according to the fundamental attribution error theory, we should be making negative personality attributions for the other person's undesirable behaviors. But, of course, we don't do this at all. Instead, we extend the self-serving bias to the other person, folding him or her into a loving cocoon of consistently charitable attributions. If our handsome new partner is acting like a total jackass, we are quick to explain this away ("it's because of all the stress he's been under"). When he treats us with kindness, our assumption is that he does so because it is in his character to be kind and sweet.

The transition from the cocaine-rush phase of the relationship to the testing phase rolls away this protective mental cocoon and we begin to see our partners in a rather harsher light. To the degree that the partner was initially granted unmerited and inaccurate personality strengths, this recalibration process can be profoundly destabilizing to the relationship. As the lovers come out from under their mutual spell and the *folie a deux* passes, they may even overcorrect and begin to see their partners in a more *negative* light than is warranted. Hugh Jackman begins to look like that guy who played the high school principal in the movie *Ferris Bueller's Day Off*. Such overcorrection results from a swing of the pendulum from a stance of "I thought she was perfect because I was always excited to see her" to "I guess I was wrong…she doesn't really look like Rose and she no longer makes me feel like Jack [of *Titanic* movie fame], so it must not be real love." It is healthier to expect the relationship to change as you progress from the cocaine-rush phase into the testing phase and to set your expectations of your partner more realistically (in other words, set yourself up to make healthy attributions). Ultimately, although no romantic relationship can sustain the endless continuation of unfounded idealization, those in successful relationships do carry over into the post-cocaine-rush phase a tendency to slightly idealize each other in a habitually adaptive manner.[48] We extend this idealization to ourselves anyway, so why not fold in the love of our lives as well? Since our intimate relationships have a huge impact on the quality of our lives, then surely, to do so would be self-serving, in the best possible sense of the concept.

De-escalating and Repairing Relationship Conflict

Several authors have written excellent books on the topics of de-escalating conflict and repairing relationships after conflict has occurred. Dr. Sue Johnson's book *Hold Me Tight: Seven Conversations for a Lifetime of Love* is highly recommended additional reading, particularly if significant trauma is an element in your own or your partner's history. See the appendix for additional resources on this topic. I join a multitude of marital researchers in pointing out that conflict de-escalation skills are absolutely critical if you want to sustain healthy long-term love. I would also add the following observations to this basic assertion, however. First, depending on how it is handled, conflict can be a powerful catalyst for growth. If you can protect your relationship at the level of *G* you will usually avoid getting stuck and will often learn new things about your partner and your relationship. Through conflicts, we have new opportunities to reflect on and redefine the implicit (unspoken) rules that guide our marriages. Conflict can be healthy. A good fight can clear the air and establish new patterns, making your relationship stronger in the long run. To solidify this concept, think of the process of growing muscle tissue. When we lift weights, we actually rip the muscle fibers and they become stronger during the repair process. In a similar way, when we make slight tears in the fabric of our relationship, the relationship may become much stronger through the subsequent repair process. In fact, this muscle-repair analogy sheds light on the trust-building process in several different types of close relationships; for example, in therapy, a slight rupture followed by a repair of the treatment alliance often leads to a much stronger relationship. I think this is because ruptures and repairs give us critical sources of information about how much we can trust each other when the going is rough.

I have also noticed that couples who are good at conflict have an ability to do what I call "zooming out." I have seen a related concept referred to as meta-cognitive processing, more simply defined as thinking about thinking. When we meta-cognate, we pull back from the immediacy of an interaction and think about the *process* of how we are interacting with someone else. We become more mindful of our emotional state of being and can slow our rate of emotional response. If you like, think of yourself as Neo from the movie *The Matrix* when he pulls back from a spray of bullets and slows time so he can avoid getting damaged. After zooming out, we can assist our partner in shifting gears by using humor or providing reassurance that although a part of us is really pissed off right now, a much bigger part of us loves them more than anyone else in the world. We begin to observe our behavior differently from this zoomed-out perspective and we start to notice some new elements of our partners' behavior and consistent patterns across conflict situations. Of course, we deploy these meta-cognitive skills from the executive functioning center of the brain, *not* the part where Mojo lives. In therapy, I often find it productive to help couples alternate between zooming out from the emotional themes in their repeated conflicts and zooming in on some core emotions they are experiencing in the moment. This practice strengthens their ability to apply a wide range of strategies in managing conflicts. The practice of pulling out and engaging the executive functioning center of the brain also converts animosity into curiosity, which is an ideal place to be in a marriage of equals.

Life Management Qualities

Become a "Two-Marshmallow" Person

Making conscious choices that allow you to live in alignment with your deepest values often requires the ability to delay gratification. In the 1960s, Stanford University researcher Walter Mischel came up with an elegantly simple method that showed the value of the ability to delay gratification. His study subjects were a group of four-year-old children. He offered each participant a large, puffy marshmallow but told them all that if they would wait for him to run an errand, they could have not one, but two, lovely marshmallows. The marshmallow was an excellent choice because it had not only the taste, but also the appearance and texture of a delectable treat. The little tykes squirmed in front of their marshmallows like dogs might whimper when told to stay while sitting in front of T-bone steaks dripping with meaty juices.

Some of the four-year-olds were able to control their impulse to snatch up and consume their marshmallows for the duration of Mischel's 15–20-minute errand (which must have felt like several lifetimes for these four-year-olds). Others could not. Mischel followed up with his subjects many years later and found that the ability to control impulses and delay gratification was associated with success in many different areas of life as an adult. For instance, those who delayed gratification were more self-motivated and more persistent in the face of obstacles. On average, they scored 210 points higher on SAT tests. Those who had quickly consumed the first marshmallow they were offered continued to have impulse-control problems in adulthood. Mischel characterized them as more troubled, stubborn, indecisive, and mistrustful, and less self-confident.[49]

When you have done the work of clarifying your values, it is important to think long-term in setting up your life. For example, instead of pursuing work that pays well now but has no intrinsic reward or personal growth potential, consider investing the time and energy to gain skills that will flower into a stimulating work life for the rest of your career. In my opinion, when you take the long view of your life, it makes the most sense to become a two-marshmallow person where your deepest values are concerned. Moreover, the discipline of being a two-marshmallow person pays off in many ways as you create an interesting life with a well-matched partner.

Pursue a Meaningful Life Regardless of Your Relationship Status

I have previously mentioned that desperation is not a healthy place from which to launch the search for a mate. The best way to avoid being perceived as desperate is to not actually be desperate. Instead of worrying about whether you'll get left behind in the mate-selection game, why not use your energy to construct a fulfilling life independent of your relationship status? As psychologist Harriet Lerner explains, "Without a life plan, our intimate relationships carry too much weight, and we begin to look to others to provide us with meaning or happiness, which is not their job."[50] A rich and meaningful existence is entirely possible whether or not you are partnered. Why not populate your life with interesting people and stimulating activities? Why not continue to work toward spending as much time as possible living into your deepest values? If you can view a new relationship from a stance like, "Life is good right now and I enjoy the freedom I have, so this person needs to be well worth it for me to give up my current level of freedom," you'll be in a much better position to make a good decision. People who study business practices talk about the walk-away factor as a core principle in effective negotiation. Robert Rubin, former U.S. Secretary of the Treasury, described it this way: "When others sense your willingness to walk away, your hand is strengthened."[51] In a marriage of equals, the two individuals hold walk-away power mutually throughout the premarital courtship period. In such a formulation, the goal is not to manipulate the other person but to establish a relationship in which neither person *needs* the other, but both very much *want* the other person, a true win-win outcome. As a side benefit, when you create an exciting life for yourself regardless of your relationship status, you convey that you value your time and are someone who might be interesting to "catch."

Let me be clear here, though: I'm talking about pursuing meaningful activities and relationships because you value them for their own sake and *not* because you are following some set of rules that manipulate potential partners' views of you. Case in point: Consider the guiding message in the catch-a-mate book *The Rules: Time Tested Secrets for Capturing the Heart of Mr. Right.*[52] Authors Fein and Schneider tell readers that their "job is to treat the man [that they] are really, really crazy about like the man [they're] not interested in—don't call, be busy sometimes!"[53] When I read *The Rules*, I reacted negatively to them and wasn't sure why until I formulated my three-phase model of relationships. That is, during the cocaine-rush phase, when you behave according to a set of rules like this, you are intentionally manipulating your partner's perception of the person you are and prolonging the period of untested idealization. For example, take the "rule" that amounts to appearing to be less available than you really are or the advice that female readers "act independent so that he doesn't feel that you're expecting him to take care of you"[54] (as a side note, isn't this entrapment?). If you have good self-worth in the first place and a tendency to create an interesting life for yourself, you don't need a set of rules like this to attract potential suitors. It seems not only dishonest, but also unsustainable to me. Research does not suggest that playing hard to get leads to happier relationships.[55] If your relationship is built on the chase, what happens when you get caught? How long before the other person figures out who you really are?

Forget the Spouse Hunt

Despite the prevalence of pop psychology books full of tips for "catching a mate," like *The Rules: Time Tested Secrets for Capturing the Heart of Mr. Right; How to Make Someone Fall in Love with You in 90 Minutes or Less; Single No More: How and Where to Meet your Perfect Mate; The Get-Your-Man-to-Marry-You Plan: Buying the Cow in the Age of Free Milk;* and *Marry Me! Three Professional Men Reveal How to Get Mr. Right to Pop the Question*, you might want to consider forgetting the spouse hunt entirely. The hunt puts a person in a mentally appetitive—and competitive—state of mind that does not often lead to good assessment of potential in others. Desirable partners often seem to present themselves with sufficient frequency to those who are not actively hunting for them. The strategy I suggest for any and all significant close relationships, from friendships to marital partnerships, is to create a full and active life for yourself and to develop relationships with others who are naturally drawn to whatever lights you both up. When you are developing a relationship with someone who has potential, remember that using coy "rules" during the courtship phase is one of many ways to artificially extend the time during which the other person over-idealizes you. Besides, instead of pretending that you are unavailable, if you are pursuing a multifaceted existence regardless of your relationship status, your unavailability at times will be a natural offshoot of such a full and exciting life, and you will attract someone who is capable of meeting you as an equal and forging an exciting life together with you. The next chapter will help you understand how to accurately identify such a person.

Chapter 4

Selecting a Partner for the Conversation of a Lifetime

This chapter is dedicated to the Lifestyle Poll participant who shared the following response to the question "What did you look for in a lifelong partner (or what are you looking for in a potential lifelong partner?)":

> I don't even know what to look for anymore! The things I have looked for have been so horribly dysfunctional that I now at least have the good sense *not* to look for those things anymore but feel stuck because I am not attracted to anything else. Things I have looked for but have decided I am not looking for anymore: brilliantly charismatic high achievers who are misunderstood by the world.

I'd like to start by taking a critical look at the frequently cited 50% divorce rate.[56] With so many experts constantly referencing the 50% divorce rate,* it's easy to stop thinking critically about the implications of this statistic. Often, this is translated as "you have a 50/50 chance of divorce anytime you get married." Consider, for example, this statement made by Dr. Phil during a relationship-advice episode: "We got a 50% divorce rate in America. I mean you got about a 1 in 2 chance of marriage working. And that is when both people are running towards each other as fast as they can get there. They want to get married. They are excited about it. They are coming together and they crash instead of mesh. So you got a

---

*Some suggest a higher rate of divorce than 50 percent of marriages. Martin and Bumpass (1989) estimate that "about 2/3 of all first marriages are likely to disrupt" (p. 49). Also, divorce rates for subsequent marriages are consistently higher than for first marriages.

1 in 2 shot if both of you are really leaning forward and excited about it."[57] I understand and agree with his underlying point that the particular woman he was advising would be wise not to jump into marriage with someone who admitted that he doesn't love her. However, this is a very good example of how the myth of the 50/50 divorce probability gets transmitted through media sources to large viewing audiences. First, there is a blatant logical error within this statement that needs to be addressed. The 50% divorce rate in America is based on ALL people who get married, not just the ones who are "really leaning forward and excited about it." Researchers who study divorce statistics do not exclude married couples who were not really leaning into and excited about walking down the aisle. It's probably true that most people are excited to get married and most people want their marriages to succeed. Nonetheless, a number of people get married for reasons that have nothing to do with love, and researchers capture these marriages in divorce-rate statistics as well. Furthermore, the general logic of the 50% divorce probability myth is like saying, "Marriage is really nothing but a game of roulette. Half the numbers are black and half are red. You drop your ball in the circle and watch it spin around and around. There is a 50% chance that it will land on a red number, and if it does, your relationship will end in divorce." Ridiculous, right?

The truth is that there are some groups of people who have an incredibly high rate of divorce and other groups who do not. One key factor that affects divorce rates is a given couple's level of financial wealth. Rates of marital dissolution are consistently associated with levels of income, such that the risk for individuals of low income (defined as those within 200% of the poverty line) is several times greater than the risk for individuals of middle- or high income. Similarly, divorce rates vary substantially across neighborhoods and states. According to national data collected in 1995, in communities with high rates of unemployment and large numbers of families receiving public assistance, the chance of a first marriage breaking up is nearly twice as large as in communities where socioeconomic indicators are higher.[58] Researchers who have specifically targeted financially distressed samples, such as couples studied in the 1930s Great Depression, have shown that economic hardship is associated with more conflict, higher levels of marital hostility, lower levels of warmth, and higher rates of divorce.[59]

My graduate school mentor, Dr. Benjamin Karney, brought this point home to me in one of our early conversations. He asked me to imagine that two different families—one with a high income and one with a low income—were facing the same stressful event: the breakdown of a car. He posed a question: How would each of these families cope with this stressful event? I thought aloud, "Well, someone in the wealthy family would pull out their AAA card and call for roadside assistance. The car would be towed to the nearest shop, and either their insurance would provide a rental car or they would probably just use the other family car. In the case of the financially strapped family, there would probably be no roadside service, and there may be no extra money available to rent a car, and quite possibly no other family car to use instead. Family members and friends would probably be called upon to help out. If help were not possible, the individual would be left to negotiate his or her commute with some form of public transit, which could significantly cut into free time (potentially a much longer, choppier commute with multiple bus transfers)." Going through this exercise was both practical and conceptually illuminating. It was obvious that what would have been an acute, very time-limited stressor for a wealthier family could very likely stretch out into a source of chronic strain for a family of limited resources. The stress load in the case of the economically constrained family would likely be much higher, whereas for the wealthier family, access to ready options would provide a buffer against the effects of this acutely stressful event. And for those with limited resources, such a high level of stress could create chronic marital spillover.

Inspired by this very practical revelation, I embarked on a process of exploring the connection between several domains of stress and marital satisfaction. My graduate school dissertation was an examination of the association between stress and marital satisfaction in more than 164,000 married individuals. After spending a year performing targeted meta-analysis across 113 studies of 300 studies I reviewed, I can pretty much boil it down to this: contextual factors like being unemployed and constantly struggling to make ends meet create an extremely challenging environment in which to sustain a satisfying marriage. If people don't feel secure in getting their most basic needs met, it is much harder for them to feel satisfied and secure in their marriages. Spillover between generally high and chronic life stress and marital satisfaction is a strong factor in divorce. High levels of stress operate like chronic environmental toxins on marital satisfaction.[60] As such, divorce is not a judgment on the character of people under severe stress, because it is largely a byproduct of the stress loads they are facing. Even in such contexts, however, some people display amazing resilience. I once worked with an inspiring couple, faced with a large number of severe chronic stressors, who said, "Our backs are always up against the wall, but we have each other's back no matter what. Sometimes, it feels like it is us against the world, but we know that we have 'us' and that's not ever going to change. We're there for each other every day."

On the opposite end of the spectrum of privilege, material comfort and resource abundance change the picture significantly. In 2008, I collected data on a targeted sample of more than 1200 of some of the most intelligent, well-resourced women of my generation. Very few of the women in this sample classified themselves as having been raised in a poor or working-class background. Eighty-five percent of the sample classified themselves as having been raised in a middle-class (37%), upper middle-class (44%) or wealthy (4%) family. Seventy-five percent of my sample had a current household income of $50,000 or greater, and 60% had a household income of $76,000 or greater. The vast majority of the respondents in my sample (98%) are college graduates, and more than half of the sample graduated from Harvard University. I asked my respondents about the divorce rate of their parents and, not surprisingly, discovered that it is nowhere near the widely cited 50% national divorce rate. In this relatively privileged sample, nearly 80% reported that their parents' marriages were still intact.

A specific example of a very satisfied marriage at the wealthiest end of the spectrum is perhaps that of Edith and George Vanderbilt (who were not participants in my study, to be clear). I'll never forget a trip my husband and I took to the Biltmore Estate in North Carolina. We were touring the house and grounds, plugged into one of those self-guided audio tours. Upon entering the sumptuously decorated private quarters of Edith Vanderbilt, we were treated to a peek at the very happy marriage of Edith and George through a written account in one of Edith's letters. George died unexpectedly at age 52 of a heart attack and Edith was reflecting on this great loss and some of the rhythms of their married life together. She concluded by saying, "We were just so happy together." They are described by the curators of the Biltmore estate:

> The young couple uniquely complemented one another: Edith, with her independent, compassionate, and industrious talents, and George, with his thoughtful, visionary, and intelligent worldview. Both Edith and George were socially progressive individuals who believed firmly in their ability to be catalysts for a better quality of life for Western North Carolina residents.

Together, they created initiatives, programs, industries, and schools that forever changed the face of this part of the Blue Ridge Mountains.[61]

I was very impressed by the account of the partnership of this early power couple. To be honest, though, a part of me was also thinking, *Yes, it follows that this couple would have been very happy together.* After all, who wouldn't be, in the context of endless parties, dips in the pool, picnics on the grounds, and intimate dinners with some of the most fascinating people in the world? Here is an account of one of the grand—and not all that unusual—social scenes of the Biltmore estate:

> An evening under the stars is always a magical experience. But imagine an elaborate, moonlit birthday party in Biltmore's gardens, colorful Japanese lanterns hanging from trees and shrubbery, an orchestra guiding guests towards midnight. This is not the stuff of fairy tales, although it seemed as such to those attending. Instead, it was the very real birthday celebration in 1925 for George and Edith Vanderbilt's only daughter, Cornelia. The event actually began in the afternoon, when employees gathered in the gardens for a tea party and dancing to Guthrie's Orchestra. Biltmore dairy employees presented the newlywed Cornelia Vanderbilt Cecil with "one of the largest cakes ever made by Biltmore Dairy," consisting of 26 gallons of ice cream with alternating layers of chocolate parfait, Lady Ashe ice cream, all covered with a vanilla mousse and studded with roses and lilies. The cake was four feet high and two feet square at the base, and the inscribed birthday sentiment was equally as grand and magnificent—"May your joys be as many as the sands in the sea." By 9:30 p.m. dancing to the Charles Freicher Orchestra was underway in a pavilion, and the whole affair was crowned with a midnight buffet. The newspaper accounts captured it best. "The beautiful array of summer gowns of the many dancers made a scene as beautiful as that of gay moths and fireflies in a fairy garden."[62]

Such a happy life is bound to spill over into the marriage of all but the most unfortunately matched couple. At the same time, I'm not proposing a linear association between marital satisfaction and financial wealth such that those at the highest levels of wealth enjoy the most satisfying marriages. I'm willing to bet that there is a U-shaped curve between material wealth and marital satisfaction, because a number of factors might increase the risk of divorce for the very wealthiest couples. As I've mentioned previously in the case of great beauty, being flush with visible assets that society values lends some interesting vulnerability factors. In the marriage market, there is likely to be keen competition for those individuals who have power, fame, and money. Some portion of ambitious singles (who lack good character) may continue the hunt for a rich spouse, even though their intended may already be married to someone else. With an ever-present coterie of people pumping up their ego, those with wealth and power are also at risk for developing both a strong narcissistic streak and a steady undercurrent of insecurity (asking themselves, in the privacy of their minds, "Why do people *really* seek me out?").

The well-publicized sequential marriages of many Hollywood stars suggest a tendency among the very wealthy and famous to repeatedly "trade up" in their marriages. So, if you value the prospect of having a good marriage, it makes no sense to pine after the lifestyle of Hollywood stars. Even though the Hollywood set appears to have won the genetic lottery, the failure to create sustainable marriages is painfully apparent within this starry tribe. With a few notable exceptions, which everyone points to as exceptions to the rule, like the marriage of Paul Newman and Joanne Woodward, a good marriage seems to be a very elusive part of the lifestyles of the rich and famous. Ultimately, anyway, I'm directing this particular writing to the majority of the people I see, who live somewhere in between constant material deprivation and anything like the Vanderbilt lifestyle.

Possession of material resources is only one way of categorizing comparative risk of divorce. In any case, I don't have the expertise to provide guidance on how to increase your level of material wealth—I'll leave that to the financial gurus out there. My expertise is central to another category of risk—the category of insight and understanding. Let's say that the statistic were instead that 50% of people who engage in the relatively new sport of wing suit flying ended up crashing and severely injuring themselves. If you don't know what wing suit flying is, imagine a person wearing a skintight suit (also called a "birdman suit" or a "squirrel suit") with fabric flaps between the legs and between the hands and hips—a cross between a superhero and a flying squirrel. Outfitted thus, the wing suit pilot manipulates the shape of his or her body to create lift and drag by changing the shape of the torso, arching or bending at the shoulders, hips, and knees and changing the angle of attack relative to the prevailing wind currents.

Now imagine two groups of would-be wing suit fliers—one group with no understanding of how to manipulate their body shapes to slow their freefall or position themselves above wind currents, and another group with a healthy understanding of the key aspects of wing suit flight. If they all jumped off the Empire State Building, perhaps 90%–95% percent of those with no wing suit flying knowledge would crash and injure themselves, while a much lower number of the other group (maybe 5%–10%) would meet the same disastrous end. I'm guessing at these figures, but regardless of what they would be, clearly, the fliers in the second category would have a much lower probability of crashing. If we averaged the probabilities of crashing across the two groups, we'd arrive at the statistic that about 50% of people who jump off the Empire State Building while wearing wing suits end up crashing and severely injuring themselves. Those who lack an understanding of the dynamics of falling in love and have a limited grasp on what it takes to sustain lasting love are like the people in category 1, whereas people with significant insight into both are like the people in category 2. Clearly, people in the latter category would have a much lower risk of divorce than people in the former. One way to dramatically decrease your own chance of divorce is to understand how to identify a partner who is capable of living into the potential of a marriage of equals. The information to come is organized in three main sections: general commentary and models for understanding the process of wise selection, specific personality characteristics to assess in potential mates, and important relationship qualities to evaluate.

A Wise Mate-Selection Process

Selection Principle #1:
Remember the Principles of Attraction

The first principle of wise selection is to understand the cocaine-rush phase of all new relationships and to understand the implications of this reality for the process of wise decision-making. To help you hold on to this level of insight, I have a challenge for you. Embedded in the hired psychological consultants' disreputable plan (Chapter 1) are more than 15 suggestions for ABC's producers that increase our attraction to potential mates regardless of their actual potential to be a good mate. Can you identify at least 10 of these principles and write them out in your own words? This will allow you to remember these insights when you are evaluating potential partners. For example, you might convert some of the text in Chapter 1 into your own words as follows:

> Physical beauty might temporarily blind me to someone's inner character.
>
> When I conquer a fear alongside someone else, I feel closer to them.
>
> When I know very little about someone else and it stays fairly superficial, I'll be more likely to form an inaccurate fantasy of who they are.
>
> When I have sex with someone, even if I barely know them, oxytocin is released, and strong biological forces will act to bind me to them as a result.

Got the principles of attraction well in hand? Let's see if you can now identify the attraction principle(s) behind a couple of scenarios. In 1986, *Newsweek* magazine asserted that a 40-year-old woman was more likely to be killed by a terrorist than to receive a proposal of marriage (and, to clarify, not more likely to be killed by a terrorist than to receive a proposal of marriage from that terrorist, but to receive a marriage proposal from any man).[63] Which principle of attraction would be heightened by such a fear-mongering article that taps into anxieties about a marriage crunch? This seems to me to be a classic example of how the scarcity principle increases the mate-seeking drive of those looking for life partners. For most people, the marriage crunch hasn't really been true since the post-WWII Baby Boom era. Most people who want to get married do get married at some point, with the exception of specific minority groups of women who do continue to face a real marriage crunch.

In a second scenario, can you interpret, in light of attraction principles, the finding that parental disapproval makes people want their partners more? My take on this is that parental disapproval often comes with parental decrees that one is "never to see that person again." If a person is viewed as unobtainable in this way, the scarcity principle once again applies. In addition, the bonding process would also get a boost from the super-charged environment of secret trysts and "Romeo and Juliet" inner narratives.[64] Another powerful psychological phenomenon called reactance theory would also be tapped. Reactance theory suggests that we will often willfully act against our own best interests if our sense of self-determination is threatened. When a parent comes down with a severe judgment of a new boyfriend as a "loser," then we may forget that we were beginning to think along the same lines before they mentioned this. (Our boyfriend has instantly been transformed from a loser into "Romeo" or a "Peter van Daan" into a "Peter Schiff"). Instead of reflecting thoughtfully on whether the negative parental evaluation has any merit, we are moved to a defensive stance (*"no one gets to tell me who to love"*) and, out of this defensive motivation, will often fiercely defend the person we are dating. Parents, this means that if you are worried about the character of your son or daughter's new partner, it is often far wiser to ask clarifying questions that help your child think about the possible limitations of their chosen partner than to issue a decree of immediate separation—easier said than done, though, I'm sure!

Selection Principle #2: Don't Make Major Decisions While on Cocaine

Of all the principles of attraction, perhaps the most important thing to remember is that when we're falling in love, it's like we just snorted crack cocaine, so it might be a good idea to hold off on making any life-changing decisions in this state of mind. When I give talks on how to make wise decisions about love relationships, the burning question that someone almost always asks is, "How long do I have to wait?" The phrasing of this question illustrates the fact that waiting can feel like working against the tide of biology and the romantic rush of falling in love and making it official. To this question, I respond that most of the things that are worth achieving in life require us to delay gratification and to prioritize restraint over indulgence in more primitive drives. Or, to put it another way, are you willing to wait for an endless supply of lovely marshmallows, or do you want to bite down, right now, on something that resembles a marshmallow but may well turn into a bag of pus once you've committed? I wonder if this explains why the Spanish word *esposas* means both "wives" and "handcuffs."

But, of course, pointing out that not rushing into a pre-mature commitment is very difficult when we're in love doesn't really address the question at hand—that is, how long is it until the cocaine-rush wears off and you can make a good decision? Some marital experts would argue that two years is a good amount of time to wait. If you are looking for a general rule of thumb, then two years is probably a good length of time for most people, but I don't personally favor any hard-and-fast rule about how long a courtship should be. I think it depends completely on the character of the people involved, how often they see each other, in what situation(s) they spend their time dating, and how intentional they are about discovering their degree of fit. In some cases, it may be wise to wait three or more years before making a decision, and in other cases, a couple may be able to make a wise decision in less than two years.

As I write this, I'm imagining that some readers may be thinking, *"Three years? Really? That seems like much too long!"* If you are thinking along these lines, the question to ask is, "When might it be wise to wait three years or longer?" To this, I would say, a lengthy courtship would be wise any time three years (or more) have passed but you still know relatively little about each other. For example, consider the case of a courtship that has played out during multiple successive military deployments. A military combat deployment is one of the most emotionally super-charged environments imaginable. Life and death may be at stake daily. The threat of loss of the other boosts attraction considerably for both partners. Lack of access to each other, paired with short-lived reunions during R & R weekends, fuels unrealistic fantasies of the true potential of the relationship. Real compatibility is hard to assess based on limited opportunities for interaction. The fantasy script of the stateside partner incorporates the potent thought, *"My partner is a hero,"* and all sorts of positive traits are then linked to this global perception. On the flip side, it's quite heady stuff to be told that you are the person a soldier holds in his or her heart amidst the chaos of war. Ultimately, this courtship context makes *The Bachelor*'s potent love-manipulating scenarios look like mere child's play, and as such, a much longer courtship may be necessary if you want to make a good decision.

Extending the courtship period in all cases will progressively minimize your relative risk of developing lasting regrets down the line. Getting married is described as a leap of faith for a reason, but when you wait a significant length of time before you "make it official," the leap is not nearly so great. In each audience that I've spoken to about marital decision-making, there is almost always someone who raises a hand and says, "My parents fell in love and got married a month later, and they've been completely happy together for the last 50 years." The core of this statement is an assertion that lifelong happy marriages are possible with very short courtships. I wouldn't disagree with this. My point is that it's a matter of relative risk. Sure, a handful of marriages might thrive after short courtships, but for every one of these examples, a *much* greater number end in divorce. So, if we were to honestly weigh the emotional, psychological, and financial costs of a bad decision, wouldn't wisdom in all cases suggest a relatively long courtship?

Instead of trying to fix a target courtship length that applies to all relationships, it makes more sense to me to gauge whether and when the relationship has transitioned from the cocaine-rush phase to the early stages of the testing phase. How would you know if this has happened? If the cocaine-rush phase is essentially about untested idealization of your partner, then during the testing phase, you would begin to notice some of the less-than-wonderful qualities in each other. Your sleep patterns would return to normal and you would start to see the rise of some conflicts in the relationship. Differences of opinion would start to surface once you both stop trying to demonstrate how similar and "made to be together" you are. All of these changes are normal, healthy, and vitally important in the process of assessing true relationship potential.

Along these lines, it feels important to mention a theme I'm seeing among young couples of faith, who often marry after a relatively short courtship (often while citing the biblical phrase "it's better to marry than to burn with lust"). As far as I can tell, the thinking is, "Since we share the same core beliefs, and we find each other very attractive, then everything else will work out according to the principle of the Great Love that commands our lives." Christian couples seem especially prone to assume multiple levels of compatibility based on mutual profession of the same belief system. For many eager couples, profession of the same belief system is treated as a kind of Hasbro Candy Land "gumdrop mountain pass" that allows the couple to skip several steps of a wise courtship process and to marry prematurely. Profession of the same belief system should not be viewed in this light. If holding similar beliefs were a true gumdrop pass, the rates of divorce would be lower for Christian couples than for non-Christian couples, and they are not. It's not necessarily the case that one or the other person is trying to misrepresent his or her beliefs intentionally but that during the cocaine-rush phase, we filter out evidence of what does not fit, and make a case for how we are destined to play opposite each other in the greatest love story of all time. We miss the things we ought to notice on other levels of fit. In fact, Christian couples are at greater risk of a variant of the soul mate fallacy, which in this case materializes as the cocaine-rush thought that the other person "must be 'the One' whom God designed just for them." This sets these couples up for a particularly devastating period of disillusionment once they are married. In some cases, this disillusionment results in a crisis of faith, a questioning of their entire belief system. So, instead of rushing into marriage, it seems especially wise for Christian couples to consider the biblical injunction to count the cost before making the leap into marriage.

Selection Principle #3: Value Yourself as Much as You Value Your Potential Mate

One of the things I've noticed in life is that people will usually treat you the way you expect to be treated. Another way to put this is that we signal through our behavior whether we treat ourselves with respect, and others will often cue off of these signals. While dating someone, we cue them in overt and subtle ways, setting a tone for how we expect them to relate to us and how we expect to relate to them. Based on this, we form a number of unspoken rules of engagement for our relationships. Valuing yourself throughout the dating phase of a relationship means making your commitment to the relationship contingent on evidence that the relationship is worth increased amounts of your time and energy. As I've mentioned previously, this is why it is so important to create an exciting life independent of your relationship status. Doing so places you in a position to evaluate the benefits and costs of deepening your commitment without feeling that you need the relationship in order to have a fulfilling life.

Holding your value high requires that you intentionally pace the development of a relationship in order to make smart decisions about its true potential. One of the most practical models I've come across for how to apply this concept is Dr. John Van Epp's Relationship Attachment Model (RAM).[65] Van Epp's RAM describes five adhesive dynamics that predictably create feelings of attachment in every relationship—knowledge, trust, reliance, commitment, and touch. *Knowledge* refers to how much you actually know the other person, *trust* refers to the extent to which you invest trust in the other person, *reliance* refers to how much you depend on them, *commitment* refers to the degree to which you commit yourself to them, and *touch* refers to the level of sexual involvement you engage in with them. Van Epp argues quite convincingly that imbalances in these bonding dynamics will lead to an unsafe over-attachment and distorted judgments. The ordering of these five elements (e.g. knowledge, trust, reliance, commitment, and touch) is important for Van Epp's central guideline for staying out of the "unsafe zone": "The degree or level of each bonding dynamic should never exceed the previous."

To apply this concept, let's look at a couple examples of how the RAM identifies unsafe over-attachments. In terms of these five elements, how would a one-night stand rate? Actual knowledge about the other person would be very low, trust may or may not be considered very high, reliance would be very low (and quite beside the point for a one-time fling), commitment would likewise be nonexistent, and sexual touch would be very high. If we were to graph this pattern of elements according to the RAM, it might look something like Figure 4.1.

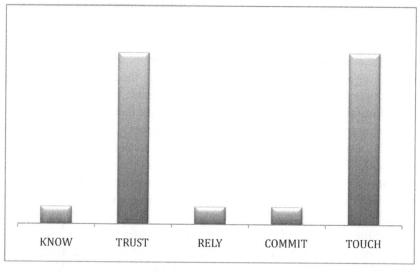

Figure 4.1. Relative RAM Elements for a "One-Night Stand"

When describing a one-night fling, I mentioned that trust may or may not be very high. My thinking is that if you were to fall in stride with someone doing the walk of shame and ask them whether they know anything about the person they just hooked up with, they would probably acknowledge that they don't know much about him or her (other than in the euphemistically biblical sense, of course). If we then asked the walk-of-shamer if they rely on or trust the other person, they would probably respond, "No, of course not, we just met last night." Such a response would indicate an instinctive understanding that you can't really say you trust someone unless you actually know them well. No matter how sexually liberated one deems oneself, I'd submit that none of us wants to roll over in the morning and have our lover say, "So, what was your name again?" Guarding your own safety means trusting someone only as much as you know them, which is an elegantly simple, but profoundly important, concept. In the case of the one-night stand, however, we might argue that the person's actual trust is very, very high insofar as they have just exposed themselves to the possibility of getting a sexually transmitted disease or conceiving a child with that person. They may have also exposed themselves to negative social consequences such as getting a reputation for having casual sex with strangers should their erstwhile lover view the hookup as ripe material for another conquest tale. So, in some ways, the one-night stand is a case of a very high level of trust placed in someone who is a complete unknown, for the temporary thrill of an anonymous sexual encounter. Now, take a look at Figure 4.2. Does this call to mind any scenario in particular?

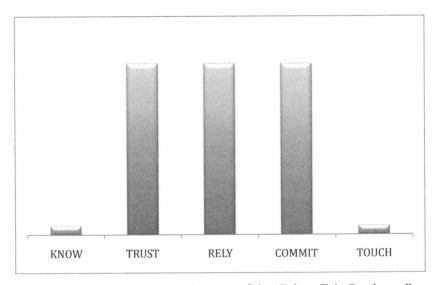

Figure 4.2. Relative RAM Elements of the "Prince Eric Syndrome"

I think of the scenario in Figure 4.2 as representing the "Prince Eric Syndrome." If you've seen the Disney movie *The Little Mermaid,* you may recall the scene depicting Ariel's experience of love at first sight. Already primed by unrealistic fantasies about how the other half lives, she pops up on the deck of a ship and sees the dashing Prince Eric cavorting with his salty dog. Shortly thereafter, Ariel rescues Eric from certain death by sea storm and gazes at him while he sleeps, entranced by his chiseled cheekbones. In the Disney book version of the story, the script reads, "Oh, he's so beautiful! At that moment, Ariel knew that she loved Eric."[66] Her eyes glaze over, and, on the basis of this solitary and completely one-sided encounter (Prince Eric might as well be a neurological vegetable for all she knows), she decides to give up her family, her kingdom, her voice, and her body so she can totally reshape herself into a woman she hopes he will find irresistible. This is a woman with an incredibly high level of trust, reliance, and commitment who has no real knowledge of who this man actually is! Really, all that she knows about him is that he is handsome and rich and has probably had it easy his whole life. Given these realities, if she were smart, she should see whether he can demonstrate, over time, that he is neither arrogant nor entitled and that he is willing to do his fair share of the more crappy chores in life.

Sadly, in real life, there are plenty of "Ariels" (both men and women) who commit themselves in radical ways to people they barely know. Real-life Ariels fly off to a faraway city to meet up with someone in person that they've just barely met over the internet. Real-life Ariels make cross-country moves to live with someone they've only ever known through internet correspondence. Real-life Ariels quit their jobs and eagerly present themselves as participants on shows like *The Bachelor.* I would hope that the emotional and physical safety issues in this approach are quite clear to you at this point. When you are willing to make this kind of commitment without any knowledge of the other person, what message do you think this sends about self-worth? What is being cued to the other person when one is willing to make a huge investment without any evidence that it is a wise one to make? John Van Epp's book *How to Avoid Falling in Love with a Jerk*[67] elaborates further on the RAM and the rule of safety; I highly recommend it as an additional resource.

A second aspect to holding your value high is to "listen eloquently"* to the other person's reasons for pursuing you. I once met a newly engaged

---

*With gratitude to my friend and colleague Dr. Regi Melchor-Beaupre, who shared this language.

couple during an airplane flight. When they learned that I was studying newlywed marriage, they spontaneously began to share their love story with me. Their courtship had been short, a six-month whirlwind sparked by stormy-eyed feelings of mutual attraction. I asked each of them what had led them to fall in love with the other person. The response I heard from the young man was very troubling. He said, "Because she's the hottest woman in the room in every room we go into…she's a lingerie model." To my amazement, this made his fiancée glow with happiness. Dark clouds were forming in my mind, and I thought about this conversation long after that brief interaction. In trying to put my finger on what was so unsettling about that statement, I realized that I can't think of any 60-year-old lingerie models. If marriage is to be forever, it cannot be based on something so shallow. What sounded like a compliment to his fiancée was, to my mind, an ominous statement about a relationship built on a foundation of shifting sand. At some point, this beautiful young woman certainly will *not* be the most beautiful woman in the room any longer, and the husband who married her for this reason will be drawn to whoever upstages her as she ages. Even if she were to continue being the hottest woman in the room, defying all odds and the realities of the aging process, a man so influenced by physical beauty will usually have a keen eye for novelty. On the flip side, trying to hold onto someone with your looks is a losing game if this is the central basis of your partner's attraction to you. As far as motivations go, this is a very shaky basis indeed for sustaining a life partnership, let alone a marriage of equals.

Selection Principle #4: Consider Information from Plenty of Sources

Before you make a significant commitment to any relationship, it is critical to view your leading man or woman in multiple lights. Long distance relationships and internet-mediated relationships are two types of courtships that are especially vulnerable to decision-making based on relatively little information over a potentially lengthy period of time. In a long distance relationship, when you visit your partner, you get to leave your normal life behind and can immerse yourself in their world, far from the stress and routine of your own life where you are typically assured of a warm, loving reception. As such, this type of relationship may be especially protected from the intrusion of mundane, stressful elements of day-to-day life. The *folie a deux* of mutual flawlessness thrives in such a context. With the distance and the lack of face time, it is relatively easy to maintain illusions of mutual perfection, thereby extending the time during which each of you project and perceive unrealistic fantasies. Because the limited time you spend together can feel so magical (remember, the scarcity principle intensifies your hunger to see each other), you may begin to feel certain that you have found "the One." It is important to bear this in mind, because people in love often overestimate the actual potential of a succession of steamy phone conversations and weekend dalliances to translate into a successful life partnership. Almost anyone can be accommodating, flexible, and attentive for a long weekend, but this says very little about how accommodating, flexible, and attentive that person will be when you see them every day, year after year.

I had previously mentioned that it would be unwise to relocate on the basis of an internet-only relationship. To be clear, I'm not saying that relationships that begin through an internet correspondence are a bad idea at all. A good number of my friends and acquaintances have met and married some high-quality partners with the help of online dating services. Some of these friends have eventually relocated to be near the person they met through the internet. Internet dating services have become main stream and are now a widely accepted forum for meeting potential partners. All things considered, you are probably more likely to meet a high-quality partner through a quality online dating service than in any singles bar scene. What I am saying is that in the case of internet-mediated relationships, as in the case of long distance relationships, proactive assessment of the other person's character is especially important. The potential for distorted perceptions and false impressions is highest when there is little to no accountability. How many people have internet profiles that read as follows?

> Plain-looking SWM of average intelligence, with boorish manners, a shrunken chest, chicken legs, and a large inheritance he did not earn seeks female that will look good as an accessory in his convertible candy-apple red Roadster.

> OR

> Sexy SWF who has no life plan, a lousy work ethic, and no earning potential seeks affluent, handsome male who will support her out-of-control shopping addiction.

Of course, these are exaggerations, but no less so than the positively biased exaggerations featured in many personal ads and online bios (in which parallel universe does this assemblage of all these "stunningly attractive, extremely successful" people exist?). Because of the tendency to over-exaggerate positive features and downplay negative aspects of the self in the world of online dating, it is especially important to separate fact from fiction, to slow down and consider information from multiple sources. You cannot do this if your entire relationship occurs over the computer. When you find yourself very emotional about something—perhaps very angry with someone—it is sometimes a good idea to write out what you want to say to them. Writing it out allows you to stop and think about how you want to present something, keeping Mojo safely at bay. Writing allows you to be strategic. In the same way, the internet allows people to be strategic in how they present themselves and how they respond to each other. When you are trying to assess the character of someone, there is no substitute for real-time information (that is, what they say in the heat of the moment, and, of even greater importance, what their body language communicates while they are saying it). So, without impulsively relocating your life to be with someone you meet online, it is important to find ways to spend a significant amount of time in the same place during the dating phase of your relationship.

The natural tendency in many long distance relationships is to enjoy each other in the seclusion of a love-nest setting when visiting each other. Recognize and resist this tendency. Seek information that helps you see the other person from different angles. For example, spend some time with the friends of this person and ask yourself whether you like his or her friends. Would these friends be people you would choose as friends yourself? Does he or she maintain a close friendship with anyone who is disrespectful and rude to other people? It's also helpful to clue in to how your love interest talks about exes and how he or she describes the breakup of past relationships. Ask them about their dating history and how their past relationships have ended. In some cases, you may need to find out whether their past relationships have actually ended! If, for example, someone says that all of their exes are "total psychos," what does this tell you about them? It may be a tipoff that they have untreated trauma. Alternatively, they may be projecting their own deficiencies onto their past partners. This kind of statement might signal an inability to take ownership for their part in past relationship problems and may predict that someday, they will regale their friends with stories of how you are the latest in a long line of "psychos" that they somehow keep picking.

It is also wise to evaluate how this person behaves under stress. Does he lash out at others in Mojo fashion, or can he generally control his aggressive impulses? Does she treat others with respect even when she doesn't see things the same way, or even when she doesn't have to be respectful? It is also a good idea to note how a potential partner behaves when he or she has messed up. Does she become defensive and immediately make a case for how whatever happened is actually someone else's fault? Does he accept a fair share of the blame, and does he take responsibility for making things right? Drs. Scott Cloud and John Townsend wrote a helpful little book titled *Safe People*.[68] They write that "safe" people admit their weaknesses, are humble, confront-able and are able to prove their trustworthiness over time.[69] Unsafe people have some clearly identifiable negative characteristics that are best avoided. To help you make accurate distinctions between "safe" and "unsafe" people, I've converted several distinguishing personality characteristics into a 10 question mini-quiz, as follows:

Mini Safety quiz*

1) Does this person admit to having some weaknesses?
    Yes   No

2) Is this person humble?
    Yes   No

3) Is this person defensive when you tell him or her that you have been hurt or offended?
    Yes   No

4) Does this person prove that he or she is trustworthy over time?
    Yes   No

5) Does this person apologize, but fail to change his or her behavior?
    Yes   No

6) Does this person admit it when he or she has problems?
    Yes   No

*Adapted from the qualities of "safe" and "unsafe" people as articulated by H. Cloud and J. Townsend in the book Safe People: How to Find Relationships that are Good For You and Avoid Those That Aren't. Grand Rapids, MI: Zondervan Press, 1995, p. 34.

7) Does this person confess when he or she wrongs someone else (e.g. own up to it?)
   Yes   No

8) Does this person treat others with a lack of empathy?
   Yes   No

9) Does this person take responsibility for his or her own life?
   Yes   No

10) Does this person blame other people for his or her problems?
    Yes   No

Answer Key:
1. Score 1 point for "No"
2. Score 1 point for "No"
3. Score 1 point for "Yes"
4. Score 1 point for "No"
5. Score 1 point for "Yes"
6. Score 1 point for "No"
7. Score 1 point for "No"
8. Score 1 point for "Yes"
9. Score 1 point for "No"
10. Score 1 point for "Yes"

(More than 2 points and you begin to wonder…more than 4 points and red flags should go up)

If you've ever been royally disappointed by a past relationship partner, would they have scored at least four points? Any behavior that signals a lack of safety or a pattern of being a jerk, as described by Cloud and Townsend or Van Epp, should give cause for serious reservations.

Another important thing to assess in the dating phase is how your partner treats you over time when you've spent a significant amount of time together. Almost everyone treats their partner with love and respect in the initial phase of a relationship. Over time, do they continue to listen with respect to your perspective and to demonstrate openness to influence? Or do they tune you out and show that they aren't really listening to you?

When you do point out a problem you have with their behavior, do they make statements like "Well, that's just the way I am," suggesting that they do not want to change? While we're on the subject, here is my roundup of the most common lines that unsafe people use after causing emotional devastation to others. Many of the following phrases appear regularly on any given season of *The Bachelor*. If you want to check this assertion, tune in to the episode toward the very end of the season called "The Women Tell All" and see what phrases the unhappy bachelor uses to defend himself:

> "I think the worst thing in the world is to live your life with regrets."
> "I admit that I'm not perfect, but I'm doing the best that I can."
> "All we really have in our lives is what we have today."
> "I want to live in the moment and enjoy life to its fullest."
> "If I could control my heart, I would."
> "I need to follow my heart—I know you can understand that."

Selection Principle #5: Assess the Other Person's Character Carefully

"Good character" involves a number of positive personality qualities. My intention is not to exhaustively review every possible way of angling in on what it means to have good character. Suffice it to say that there is good convergence between my view of good character, the concept of safe people described by Cloud and Townsend, and the concept of someone who is *not* a jerk according to Van Epp. In addition to referring you to Cloud and Townsend's *Safe People* and John Van Epp's *How to Avoid Falling in Love with a Jerk,* I want to call your attention to another excellent book—Albert Bernstein's *Emotional Vampires: Dealing with People Who Drain You Dry*.[70] With humor and clarity of mind, Bernstein describes the vampirical energy of people with various personality disorders. (For any *Twilight* movie fans in "Camp Edward," this is *not* a good thing in this case). A personality disorder is a clinically diagnosable condition with a very poor prognosis. Personality disorders are "ego syntonic," as opposed to "ego dystonic." That is, an individual with the personality disorder tends to feel, "*this is just the way I am*" and does not see his or her own behavior as problematic. In fact, from this person's perspective, if others were not such complete asses, there would be no problem at all. If one's goal as a therapist is to extend unconditional positive regard to patients, then as a therapist, you have to dig really deep when you are sitting across from someone with a personality disorder. The personality-disordered patient is often urged by others to seek treatment but does not stay in with treatment because he or she often lacks intrinsic motivation to make changes. He or she may be temporarily motivated by acute distress, but typically, when the distress subsides, it's back to business as usual. Bernstein puts each of the psychiatrically classified personality disorders on display with a great deal of wit and candor. For instance, in reference to individuals with narcissistic personality disorder, he says, "Just as sharks must continually swim to keep from drowning, narcissists must constantly demonstrate that they are special, or they will sink like stones to the depths of depression....Narcissistic vampires' greatest fear is of being ordinary."[71] Your ability to assess others' characters will be immeasurably improved by a close read of Bernstein's book.

In addition to referring you to these three key reference books, I want to highlight the seven personal qualities I feel are most important for achieving a marriage of equals: trustworthiness, dependability, emotional maturity, personal growth orientation, sense of fairness, openness to influence, and a healthy level of self-worth.

Trustworthiness

I previously mentioned that self-worth is a function of the alignment between what you say you value and what you actually do with your time, energy, and physical resources. In a parallel way, trust in a relationship is a function of the alignment between what a person says he or she will do and what he or she actually does. Trust builds when a person shows that he or she is safe. My current job involves helping U.S. military veterans repair their marriages after the psychological ravages of a combat deployment. The process of building trust with veterans and their spouses must be attended to as first priority, or treatment will never work. I explain to veteran patients that I imagine that their trust may have been shaken or completely destroyed and that I am not seeking their blind trust as we begin treatment. I let them know that building trust occurs over time when a person is able to see that someone is worthy of trust. I suggest that perhaps they might be able to take a very small risk in telling me something they feel fairly comfortable sharing to see how I handle it. Over time, as they progressively disclose the nature of their experiences to me and I respond in safe and respectful ways, trust builds. Similarly, in a new relationship, trust forms as a function of how you handle each other's vulnerabilities. From the perspective of assessing a potential partner, you can take a similar strategy—take a small risk and see how your partner handles it, and then increase the level of risk over time. In this regard, Van Epp's RAM is a helpful model to consult in thinking about safe ways to develop trust and to assess another's trustworthiness.

Dependability

Dependability is closely related to trustworthiness. We live in a society of increasingly flaky people. Have you noticed that people nowadays do not like to be pinned down by specific plans and are often quick to change social plans when a more exciting invitation comes their way (or when they just don't feel like going out)? I recently read a compelling book entitled *Generation Me: Why Today's Young Americans Are More Confident, Assertive, Entitled—and More Miserable Than Ever Before*[72] by psychologist Jean Twenge. Twenge argues that the self-esteem movement of the 1970s has directly fostered a culture of self-centeredness. If the self-esteem movement prioritizes self-love and self-interest above all else, then it naturally follows that the stock of values like dependability would decline correspondingly. Twenge has assembled an impressive array of research to show that pro-social traits like dependability and respect for others have become less a priority in relation to self-actualization and fulfillment of personal dreams and desires. All this makes me wonder whether I'm out of sync with many of my contemporaries, who, Twenge argues, would view dependability as an outdated value aligned with an "old school" way of behaving. But it's hard for me to imagine forming a successful life partnership with someone who isn't dependable (or to imagine that one would be an attractive partner without also being a dependable partner). It's a trait that I actively screen for in forming friendships, and it says something to me when a potential friend is always late to meet me or shows a pattern of changing plans at the last minute. To me, this communicates that the other person doesn't respect my time or my feelings nearly as much as his or her own. In the context of close relationships (or even working relationships with colleagues), dependability communicates respect. Dependability builds trust and a sense of safety. Dependability allows you to rely on others and lets others know that they can rely on you. What storms lie ahead during the transition to parenting for those who have not developed a pattern of being dependable? So, even if I am behind the times, from my perspective, dependability is a vitally important quality to bring to a marriage.

Emotional Maturity

Author Howard Halpern, who wrote *How to Break Your Addiction to a Person*,[73] criticizes the concept of the strong, silent type, asserting that "one of the most common forms of malignant idealization...is misconstruing the other person's inability to be loving, giving, and supportive as evidence of his strength, rather than as a crippling weakness."[74] Another important dimension of character to assess has been labeled with various related terms like emotional intelligence, emotional maturity, or theory of mind development. Emotional intelligence (sometimes called EQ) refers to an individual's ability to understand his or her own, and others', goals, intentions, responses, feelings, and behaviors. Daniel Goleman, author of the book *Emotional Intelligence*,[75] defined five domains of EQ, which are knowing your emotions, managing your emotions, motivating yourself, recognizing and understanding other people's emotions, and managing relationships (i.e., managing the emotions of others). EQ is related to emotional maturity, which some people have at an early age, some develop at a later age, and some fail to develop, ever. In the field of psychology, "theory of mind," has been described as "one of the quintessential abilities that makes us human."[76] Theory of mind refers to "a person's ability to understand the thoughts, intentions, beliefs, and feelings of others (and themselves)... [which is] a consequence of the mind's ability to reflect on itself."[77] The key here is a person's capacity for self-reflection, empathy, and insight. In light of my commentary on dependability, I would guess that people with high levels of emotional intelligence are more likely to be dependable as well. How do you assess EQ or theory of mind? There is no substitute for a large number of conversations about how each of you thinks and feels about various topics. To return to an earlier concept, if you think about marriage as a really long conversation, you should ask yourself during the dating phase if this is the person with whom you would want to have the conversation of a lifetime. See if you can correctly perceive and demonstrate that you understand each other's points of view, especially when you disagree. Your ability to see each other's points of view and to empathize with each other's emotions will lubricate your future conflict discussions.

Personal Growth Orientation

A well-developed EQ (or a healthy theory of mind ability) is usually paired with a personal growth orientation. Personal growth orientation is what allows two people in a marriage to become perfect for each other over time (given that there is no such thing as a soul mate). Personal growth orientation is also the quality that allows people to create lemonade when their early lives have left them with a basket of lemons. When you are assessing a potential partner by exploring their early background, do this with an open mind. Some of the best people I've known have grown up in terrible family situations. Traumas shape people in powerful ways. Take, for example, someone who was raised by an alcoholic parent. Research tells us that people who were raised by an alcoholic parent are more likely to become alcoholic themselves. So, at first blush, we might consider alcoholism in the family of origin to be a huge red flag. What is also true, however, is that people who grew up in an alcoholic environment are also more likely to become teetotalers (people who don't touch the stuff on principle).

Related to marriage, take the example of someone who has divorced or separated parents. Statistical figures might suggest that this person is more likely to end up divorced. If this person has insight and a personal growth orientation, however, he or she may become capable of creating a truly beautiful union if he or she is determined to forge a new path. As a general rule, trauma often pushes people to the extreme ends of the behavioral spectrum. Those who lack the capacity for insight and the motivation to change the pattern in place often blindly play out the same script. Others reflect on their family of origin experiences and tell themselves, *"There is no way on earth I'm going to do my family the way family was done to me!"* With this character-defining stance in place, these individuals actively work to become much better partners and parents to their children, despite having had very poor models when they were young. This goes for all kinds of human behaviors and predicts all kinds of decision-making in the areas of life planning, mate selection, and parenting style. The key here is to make sure that the person you are dating has insight into the destructive patterns in his or her past and can articulate a clear vision for how to do things differently going forward.

Sense of Fairness

Assess your partner's sense of fairness before you get married. Full stop. Does your partner have a sense of justice, and is he or she moved to correct injustices that are in his or her control? Does your partner consider men and women equal? If so, how does this value show up in how your partner treats the opposite sex? Does your partner have a good work ethic, and does he or she make efforts to do a fair share of the chores and the most boring tasks you have to manage together while dating? Speaking specifically to any female readers, if your partner does not place a high value on fairness, and does not have a belief in true gender equality, you are much more likely to end up cleaning all the toilets in the house for the rest of your life. If I could make two additions to Albert Bernstein's vampirical canon, I would add "GLUMS" and "princesses." GLUM stands for a "good looking, under-functioning male." In the world of a GLUM, all that ought to be required of him is to radiate his obvious studliness. Charming and smooth, with beguiling looks, the GLUM is least likely to be found in any place where chores are actively being completed. When it's time to do the dishes, he backs out of the kitchen with a boyish smile while saying, "I know better than to get between a woman and her kitchen!" GLUMS look to the women in their lives to do not only the chores but also the mental work of managing the family's needs. The result for their wives is that the GLUMs begin to feel like additional children to manage and tend, which is a far cry from participating in a marriage of equals.

The female counterpart of a GLUM is a princess. From the perspective of a princess, all that ought to be required of her is that she continues to look fabulous. A princess doesn't mind being patted on the head by someone from time to time as long as that someone continues to pay her shopping bills. A princess doesn't hold down an unrewarding job or contribute substantially to the work of running a household. She's likely to recruit maids, cooks, and nannies to do the heavy lifting. Marry a princess at your own peril. Less an adult than an overgrown child, she is a play-at-home wife who spends all day frolicking in the garden with her golden ball (or getting her hair done, chatting with friends at Starbucks, and doing the downward dog before the admiring eyes of the creepy guy in the back row of her yoga class) while your own butt gets bigger from all the hours you log in the office, supporting her self-indulgent lifestyle. And do be careful, men, because a certain portion of the female population is using books like *The Rules* as a dating guide, and these women have been pointedly instructed to "act independent so he doesn't feel like you are expecting him to take care of you."[78] It's always a shame to see a good man get duped by a princess.

Openness to Influence

In my opinion, one of the most important character traits to assess is openness to positive influence. Openness to positive influence is highly associated with the value of respecting others. Openness to positive influence goes hand in hand with a personal growth orientation and the emotional flexibility that allows us to create wonderful, mutually satisfying marriages. Openness to influence is the antidote to the "seeds of dissolution" referenced by May Sarton's discontented wife, who asked whether people can be expected to keep growing at the same rate.[79] Furthermore, while it is true that the best predictor of a person's future behavior is their past behavior, openness to influence can change the equation significantly. I was once approached after a talk by a young woman who was deeply troubled by the notion that the best predictor of future behavior is a person's past behavior. She explained, "I'm really concerned about that idea. My boyfriend has slept with a number of women in the past, before we met. I told him that I want to wait till marriage, and he respects this. We've been dating a little over two years, and he hasn't pressured me, but this is his past behavior. Should I be concerned about his past sex life?" I couldn't really give any informed counsel based on such limited information, but I was happy to point out that in this case, her boyfriend's past behavior also included a proven ability to change his previous pattern and to demonstrate sexual restraint so that their relationship could develop in a way that felt safe to her.

People can and do change, and the dating period is the time to assess their ability to make and sustain positive changes. To assess your partner's openness to influence, when you are starting to discuss the possibility of marriage, a key question to ask your partner is "Would you be willing to go through premarital counseling with me?" You could arrange to do this with a professional counselor, or perhaps with a minister in your church, or even informally with a successfully married older couple who can then mentor you through the tough patches in the future. Your partner's answer to this question communicates information you would be wise to note. If a person is willing to engage in a course of some form of premarital counseling and actively participates in the process that follows, this would demonstrate openness to influence and a personal growth orientation. If the answer is "I don't think we really need to" or "I'd rather not talk to a stranger about our problems," this may not bode well for the future you may have together.

Healthy Level of Self-Worth

All of these good character qualities promote healthy self-worth, which is the final key element to assess, in my opinion. As I have mentioned previously, strong self-worth gives us room to give and receive feedback about the impact of our behaviors on others. With the anchoring of good self-worth, based on a life of living into your deepest values, you are much more likely to hear negative feedback at the level of s, and not G. In addition, someone who *"wants"* you but doesn't necessarily *"need"* you is also more likely to give you honest information about how you can become a better partner.

Selection Principle #6:
Be Intentional in Getting to Know a Potential Partner

As I stated earlier, I don't favor any hard and fast rule about how long a courtship should be. Critical thinking requires a more sophisticated analysis of the multiple factors in any equation. In addition to the character of each partner, one of the key factors in marriage readiness is how intentional you are about discovering your actual degree of fit. Because they are so dependent on verbal and written communication, long distance relationships can prompt us to become more verbally assertive rather than falling into mind-reading expectations that often surface when two people are with each other all the time. Long distance relationships also offer a unique opportunity to learn about our relationships in the zoomed-out, meta-analytic way I described in Chapter 3. Perhaps we might think of being in a long distance relationship as akin to losing one or two of our senses—maybe our sense of sight and touch. In response, we might hone our other senses, sharpening them in a compensatory manner. That is, long distance relationships may maximize opportunities to become eloquent listeners.

The relationship of one long distance couple I worked with illustrates intentionality in the dating phase. The couple had to separate geographically because of a job opportunity for one partner. They were still very much in love and wanted to keep their relationship going strong, despite the distance. They enlisted my help with this purpose in mind. As we thought about the unique properties of the long distance relationship, it soon became clear that they might be able to not only maintain, but also to strengthen, their relationship by focusing attention on how they communicate with each other and where they get off track. With the permission of both partners, the one who had stayed in place brought to sessions transcripts of particularly tense or conflict-filled instant message chats between the two of them, and we phone-conferenced with the other. This source of information was a wonderful, and productive, addition to the sessions we had already had.

In regular therapy sessions, it is typical for one partner to raise a problem and explain how they behaved in some problematic interaction. Efforts to discover exactly what each partner said and how they said it are obscured by each partner's tendency to cast him- or herself in the best possible light while making compelling arguments for each other's unreasonable attitude or lack of emotional sensitivity. So, what I usually hear are distorted portrayals of what actually happened. We can simulate a tense conversation in sessions, and this is often productive, but a therapist's presence in the room changes the couple's behavior somewhat—people somehow show themselves more capable of emotional sensitivity in the presence of a counselor than they do at home (hence the commonly uttered statement, "Yeah, OK, we made some progress on this issue today, but this is NOT how he/she talks to me at home!"). The key factor appears to be the presence of a third person in the room. When couples are filmed during conflict interactions, they seem to quickly forget about the camera in the heat of their conflict. It's an "out of sight, out of mind" phenomenon. In the case of this long distance couple, the transcripts of their communications proved to be a precise record of how they speak to each other when I'm not present, a kind of freeze-frame sequence of how they had pressed each other's buttons and what types of implicit rules each had violated that had hurt the other person. Given that I had worked with this couple and had developed a good understanding of their particular sensitivities and hotspots, it was possible for me to then pinpoint specific places in their interaction where they had become derailed. Focusing on these problematic points led to some really productive conversations about themes in how they communicate with each other when each feels threatened.

This experience suggests some interesting potentials for the creation of a healthy, lasting marriage. I've often thought that in my role as a counselor, if I could get this kind of information from more couples, it would be an incredible source of insight. If you are working to create a sustainable marriage, you might consider tapping this source of insight for yourselves. That is, even if you are not in a long distance relationship, you might intentionally begin to communicate about some of your most difficult topics in a manner that allows you to store an accurate record of exactly what you said (not what you wish you had said if you were as loving and responsive as you would like to believe you had been). In fact, some researchers at the University of Washington have built illustrious careers from using the method of taped replays to study how couples interact during conflict.[80] In Dr. John Gottman's Love Lab, couples are hooked up to electrodes that measure tiny signs of stress and are asked to sit in chairs that register the shifting of their posteriors during uncomfortable moments. Each couple is asked to have a discussion about one of their most heated, unresolved conflicts, and their interactions are recorded. The couple is then prompted to review the tape of their conflict discussion and to identify emotional shifts and the thoughts that accompanied those shifts. This methodology has proven very fruitful in understanding the anatomy of healthy and unhealthy conflict discussions. Gottman's book, *Why Marriages Succeed or Fail*, listed in the appendix, is recommended for further reading on this topic.

Given that this method is so fruitful, why not tap into a very inexpensive version (that is, transcripts of your instant messaging, or a home video of how you argue) to become a better student of your own relationship? What would you have to lose, really? If the camera's presence does dampen some of the usual animosity, would it be so bad to exercise your self-restraint muscle? If you can store your texts to each other in some secure way, or jointly agree to privately maintain some record of your instant-messaging communications, you can sit down and review them later with an eye to what was said and how you perceived it. You could highlight areas in your communication that were associated with strong feelings. You could then identify the feeling that you had/are having and make a clear association with what was said (e.g., "When you told me that you didn't see what the big deal was, I felt crushed and put down because it is a big deal to me, and I'd like you to understand that I feel strongly about this issue"). There is also great potential to look at attack/counter-attack strategies in the escalation of conflict situations. For instance, take the common argument that most often boils down to the following exchange:

> Partner A: "And then my boss told me that flex time isn't going to happen for me even though everyone else in the office has some flex-time arrangement set up!"

Partner B: "What you need to do in this situation is [insert sage advice]."

Partner A: "I don't need you to tell me what to do. I just need you to listen!"

If these partners were reviewing this script, Partner A might identify his or her feeling state as something like feeling disrespected or belittled. In identifying this feeling, this couple would possess the answer to the age-old mystery of why this conversational pattern is such a common source of conflict in relationships. Partner A's first statement is actually code for "My boss is such an ass—can you believe he said that to me?!" In this scenario, Partner B is only trying to be helpful, of course, but by responding to Partner A's statement in an advisory capacity, Partner B is unintentionally sending the message to Partner A that he or she doesn't trust Partner A to come up with a good solution on his or her own (and this makes Partner A feel disrespected, belittled, and the like).

On the more positive side of things, by reviewing records of conversations, you could also identify instances in which one of you successfully de-escalated the conflict to a productive level. Specifically, you could identify behaviors that protect the relationship at the level of G (global perceptions), such as providing reassurance of love, affirming each other's good character, or using humor to shift gears. You'd probably gain a wealth of understanding about your own hotspots, your partner's hotspots, and how you move strategically (and often less than kindly) when each of you are feeling threatened. Engaging in this kind of exercise would be a powerful way to begin to think like a counselor—to look at not only what is said but how it is said, and how it triggers old traumas and mimics age-old conflict scripts in families of origin. Armed with this knowledge, you can gain insight into how to protect your partner in the midst of a conflict and ultimately how to keep the foundations of your relationship safe without avoiding things that you need to confront together.

Selection Principle #7: Assess Your Ability to Tackle Challenges Together

At this point, I imagine that you may be thinking, *"It will be impossible to find someone who meets all these criteria! Such a man or woman does not exist!"* If you are thinking this, I would want you to know that such people do in fact exist, and you don't need a whole harem of them—you only need to find one really good one (who didn't get blindsided by a GLUM or duped by a princess). I would also add, though, that we're all flawed and the most important thing, if you have to boil it all down, is to identify someone with good character who is also open to influence. Because this is a chapter about the multiple levels of assessment of a relationship's potential, however, I'd be remiss in failing to include some commentary on some of the more critical relational qualities.

I previously suggested that you evaluate whether a potential partner is fundamentally trustworthy. In addition to your partner's trustworthiness, there is the bigger question of whether you can trust yourselves as a couple to weather the storms that will come. Theorists and researchers refer to this as relationship self-efficacy. In other words, do you, as a couple, feel confident that you can work through conflict productively? This may seem obvious, but it's a very important point: *You can't know the answer to this question without having had some conflict.* A major reason to wait out the cocaine-rush phase of the relationship is to date each other long enough so you weather a few storms before you take the final plunge together. The transition between the cocaine-rush phase and the testing phase is reliably paired with the emergence of waves of conflict as each person begins to perceive areas of incompatibility. Often, people marry on the crest of a shimmering wave of ecstasy after a short dating period. A few months into the marriage, these are the people most likely to report feeling dragged under and nearly drowned by the waves of conflict that follow. This is a lonely and terrifying place to land. Like suffering castaways, such newlyweds face a mounting sense of panic as they begin to wonder, "What have I done?!" and "How will this affect the rest of my life?!" In fact, given the tendency for many couples to marry during the cocaine-rush phase of their relationship, perhaps the more impressive figure is not that 50% of marriages end in divorce, but that, remarkably, half of marriages survive!

Pamela Paul, author of the well-researched book *The Starter Marriage and the Future of Matrimony*, suggests that "a typical marriage follows a certain course. The first year is the hardest, as the saying goes."[81] I haven't studied this in any formal way, but in my role as a marital counselor, I often hear that the first two years of marriage are experienced in one of two extreme ways. That is, some couples experience consistent moments of sublime bonding that lead others to observe that they have "that newlywed glow," while other couples acknowledge that the first two years were "a rough transition." Of course, in the latter case, the couple is at a double disadvantage because the reality of their situation is out of line with both their own expectations and societal expectations of how newlyweds should feel about each other.

For this reason, I strongly recommend that you proactively set off some hidden land mines before you consider marriage. If you set off some land mines up front, you will benefit from some of the protection that comes from the tendency to idealize each other in the first stage of love. Motivation to overcome barriers and find common ground will also be at peak levels before you are legally bound to each other. Even so, it may be wise to do this with the help of a skilled psychologist. A trained professional can listen eloquently to your formative stories and can help you identify probable areas of future conflict. A competent counselor will create a safe space for discussing areas of incompatibility, will help you define respectful rules of engagement, and will identify destructive behaviors that need to be eliminated from your interactions. If you engage in such an endeavor, with the help of a counselor or on your own, you will each gain a rich source of information about the process of how you fight and whether you can learn to have conflict without weakening your bond. Only in the context of conflict will you be able to see whether each of you can do things like...

- Zooming in and out between discussion of specific behaviors (s) and the global (G) level of perception

- Bending before the bullets, slowing time, and de-escalating your own emotions

- Helping de-escalate your partner's hot emotions

- Understanding each other's perspective even when you don't agree

- Protecting each other on the global level (G) while fighting about specific problems (s)

- Strengthening your bond through the process of post-conflict insight and repair

How you work through problems is in many cases even more important than the actual issue(s) you resolve. Successful couples show core respect, recognize the validity of each other's thoughts and feelings,[82] and make generous attributions for each other's behavior.[83] So, specifically, ask yourself, on the far side of a conflict, do you both feel heard and respected? Does each of you feel like you had influence on the other person and on the decided outcome? Being mindful of how the process of conflict feels is critical to assessing the true potential of a developing love relationship.

Compatibility of personality, beliefs, core values, and goals also shows up with greater clarity during conflict. When you are beginning to form a strong attachment to someone, don't avoid asking the hard questions up front. This is not an exhaustive list, but here are some hard questions to get these types of conversations moving (of course, don't ask these questions until you are both seriously considering a long-term commitment):

- When you are in a committed relationship, how you deal with your attractions to other people?

- Have you ever been unfaithful in the past? If so, what do you think led you to be unfaithful at that time?

- How were chores split up between your parents when you were growing up? How would we do chores? How would we split up roles if we were to get married in the future?

- Do you believe that women are just naturally better at some things and men should do other things? If so, in what areas do you believe this is true?

- What is your credit score and how much debt do you have (if any)? What is your plan for paying down this debt?

- How do you feel about having children? How might this expand or limit the experience of a life without children? What do you imagine are the biggest challenges in the phase right after having a child?

- What is one model of good parenting that you've seen, and what role would you see yourself playing as a parent? How would you like to be involved on a consistent basis in childcare?

- What's your philosophy on bachelor/bachelorette parties, and what kind of pre-wedding party would you like to have?

I risk being labeled prudish on this one, but I feel pulled to say more about this last question. I'm not speaking from any personal pain on this issue but from the distress of many a newlywed I've counseled who gets wind of his or her partner's "totally wild" last night of freedom. In my (rather strong) opinion, there could not be any wedding-related tradition more stupid than a bachelor or bachelorette night filled with strippers. Where in the world did we get this tradition, and how has it persisted for so long? If your goal is to kick off your marriage in a veil of secrecy and suspicion, a night of carnal pleasure with strangers would be a wonderful way to achieve it. If your goal is to undermine your partner's sense that you only have eyes for him or her when he or she most wants to bond with you, then a trip to a few strip clubs ought to do the trick nicely. If you'd like your future spouse to see that after all that practice in high school, you still haven't figured out how to stand up to peer pressure, then by all means, get wrangled into going to a strip club, and deflect your partner's pain by blaming it on one of your friends ("My best man sprung that lap dancer on me unexpectedly, and she was grinding on me before I even realized what was happening"). (Really?!) If you want to send your beloved a message that you are entering the marriage with mixed feelings and a sense of loss, then by all means, you should participate in a custom that suggests you need to have one last go at sexual intimacy with a stranger because you'll be deprived of such opportunities in the future. What a beautiful way to herald the sacred vows between yourself and the self-professed love of your life!

I know that some people are more philosophical than I am about this whole stripper thing, so I'll even take that into account. Overlooking the possibility that you could be one of the rare people who is not at all bothered by the thought of some random human pressing his or her naked sexual parts against your future spouse, one question you still may want to ask is "If I told you that I have a problem with strippers at your bachelor or bachelorette party, how would you respond?" This very telling question is code for "Will you hear me and understand my concerns even if you don't feel the same way? Do you understand that, within reason, when one of us has a problem, it's a problem we both need to address? Can I depend on you to stand up for us even if you get ragged on by some of your friends sometimes? Can I depend on you to protect what we have and to treat me with respect whether I'm in the room or 3,000 miles away? Am I, and are we, now your top priority? Are you open to influence when I tell you about something that causes me pain?"

In addition to having some hard conversations up front, it is also helpful to simulate some elements of how you might do life together. For example, see if you can be two-marshmallow people together by jointly saving up enough money to do something really special. Or decide to do something really challenging together and see how you handle it as a team. When my husband and I were dating, I don't think we consciously thought, *Let's challenge ourselves in order to test our relationship's potential,* yet that is exactly what we did. When we began to talk about getting serious, we decided to apply for a grant to help lead a community service initiative in Chile, South America. We co-wrote the grant application and funded our travels with the money we were jointly awarded. With a team of eight people, we travelled to Pachica, Chile, to live within a community of Aymaran Indians in the Atacama Desert, where it has never rained. We lived in fairly primitive conditions, bathing in a freezing aqueduct and coping with ongoing (and very unsexy) gastro-intestinal issues. We integrated into the life of the Kusayapan community for a time and shared in their festivals of celebration. We formed bonds with our team members. We shimmied along a shale-stone cliff and saw the remains of someone who had fallen there previously. We waited for help on a dark highway in the middle of nowhere when we punctured a tire. We shoveled loads of rocks and sand, poured and mixed concrete, and helped build the foundation for a laundry facility for the Kusayapans. We also built the foundation of our future marriage. This experience has often led me to wonder whether a two-month rustic adventure like this would tell people more about their compatibility than two years of dating would. Whether you take our approach to assessing potential or not, please consider the fact that you cannot tell where future cracks will appear unless your relationship is significantly stressed. Instead of avoiding conflict and discomfort, consider accelerating directly into it. It is good to be stressed together during the dating phase of your relationship so you can see how you would handle it, how you would negotiate and work through things together. Remember, we strengthen our muscles by first ripping them.

Chapter 5

Profile of a More Perfect Union

Emerson Eggerichs, best-selling author of *Love and Respect*,[84] asserts: "Women need love. Men need respect. It's as simple and as complicated as that."[85] The foundation for his platinum-level former book-of-the-year is a theorized gender difference he identified by posing this question:

> If you were forced to choose one of the following, which would you prefer to endure…to be left alone and unloved in the world, or to feel inadequate and disrespected by everyone?

In his original sample of 400 males, 74% said that if they were forced to choose, they would prefer feeling alone and unloved rather than feeling disrespected and inadequate.[86] He collected data on a female sample and found that a comparable majority would rather feel disrespected and inadequate than alone and unloved. Based on this data, Eggerichs concluded that a wife "needs love just as she needs air to breathe" and a husband "needs respect just as he needs air to breathe."[87]

As early as page 1 of his book, Eggerichs begins to shape the argument that wives' failure to show respect to their husbands is the reason that many marriages end in divorce. As he explains, "What we have missed is the husband's need for respect. This book is about how the wife can fulfill her need to be loved by giving her husband what he needs—respect."[88] A few pages later, he asserts, "Husbands are made to be respected, want respect, and expect respect. Many wives fail to deliver. The result is that five out of ten marriages land in divorce court."[89] Next, he takes the reader through a series of challenges in his own marriage to illustrate how his wife has missed opportunities to "respect" him, and how he has missed opportunities to show "love" to her. As I read these examples, I was confused by how he ended up labeling his own behaviors as "unloving" instead of "disrespectful." For instance, he says that it is unloving (as opposed to disrespectful) when he neglects certain duties, leaves wet towels where they don't belong, leaves loaves of bread on the counter, leaves the cupboard doors open, and leaves books stacked on the living room floor. It seems to me that this set of behaviors is not so much about lack of love as it is about disrespect. If your assumption is that you can leave a messy trail all over the house, doesn't this suggest that you view your wife as something like a personal maid who should clean up after you? To be fair, I do not think that many men who are inclined to leave trails are *intentionally* setting out to disrespect their wives; it's more likely a large blind spot when a good-willed husband doesn't realize that the likely outcome in this case is that his wife will feel disrespected if he continues to imitate the behavior of a small child rather than that of a fully capable adult who picks up after himself. A few pages later, I once again wondered how Eggerichs can say that it is unloving (as opposed to disrespectful) when he makes his wife feel as if he doesn't value her input.[90]

At times, I thought that Eggerichs might begin to see how disrespect is at the core of many marital problems for wives as well as for husbands. For example, he says that a wife "yearns to be honored, valued and prized as a precious equal"[91] and that wives "fear being a doormat,"[92] and informs his male readers that a wife will feel "esteemed" when "you are proud of her and all that she does" and when "you value her opinion in the grey areas as not wrong but just different and valid."[93] Why not just substitute the word "esteemed" with the word "respected?" Other elements of his message range from the condescending, to the benevolently sexist, to the blatantly sexist. In the condescending category are comments like "that a husband values respect more than love is very difficult for many women to grasp. God has made you to love, and you see life through pink lenses that are focused on love"[94] and "the problem with many women today…is that they want to be treated like a princess, but deep down they resist treating their husbands like the king."[95]

In the category of "benevolent sexism," he says that "it is the male's responsibility to place himself over the female and protect her."[96] This particular assertion brings to mind a recurring dream I had many, many times as a teenager, a variant of the classic romantic rescue scenario pictured in so many movies. In the dream, I am walking in the woods with whomever I am dating at the time and we are attacked by a bloodthirsty mountain lion. Instead of my boyfriend standing in front of me, or depositing me on a tree limb out of reach, we defend ourselves, together, against our fearsome foe.

In the dream, I once pictured my boyfriend at the time insisting that I should not join the fight because he was there to protect me. Rather than finding this romantic, I distinctly remember feeling that he did not understand who I really was. I am not a princess type but instead am the type of human who likes to be in the fray and who was created to fight alongside my partner rather than to seek a protected position. From early childhood to the present time, the desire to develop myself to the fullness of my potential, even if this requires me to fight for what I want out of life, is core to who I am. I have always wanted to find an equal partner and to adventure through life alongside (not protected behind) my husband. Assembling the data of several hundred accomplished women who also wish to be married to an equal confirms that I am not so odd among women, but am a kindred spirit to those humans—whether male or female—who are front-line fighters.

Beyond mere benevolent sexism, the blatantly sexist elements of *Love and Respect* include the assertion that men should be in authority over women because "man was not created for woman's sake, but woman for the man's sake."[97] To my ear, this is like saying that the one who was first endowed with the physical resources of a kingdom should be in authority over the other—or, to put it another way, as many a dominant culture has maintained, "because we arrived first and consolidated our power, everyone else should answer to us." Ultimately, Eggerichs argues that it is impossible to have a successful marriage of equals. In his view, "no smoothly running organization can have two heads. To set up a marriage of equals at the head is to set it up for failure. That is one of the big reasons that people are divorcing right and left today."[98] The *highly* successful marriages of several hundred equality-seeking women (described later in this chapter) in the Lifestyle Poll sample demonstrate how utterly off-base Eggerichs is in making this assertion.

Despite these issues, I don't want to throw the best-seller out with the bath water. Even though I have roundly criticized the sexist underpinnings of the book (as I see it anyway), I also feel that Eggerichs states some profound truths with great clarity. For instance, he points out that in our culture, there is a notion that it is desirable to love others unconditionally: we attempt to love our children, our spouses, and our most interpersonally challenging family members unconditionally. Eggerichs then points out that there is no parallel notion that we ought to work toward treating our loved ones with unconditional respect. He argues very persuasively that respect is a core, and absolutely necessary, element of a good marriage (albeit more for males than for females, in his view) and provides a number of compelling illustrations to show how a shift toward unconditional respect can give new life to a marriage. I agree wholeheartedly with many aspects of his message. Below, I briefly quote some areas of agreement, with some adjustments for gendered language:

1. There is no justification for a ~~husband~~ partner to say, "I will love my ~~wife~~ partner *after* (he or) she respects me" nor for a ~~wife~~ partner to say, "I will respect my ~~husband~~ partner *after* he (or she) loves me."[99]

2. Thankfully, some ~~women~~ partners are becoming aware that negative confrontation doesn't work.[100]

3. A ~~wife's~~ partner's softened tone and facial expressions can do more for (his or) her marriage than (he or) she can imagine.[101]

4. The typical ~~wife~~ partner would be up in arms if (he or) she heard, "I respect you but I don't love you."[102]

5. You cannot motivate your partner to give you what you need by withholding what (he or) she really needs.[103]

In addition, when Eggerichs talks about something he calls "the crazy cycle," he is referring to the idea that without love from her husband, a wife reacts without respect, and that without respect from his wife, a husband reacts without love. Instead of this formulation, I would suggest that the crazy-making pattern is that when one partner fails to meet the other partner's deepest needs for both love *and* respect, the second partner will react defensively and fail to meet the first partner's deepest needs for both love and respect in return.

Despite significant areas of agreement, the irritating reaction I had to Eggerichs' book was the seed that started me thinking about the book you are now reading. I took this grain of sand under my shell on a walk with my husband, who is also in the field of psychology. As we were walking, I wondered aloud what would happen if I were to assemble a set of thought-provoking questions and pose these questions to an intelligent and interesting group of women. In addition to my intrinsic interest in women's issues, when I was conceptualizing the Lifestyle Poll project, I thought about the "tradition of remarkable women" at Harvard-Radcliffe and the many amazing women I have met in my life after Harvard. To test my theory that respect is equally critical for many women as for many men, I set out to profile the marriages of some of the smartest women I have known and their equally capable friends. Based on my strong interest in personal growth and my belief in the value of self-examination, I designed the Lifestyle Poll to operate simultaneously as a data collection tool and as a stimulus for the personal growth of my research participants. I assembled more than 200 questions and recruited participants primarily through unofficial networks of Harvard graduates. Word of the project spread organically, mostly through word of mouth and invitations between friends. My goal was to see if I could get 500 respondents within one year. In fewer than eight months, more than 1200 women had completed the poll.

This is the data that I am now drawing from to provide insight into the inner workings of a marriage of equals. In selecting questions for the Lifestyle Poll, I made sure to include the "love and respect" question raised by Eggerichs; I tracked these results with particular interest. The first phase of data collection was based heavily on a Harvard college graduate sample. In this group of 300 women, 75% reported that they would rather feel alone and unloved than disrespected and inadequate. In other words, within this group of highly educated, accomplished women, <u>the tendency to favor respect over love *was equivalent in degree* to the preference expressed among males that was used to launch a best-selling book predicated on what now seems to be an inaccurate assumption of a consistent gender difference</u>. Because word of the Lifestyle Poll project spread through informal social networks, the overall composition of the sample remained highly educated and very accomplished, but as time passed, the sample became less homogeneously Harvardian. Even in this somewhat more diversified sample[*] of more than 1200 women, however, a definite majority (65%) reported that they would rather feel alone and unloved than disrespected and inadequate. Of course, I'm not saying that *all* women would prefer to feel alone and unloved any more than I'm saying that all women would prefer to feel disrespected and inadequate. My sample is a highly targeted sample, and I can no more generalize my results to all women than anyone studying a unique group of people. What I can do, however, is profile the marriages of a fascinating group of women, and this is where things begin to get really interesting...

---

[*]See the appendix for demographic characteristics of the Lifestyle Poll sample.

Profile of the Lifestyle Poll Sample

If I were to profile the Lifestyle Poll participants in one sentence, I would say that they are extremely accomplished, thoughtful strategists aiming to create marriages that place a high value on equality, autonomy, and personal growth. The following sections delve into each of these sample traits in much more detail.

Accomplished Individuals

It is quite possible that the Lifestyle Poll sample represents one of the most comprehensive polls of accomplished females to date. I make this assertion based on both the unique design of the survey (which was geared toward stimulating *intrinsic* motivation for participants) and the unique demographic characteristics of the respondents. I doubt that the usual extrinsic motivators—money and entry into a lottery for a lump sum of money—would have been motivating for my sample. Data collection for the Lifestyle Poll was initiated and completed in 2008, before the start of the post-millennial U.S. economic crisis. Take a look at Figure 5.1, which shows the annual household income of Lifestyle Poll participants and the average national household income for a similar time period (two years prior).

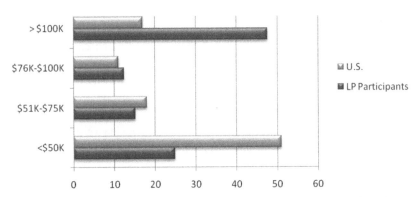

Figure 5.1. Household Income for U.S. Population vs. Lifestyle Poll Participants

In Figure 5.1, the darkly shaded bars show the income levels of the Lifestyle Poll participants and the lightly shaded bars show the average household income in the United States in 2006, also before the crash of the US economy. Clearly, the Lifestyle Poll respondents enjoyed a much higher than average household income. Ultimately, the personal budget limitations that pushed me to get creative became an asset insofar as I was able to attract a sample for which monetary compensation for participation may not have been a compelling incentive.

Regarding education levels of Lifestyle Poll participants, 98% are college graduates. The majority are graduates of highly competitive private universities. Sixty-two percent are graduates of one of the Ivy League Universities (Harvard, Columbia, Cornell, Dartmouth, Yale, University of Pennsylvania, Princeton, and Brown) and the majority of the remainder of the sample have been awarded degrees from other highly competitive universities (e.g. Stanford, Oxford University, the London School of Economics, Massachusetts Institute of Technology) and top state schools with rigorous admissions standards (UC, Berkeley, University of Florida). Harvard graduates make up the largest part of the Ivy League portion of the sample. It may not be surprising that the respondents are more highly educated than their mothers, given increasing opportunities for women to pursue advanced degrees. What is striking is that they are more highly educated than their *fathers*, men of a generation who were often expected to be highly-accomplished sole wage earners. Seventy-five percent of the Lifestyle Poll sample had graduate degrees or were in the process of completing an advanced degree (most often in law, medicine, or business), whereas slightly more than 60% of their fathers held advanced degrees.

Not only did the participants report a high level of education, but the vast majority (87%) reported that they liked their jobs. When I calculated this result, I was amazed to find such a high proportion of people who like their jobs. When I cross-checked my data against the official Harvard Class of 1997 Survey compiled by M. Talusan in 2007, I found that 88% of the class of 1997 poll respondents reported that they enjoy their jobs. Two more remarkably similar results between the Lifestyle Poll sample and the Harvard class of '97 were that the same proportion held graduate degrees—74% of the respondents of the Harvard class of '97 versus 75% of the Lifestyle Poll sample—and that for those who had life plans in mind, 93% of the female graduates of the Harvard class of '97 hoped to become mothers at some point, compared to 92% of the Lifestyle Poll respondents. These striking areas of convergence in my data—which involved several hundred participants from Harvard graduating classes spanning the years 1995 through 2002 (see Figure 5.2) and the official reunion survey data for the Harvard Class of 1997—further confirmed the integrity of my results.

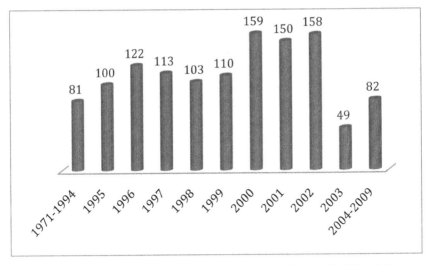

Figure 5.2. Graduating Class Distribution for Lifestyle Poll Participants

Thoughtful Strategists

In addition to being a highly accomplished group, the women in the Lifestyle Poll sample are thoughtful planners and strategists. They do not leave their futures—including their marriages—up to chance, but instead proceed through life in a very intentional manner. The Lifestyle Poll participants are two-marshmallow people (i.e. gratification delayers). Many have delayed receiving their relatively high incomes for several years to pursue graduate degrees. Similarly, the married respondents indicated that they spent an average of 3.6 years dating their husbands before committing to marriage. This is much longer than the 2 year relationship trial period suggested by some theorists. These quite happily married women knew what they were looking for and spent considerable time building their relationships before making the decision to partner for life with their husbands. Within the Lifestyle Poll sample, the average age at marriage was also significantly higher than the average age of marriage for the population at large. Specifically, the average age at marriage for women in the Lifestyle Poll sample was 27.17 and the average age for their husbands was 28.94. The average age of marriage across the United States for the same time period was 23.6 for women and 25.8 for men, so the men and women in this sample were 3 to 3.5 years older on average at the time of marriage.[104]

I suppose the relatively high average age of marriage in the Lifestyle Poll sample would explain a curious personal experience that I once had that has never been repeated at other weddings I've attended. I was attending a close friend's wedding at the Harvard Club of New York, an elegant "Harvard on Harvard" marriage. When the bride threw the bouquet, the cluster of single women immediately jumped away from it and the unclaimed bouquet landed on the floor. I believe it may have ricocheted off my hand, because someone handed me the bouquet (now that I think of it, I realize I was, in fact, the next to get married). This bouquet toss experience was illuminated when I reviewed responses to the open-ended question "At what age or stage of life do you feel is the optimal time to get married and why?" Here are some representative answers to this question:

- I believe you should not get married before your late 20s at the very earliest. Any earlier, and both people are still figuring out who they are. They are starting to establish themselves in the working world, they are still maturing emotionally. What's the rush? If two people really love each other and are committed, why not wait a few years to get married? Plus you can usually afford a better wedding and honeymoon.

- 30. Before, you are too young to be sure you're choosing someone for the right, long-term reasons. Later, and you're behind schedule for having kids.

- Late 20s/early 30s. You have had "fun" as a young adult, established your independence socially and professionally, and you really know yourself better. I thought I really knew who I was just after college...but it has taken me years to become more comfortable in my own skin. I am SO glad I did not marry the person I thought I would marry when I was 21...we would be divorced by now.

- 30–33. You are a full grown-up and know yourself better than you did in your 20s. Your education is finished, and your career is far enough along to have established professional credibility and worth, such that employers will be more flexible when it comes to children/family.

- I don't think there's any particular age—it's more a matter of maturity. But if I were to peg an age, it would probably be around 30—

old enough to know yourself, but young enough to grow with someone.

- I think the best time to get married is when you are in a good place emotionally, professionally, personally, financially because by then it should be clear to you that you are able to do great on your own, but life is just that much sweeter married to this one person.

- Your early 30s because people are more aware of what they want and have grown up—remaining independent and less likely to project unhappiness onto their partner.

- I think the 30s are good, when you have a sense of yourself and what you want to do with your life.

- I don't feel like there is an ideal age to marry; however I do think that one should spend time on his/her own and allow for plenty of maturity to take place before deciding to share one's entire life with another person. It's important to be "enough" with who you are while living on your own, first and foremost.

- I think biologically it makes sense to get married relatively young (early 20s, perhaps), but in terms of maturity and career choices, I understand why this gets pushed back more and more. Personally, I'm only just feeling ready (at 28), and having children still seems like something far off and rather unfair (that I as a woman have no choice but to put up with 9 months of suffering if I want to have children).

- I met my husband at a very young age, when we were both college sophomores, so to be honest I wasn't looking for anything like a life partner. I thought he was cute, and funny, and he was a jazz musician, so we shared that common interest that was not necessarily common among the other friends that I had. When we finally did get close to settling down I already knew that he and I were compatible as individuals—what I required from him was the promise that he was really ready to be committed to the intensity of a serious relationship (we had broken up a few times, mostly because he felt unready to be serious...not so surprising considering how young we were, and [in] retrospect, the times we had apart from each other were very valuable, they allowed us to do more "growing up" on our own before getting married).

As illustrated above, the clear consensus in the open-ended responses was that personal and professional development should be fairly well established before marriage.

The collective wisdom of the Lifestyle Poll participants to wait until the late 20s or early 30s before marrying fits with clear consensus in the literature. Author Danielle Crittenden warns that "by waiting and waiting and waiting to commit to someone, our capacity for love shrinks and withers."[105] Crittenden's statement could apply well to the experience of diminishing returns when individuals pursue a series of dead-end relationships. We might even see a parallel between indulging in the cocaine-rush of falling in love with a string of unsuitable partners, and taking ecstasy, because both decrease the range of maximum enjoyment in all future cases. The results of the Lifestyle Poll, and the research of several widely cited demographers, suggests, in contrast to Crittenden's assertion, that any association between age and capacity to love or to create a beautiful, sustainable marriage is utter nonsense. Demographers Teresa Castro-Martin and Larry Bumpass assert that "the inverse relationship between age at marriage and the likelihood of marital disruption is among the strongest and most consistently documented in the literature."[106] Dating for a long time allows us to establish a stronger sense of self and to define a set of life goals and priorities. I also believe that the later age of marriage and more lengthy courtship directly relates to the high levels of marital satisfaction reported in the Lifestyle Poll sample. In 3.6 years, the average time before marriage for this sample, there is plenty of time after the cocaine-rush phase for two people to carefully evaluate each other's character, assess compatibility, set off future land mines, and figure out how to work through conflicts together.

Some journalists and family researchers bemoan the lower rates of marriage as women and men wait longer until they get married and more people stay single until later in life. This kind of thinking suggests that what society needs is more marriage. During the Bush/Cheney years, millions of dollars in government money were diverted to programs encouraging marriage and teaching basic relational communication skills. More marriage might be a good goal, but *only* if those marriages are also healthy and sustainable. Kids growing up today need more examples of unsustainable marriages like they need two extra pairs of lips on the soles of their feet. We don't need more marriages as much as we need more *good* marriages. Working to increase the proportion of married people in the United States would be like saying, "People aren't forming enough small businesses—we need to teach them some basic tools so they can get more businesses going." It doesn't do any good to teach a few basic business skills and then offer some business-friendly tax incentives if these small businesses will soon fail because of a lack of long-term strategic planning. Promoting marriage for its own sake, reducing the complexities of a successful marriage to a few basic relationship skills taught in government-sponsored seminars, and encouraging young people to marry when the fancy strikes them is encouraging a boom-and-bust "bubble economy" in the marital sector. Successful businesses require significant planning—you get clear on your mission, make a detailed plan of how you will execute your vision, pick the right people to run your business, and then invest considerable attention (particularly on the front end of your launch) improving whatever is not working. This is not so different from the process of creating a successful marriage, and anyone who encourages couples to seal the deal quickly or to skip steps in the assessment and planning phases of marriage-building is not using good common sense.

The Lifestyle Poll respondents were intentional not only in their process of getting established before marriage, but also in selecting mates who would be their equals. Intelligence, compatibility of values and goals, good character, personal growth orientation, equality and mutual respect surfaced repeatedly in the responses to open-ended questions about what respondents sought in a mate or what they believed makes a marriage work. Let's examine some of these responses.

Qualities Desired in Potential Partners

Similar Level of Intelligence

Lifestyle Poll participants place a high value on finding an intelligent spouse, a partner who is an intellectual equal. Several researchers have shown that partners tend to match best with others who have similar IQs and educational levels.[107] Along the same lines, Dr. Gregory Neimeyer found that marital satisfaction is positively related to partners' similarity in cognitive thinking ability (what he calls "cognitive complexity").[108] What is the practical application of this research? Let's return to the concept of marriage as a really, really long conversation. I imagine that we all know people who are fabulous conversationalists, in small doses. Like fireflies of the party scene, they glow and flit about, regaling others with rehearsed stories, but they burn out after a few hours because they lack the ability to keep the conversation going once they've used up their material. They are not spontaneously witty or even great conversationalists, but instead are able to mimic the appearance of spontaneity and wit by learning their lines ahead of time. There are lots of reasons why two people who have been married a long time might sit silent at a restaurant table, but I wonder whether one of the main reasons might be that one or both were not really good conversationalists in the first place.

In a healthy marriage, you will continue to have lots of interesting conversations with family members, close friends, and colleagues throughout your life. However, when you live with someone daily, the most consistent conversation you have will be with your spouse. It is an incredible blessing to have your marital conversation not only be your most consistent conversation, but also your *deepest* conversation. When you are considering marriage to someone, ask yourself whether this is the person you want to debrief with (in the psychological/emotional sense) after a horrible day at work. Ask yourself whether this is the person with whom you want to brainstorm your most exciting dreams and visions. Do conversations with this person deepen your understanding of your own experiences and help you make connections you could not have made yourself? Does their intelligence challenge you and stimulate you to reach higher levels of insight? Speaking from personal experience, having a partner who is capable (and willing) to do this enriches life immeasurably. In my opinion, to marry someone who cannot do this with you, even if they look like Hugh Jackman or have a huge inheritance, is to forgo one of the richest blessings in life.

At the risk of beating a dead horse, I would say that the best way to figure out whether this is the person you want to have a lifelong conversation with is to have a lot of long conversations with them over a long period of time before you get married. Because marriage is the longest conversation you'll have (ideally), it seems wise to choose a spouse that you will find interesting and intellectually stimulating. Here are some representative responses to illustrate the importance of intelligence as a key mate selection criterion for the Lifestyle Poll sample (with relevant portions emphasized in bold):

- **I would love someone who I can appreciate intellectually**, is affectionate and sexually active, and with whom I can share travel and other hobbies.

- Compatible values and religion, strong family background, **intellectual/educational compatibility**, physical attraction, trust.

- That they're funny, **smart, educated**, goal-oriented, come from a similar background, **worldly/well-read**, personable, attractive, take care of themselves, that our personalities compliment each other's, and that he supports my goals in life.

- **Intelligence (and respect for intelligent women!)**

Good Character

In addition to seeking intelligent mates, Lifestyle Poll participants also recognize the importance of good character. As I've mentioned previously, if you had to boil it all down, the most important thing when deciding on a spouse is to identify someone with good character who is also open to influence. It strikes me that if a marriage of equals is based on good character, then identifying good character is *especially* important in a more traditional model of marriage, particularly for the financially dependent partner in the marriage. Let's take the example of one type of very traditional marriage that is fairly well represented to this day — the very traditional Christian marriage advocated by Emerson Eggerichs, the author of *Love and Respect*. In this marriage, the husband is the head of the home and the wife is the "help meet" (which roughly translates as "a help answering to him"). As Eggerichs puts it, this type of wife "wants to be cherished as a princess, not revered as a queen"[109] and the husband "wants [her] acknowledgement that he is the leader, the one in authority."[110] In the most traditional type of Christian marriage arrangement, the husband reports to God and the wife reports to her husband, as illustrated in the chain of command depicted in Figure 5.3. In other words, as Eggerichs puts it, "when women follow the lead of their husbands [to quote a verse in Titus 2:5, NIRV], they trust God to guide their decisions."[111]

A marriage with this type of organizational hierarchy potentially places the individual at the bottom in a very vulnerable position. The one who makes more money often has greater power. The financial dependence of the other creates a situation in which challenges to the status quo may be relatively limited. The one with less power is more vulnerable to remaining in a dissatisfying marriage because she "has to" rather than because she "wants to." As psychologist Harriet Lerner has put it, "if we are truly

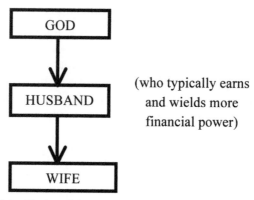

Figure 5.3. Chain of Command Associated with Traditional Christian Marriages

convinced that we cannot live without our husband's support...our own bottom line position may be togetherness at any cost...In such circumstances, we may find it impossible to initiate and sustain courageous acts of change."[112] Marriages with this type of hierarchy, which were relatively common in past generations, may have kept the divorce rates lower than if divorce had been a more viable option. Moreover, from a Christian perspective, in this type of very traditional Christian marriage, a man would answer to God, who is the source of perfect love and justice, while his wife would answer to her husband, who is *not* the source of perfect love and justice (but, if she chooses wisely, may be a good man who aspires to move ever closer to this ideal). For a couple of the same spiritual persuasion—that is, a Christian marriage of equals—there is a chain of command that looks more like Figure 5.4.

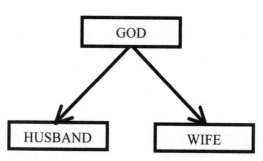

Figure 5.4. Chain of Command in a Christian Marriage of Equals

In this arrangement, both partners answer equally to God. Mutual submission replaces male headship. Of course, while this may not typically be the case, a marriage with a more traditional role distribution can certainly also be a marriage of equals. The lack of a conventional role distribution is not the defining feature of a marriage of equals. Instead, the defining feature is the presence of the foundational values of equality, respect, and flexibility. Because a marriage of equals *attends to respect* as well as to love, there is a built-in mechanism for avoiding the most serious levels of marital dissatisfaction. That is, in a marriage of equals, there is enough flexibility and respect for one of the partners to say something like "I'm feeling resentful about how we are dividing up our chores. This isn't working for me. I'd like to talk with you about a way to do this differently." The couple then openly discusses the problem with the current arrangement (sometimes with some "energy," but hopefully not in Mojo mode, i.e., primitive emotional aggression) and negotiates a redistribution of responsibilities. If each partner in a marriage is happy with the arrangement they have, then there is nothing to negotiate. In this scenario, whether their arrangement is traditional or non-traditional, if they value each other's respective contributions equally, and are responsive to each other's requests for change in order to preserve equality and mutual respect, then it's a marriage of equals.

The following are some representative responses to highlight the value of good character as a key element sought in a spouse by Lifestyle Poll participants:

- Here's what I thought I wanted: ambition, brilliance, focus, and intellectualism. But then I met my partner—and while it wasn't love at first sight, it was "I totally have been looking for the wrong thing in my life." **He is generous, loyal, creative, relaxed, tender, wise, and kind.** While he's extremely smart as well, he will never be some of the things that I thought I wanted—but what I wanted was wrong for me, and I'm lucky I realized what was actually going to make me happy when I had the chance to get it.

- Intelligence, **commitment to commitment (if that makes any sense!), kindness, a kind of nobleness (desire to make the world a better place).**

- Someone with **compassion**, competence, and love for me, who is **responsible, faithful, trustworthy**, and has **good character**.

Compatibility of Values and Goals

Participants also expressed that they were willing to wait in order to find someone who has compatible values and goals. In the married portion of the sample (about half the sample), 94% reported that they had either the same religious or spiritual beliefs or the same core philosophies of life. Representative responses articulate this third shared value:

- I got married at 32. I had dated a fair amount, but only one serious relationship that lasted less than a year. I was fairly selective about dating, though. **By the time I met my husband I had established that compatibility of personalities was really key for me...the way each person deals with conflict, together and individually.** Also, shared values like family...not just in a vague sense but caring for elderly parents, goals for your children, etc.

- **Having a relationship with God is something we MUST have in common, and I want my family to go to church together (my husband should be an example for his family and initiate this—I consider him the priest of the household). Family should be very important to him.** It's important that we were friends first. I want him to communicate well and address issues quickly. He should be affectionate. I want him to keep our marriage a priority, e.g. we should still date and travel without the children. He handles money wisely—he doesn't have to balance the checkbook but he understands that he must first provide for the needs of the family, save for the future, and then he can do what he pleases. Of course, he must be monogamous.

- **Compatible values and religion, strong family background, intellectual/educational compatibility**, physical attraction, trust.

- **Someone with similar life goals**, someone who has a bit of the devil in him, hot abs!

Personal Growth Orientation

In addition to valuing compatibility, respondents actively search for (and expect) marriages that catalyze mutual personal growth:

- **I want someone who truly believes in marriage and would strive to make it work.** I also look for someone who is smart, fun, playful, and who wants to travel. At this point in time, I also think that someone of my race and religion generally would be ideal.

- Someone with shared theological beliefs who is also **in process (constantly growing) as a person.**

- **Someone who has his own strong career interests and life journey, who will bring all that positive energy to our relationship.** Someone loyal and intelligent, with a good sense of humor. Perhaps someone with some experience of loss, so he knows how precious and short life is and how we need to make the most of it.

- A sense of humor. **A love of trying new foods and traveling to new places. Someone willing to go on adventures with me. A good teammate.**

- **Someone who has a few similar interests as me but also different ones so that we complement each other but expand each other's horizons.**

- **Someone who could communicate and push me emotionally to be more honest. Someone who would encourage my work and understand it. Someone who would help me have fun and who is socially well adjusted.**

In the Lifestyle Poll, I also wanted to assess the destiny (soul mate) vs. growth orientation of the respondents. To do this, I asked participants to indicate their level of agreement with the following statement: "Most of us could sincerely love a number of people equally well." The vast majority (81%) of the participants reject the philosophy of the soul mate, favoring instead the possibility of more than one potentially well-suited partner. Within the married portion of the sample, although 91% would marry their husbands all over again, 96% felt that "it is possible that there are many other men [they] could be happy with." In both the married subset and the overall sample, the belief in more than one potentially exceptional partner is generally paired with the ideal of marital commitment for life. That is, I posed the question "Because of the high divorce rate, some have adapted their marital vows to reflect the reality that love often does not last. How do you feel about the alternative wedding vow 'As long as we both shall *love*' as opposed to the more traditional vow 'as long as we both shall *live*'?" The vast majority of respondents (87%) agreed with the statement, "I don't like this—marriage should be forever," while a much smaller proportion (13%) agreed that "this makes sense—it's practical/reflects the current times." Thus, although these women feel that they may be able to find happiness with a number of different individuals, they nonetheless voice a strong level of commitment to maintaining lifelong partnerships.

Equality and Mutual Respect

Of all the qualities sought by this group of thoughtful planners, by far the most common themes centered on the desire for equality and mutual respect. These values came up with such frequency that they inspired the central theme of this book. As such, I want to tell this part of the story in good detail. In the quantitative portion of the Lifestyle Poll, I asked participants to indicate their level of agreement with the following statement: "In case of conflicting demands, a professional woman's responsibility is to her family." About one third of the sample (34%) strongly agreed with this statement, and an additional 43% somewhat agreed with this statement. Given that a total of 77% agree that a professional woman should prioritize her family, it seems that family values run strong in this group of women. I then asked the same question, substituting the word "man's" for "woman's" (i.e. "In the case of conflicting demands, a man's primary responsibility should be to his family"). In this case, nearly the same proportion of respondents strongly agreed (34%) and somewhat agreed (47%). The message I read from these responses is a rejection of the double standard that wives should take a bigger hit than husbands when their families need them. Happily, in the married portion of the sample, the vast majority seemed to feel they were living into this ideal of equality. Seventy-two percent reported that they were "getting an equal deal." An additional 10.6% felt that their husbands were getting "a slightly better deal," and an additional 7.3% felt that they were getting a "slightly better deal" than their husbands. The group of women who felt that one partner was getting either a "somewhat" or "much better" deal than the other totaled only 10.6% of the married portion of the Lifestyle Poll sample.

Let's look at the bigger picture again, at the responses of the larger group, the unmarried and married respondents together. Responses to the open-ended question about what participants want in a spouse also carry very strong themes of equality seeking:

- **Someone who believes in equality in the marriage partnership and who will make a great, loving and participating father.**

- **I'm looking for a dynamic relationship between equals—if I push, I want him to push back, and vice versa. We can support each other, and depend on each other.** I'm also looking for intelligence, a positive outlook, and a sense of humor. I don't think this is unrealistic (though probably pretty rare), because I do know couples who have this kind of relationship.

- **The thing about us that's different than any relationship I've been in before is that we both put the other person first and both would rather let the other person have what they want than to fight about it. This is born out of respect that our wants deserve to be taken seriously** and trust that we won't be taken advantage of.

- [My partner] is kind, intelligent, educated, giving, and gentle, **with a supersized sense of self-esteem that stands up to my own often-large ego quite well! I feel like we can hold our own against each other, that neither of us is going to end up pushed around by the other.**

- I wanted someone I wouldn't have to "fix." Someone who could take care of themselves and had his life in order so that maybe he could take care of me a little. I wanted a man of action, not someone who waits for life to happen, but someone who goes out and actively works toward his goals. I needed those things because in marriage **I knew that I must respect my partner, and I need these things so he will earn my respect.**

- **Someone completely different than my father.** Someone who would be gentle, not willing to fight with me when all I want to do is fight. **Someone who understands that my opinions do matter.**

- Shared values and family goals, **respect**, appreciation, love, warmth, consideration, ability to manage emotions.

- 1. Someone who understands me and **respects me** 2. Is responsible and trustworthy 3. Is not a pain in the ass around the house (i.e. excessively noisy, messy, attention-needy, etc.).

- **Respect**, honesty, stability, same moral background.

- My best friend; **someone I admire**; someone with a strong sense of family.

- I have been in my current relationship for 5 years and, although we are not yet married, we have made a lifelong commitment to each other. I think that we have remained together because **we respect each other, are attracted to each other, love each other, and are interested in what the other one has to say. We are also willing to compromise and negotiate with each other.** We share many of the same views but also challenge each other to think about why we have the beliefs we do.

- We're very happy, primarily because we have similar senses of humor, values, and long-term plans. We talk honestly with each other and try to have realistic expectations of each other. **We are very different in many of our interests and habits, but we respect each other.**

As I mentioned previously, I also included the question that was the basis for the (apparently false) assumption of a consistent gender difference in the book *Love and Respect*. To briefly review, the author, Dr. Emerson Eggerichs, reported that 74% of males in a sample of 400 said that if they were forced to choose, they would prefer to feel alone and unloved rather than to feel disrespected and inadequate. Eggerichs collected data on a female sample and found that a comparable majority would rather feel disrespected and inadequate than alone and unloved. On this basis, he formed the theory that a wife "needs love just as she needs air to breathe" and a husband "needs respect just as he needs air to breathe."[113] Eggerichs certainly acknowledges that some people don't fit this pattern, but ultimately, he concludes that a wife can cope with disrespect better than her husband can and that a husband can cope with lack of love better than his wife can. As I've mentioned, when I posed the same question to my sample of 1200 women, the majority responded to the contrary of Eggerichs's contention. Interestingly, when Lifestyle Poll respondents reflected on their own personality characteristics, they described themselves as high in a number of both "masculine" and "feminine" characteristics. For example, the majority of respondents described themselves as independent (81%), pleasant (67%), affectionate (61%), self-confident (59%), active (54%), and emotional (55%). They did not, however, generally view themselves as being traditional, as only 21% of the sample endorsed this personality trait in themselves.

In the supplemental open-ended questions, I probed further, asking, "In the Lifestyle Poll, there is a question that reads, ...'If you had to choose between feeling alone and unloved by everyone in the world or feeling disrespected and inadequate by everyone in the world, what would you choose?' Can you comment on which situation would be WORSE to bear and why?" As a gut reaction, many Lifestyle Poll respondents pointed out the ridiculous nature of this question. That is, how can one separate the two? How in the world is it possible to feel loved when one is treated disrespectfully (and, further, in which parallel universe would anyone ever have to make such a depressing choice)? The thing is that this question was not designed to evoke the state of things in the natural world—it was designed to illuminate a theorized difference between men and women in terms of driving psychological needs. To provide a fair sense of balance in the responses that were submitted, I have included some thoughtful responses from some of the women who would rather feel disrespected than unloved (in a way that mirrors Eggerichs' theory of gender differences):

- I would rather be disrespected and made to feel inadequate. My biggest insecurity revolves around not being loved (particularly in a romantic fashion). I think I could not live without love and knowing someone accepts me as I am.

- I think it would be worse to be alone and unloved, unless of course the people who loved you also made you feel disrespected and inadequate. I hope I would somehow find the strength to bear the criticism of the world, as long as I thought I was on the right path, whereas the idea that no one loved me would be horribly isolating and life would have a lot less meaning.

- They'd both feel pretty awful, but I think humans really need love to survive. Love from someone who disrespects you and believes you to be inadequate might be hard to take—I'd question whether that actually is love. But I'd still take lack of respect over complete lack of love.

As I've mentioned, the majority of the respondents in the Lifestyle Poll sample, however, would rather feel unloved than disrespected. Here are some of the thoughtful responses from participants who voiced this preference:

- Disrespected and inadequate would be worse to bear because it implies you're "useless" in the world. But if you were feeling alone and unloved, it implies that this is due to your own interaction with others and you can still be respected for something that you might have contributed to the greater good of society.

- Worst scenario for me: Feeling disrespected and inadequate by everyone in the world. I never want to not be an asset or of assistance to another or a group, especially if I have a talent or skill to elevate the group or project.

- Respect for yourself and others is key. My family has always valued education and independence. So being alone isn't that scary to me. It's not ideal, but I'd rather be alone, successful in my career, and making a difference in society than be with someone who disrespects me and makes me feel inadequate. I have worked too long and too hard, and I am proud of my accomplishments, so no one should make me feel bad about myself!

- This was a very difficult question! I think I chose to be alone and unloved, because I assumed that at least I would love myself in that situation. In the second scenario, there was a comment about "feeling inadequate"—I wouldn't want to have internalized others' disparagement of me.

- I feel like I would choose being alone and unloved, mainly because the situation of being disrespected and made to feel inadequate by everyone but being loved by them doesn't even make sense given my understanding of love. In other words, alone and unloved is inherent in both of those choices. So I'd rather be alone and unloved and respected and not made to feel inadequate (so that I can love myself).

- Feeling disrespected and inadequate is much harder...especially disrespected...I have a strong personality, so that one would be much harder for me.

- Though both situations are bad, I chose the first because it represents a bubble around you, which I think is easier to manage; the second situation represents a constant bursting of that bubble by people. In the first situation—being alone and unloved—you are alienated, but the second one—being disrespected—is intrusive, aggressive and also alienating.

- The worse situation would be being disrespected and made to feel inadequate by everyone. As a woman, I consider RESPECT to be an extremely important characteristic. If you don't have respect, people will always think of you as inadequate, not worthy, etc. Eventually this would impair your own sense of self-worth and self-confidence.

- That's interesting...I think I would choose to feel alone and unloved...because in my heart of hearts I know it could never be true because God is omnipresent and He loves me beyond what anyone in the world could fathom. I don't think I could tolerate being disrespected by everyone...

- Being disrespected and made to feel inadequate by everyone would be horrible. It would affect your career and self-esteem, and you'd get no satisfaction in life.

- I don't see how these are different. If a person is belittled, that person is not loved. And yes, I would rather be alone than be with others who made me feel like that.

- If you're being disrespected and made to feel inadequate, it doesn't sound like you're being loved, either. I don't mind being alone; it's not the best thing, but sometimes togetherness grates on me too. I don't think it's tolerable to be constantly belittled.

- This is a silly question because each choice can't exist by itself. Feeling unloved makes you feel inadequate. The only way I am informed to answer is that I've felt lonely at times and it didn't kill me, so I'd say the other thing—no respect—is worse.

- I think if the people who "loved" me made me feel disrespected and inadequate, I could not call that feeling "loved."

Overall, no matter which preference was indicated, the underlying message is clear: *there is no love without respect.*

In summarizing the profile of the Lifestyle Poll participants as a whole, I would say they are *romantic non-traditionalists*. That is, they are highly accomplished, thoughtful planners who delay marriage until they have identified partners with certain desirable personality traits and values in order to create a partnership that is grounded in equality, love, and mutual respect. Dan Mulhern, professor of business and law at UC, Berkeley, wrote a recent editorial in the form of a letter to his son that eloquently describes the character of a husband within a marriage of equals:

> "My dad, like so many men of his generation, could tell his wife what to do. He could tell his staff. And his boss could tell him. You and I need a more nimble strength. For example, you will have to stand up to your woman. You will honor her when you treat her as an equal, neither unduly backing down nor asking her to give up her principles and experience. You won't have clear social roles to inherit. Instead, you'll have to talk, negotiate, sacrifice, and make it up as you go along. A modern warrior prevails not by sheer physical strength but by exercising his values with discipline."[114]

Let's now drill down further from the responses in the larger sample of more than 1200 women to the married subsample (626 women, about half of the total sample).

Profile of the Lifestyle Poll Participants' Marriages

Throughout this book, I've identified the marriages of the women in the Lifestyle Poll as very successful—hence the title of the book, *Marriage for Equals: The Successful Joint (Ad)Ventures of Well-Educated Couples*. Just how satisfying are the marriages of these romantic non-traditionalists? They are strikingly satisfying by any standard. The vast majority (86%) described their marriages as either "very happy" (24%), "extremely happy" (51%), or "perfect" (11%). An additional 8% said that they are "happy," and the remaining 6% said that they are "a little unhappy" (4%), "fairly unhappy" (2%), or "extremely unhappy" (<1%). The huge majority (91%) would marry their current husband again, and nearly the same proportion (89%) "rarely" or "never" wish that they had not married their husbands. When I first read these results, I immediately checked the average length of these relationships to make sure that these reports of such high satisfaction were not generally based on relationships still within the cocaine-rush phase. However, as I've mentioned previously, Lifestyle Poll participants dated for an average of 3.6 years before entering marriage. The average length of the relationships (courtship plus marriage) in the married portion of the sample was 7.9 years, which is *well* beyond the cocaine-rush phase of any romantic relationship. Post-courtship, then, the average length of the marriages in this sample is 4.3 years. Not only is 4.3 years also well beyond the cocaine-rush phase of a relationship, it is interesting in light of fact that the third year of marriage is generally associated with the highest risk of divorce and nearly all of the married women in the sample have not divorced or separated.[115] It seems reasonable then to conclude that cocaine-rush attributions do not explain respondents' reports of very satisfying marriages.

Since cocaine-rush fantasies would have long subsided for the majority of wives in the sample, I then wondered whether social desirability might explain the report of extremely high levels of satisfaction. Social desirability refers to the tendency to respond in ways that make us look good to others. A couple things suggested, however, that social desirability was probably not a driving factor in my sample. First, people are most likely to give socially desirable responses when giving face-to-face reports (e.g., the tendency of many patients whose medical charts show alcohol-related liver failure to report that they have been drinking "only one or two glasses of wine once or twice a week at most"). Social desirability is much less likely to influence anonymous participants like the women who responded to the Lifestyle Poll. Second, if participants had strong social desirability motives, they would not apply it to only one area of their self reports; by logical extension, they would have also concealed many of the non-socially desirable struggles they reported. In the context of the Lifestyle Poll, participants spoke openly about past traumas, ongoing personal struggles, and a number of specific problems in their marriages. This frank responding style shows up in the admission that nearly 60% of the sample had feared that their marriage might be in trouble within the past three years (despite their sense of strong satisfaction with their marriages at the time they were sampled). In fact, given the predictable trials that couples encounter in the first critical phase of their marriages, and the generally higher risk of divorce during these initial adjustment years, this report of concerns makes sense. Based on this, I think it's safe to conclude that these marriages, while not perfect, are in fact very satisfying to those who are evaluating them.

That a large number of women in such non-traditional marriages could be so satisfied is very interesting given existing data on the effects of masculine and feminine traits on marriage. That is, the Lifestyle Poll respondents are clearly a unique sample of high-achieving women with a number of qualities that have traditionally been considered "masculine" traits. Remember, respondents are more educated that their fathers, who were typically expected to be highly accomplished, primary financial providers. Seventy-five percent of the women in the Lifestyle Poll sample had a graduate degree or were in the process of completing one, typically within a variety of traditionally male-dominated fields such as law, medicine, or business. In the larger sample of more than 1200 women, less than 1% reported that they hoped their future lives would involve no formal employment and no children. The vast majority (almost 95%) hoped that their lives would include some amount of work outside the home, while the other 5% hoped to be full-time stay-at-home mothers. Of those who were currently mothers, most (82%) continued to work outside the home; more often than not, this was because they "wanted to work" (67%) instead of because they "had to work" (33%). The presence of so-called "masculine" traits helps make sense of the importance that Lifestyle Poll respondents place on respect, demonstrated in responses such as "being disrespected and made to feel inadequate would be worse to bear because it implies you're 'useless' in the world" or "I never want to not be an asset or of assistance to another or a group, especially if I have a talent or skill to elevate them."

Sometimes, "instrumental qualities" are seen as overlapping with traditionally masculine qualities. That is, when researchers refer to "masculine traits," they are most often referring to traits that are also "instrumental," such as being independent, assertive, self-confident, and active. When researchers use the term "feminine," they are most often referring to traits such as being sympathetic, nurturing, affectionate, and emotional. Bradbury, Campbell, and Fincham specifically examined associations between masculine and feminine traits and marital satisfaction.[116] In reviewing the literature, they suggest that researchers who employ cross-sectional designs (i.e., "snapshots in time") most often tend to conclude that feminine traits like being affectionate, sensitive to others' needs, and eager to soothe feelings are some of the most important ingredients in marital happiness.[117] However, they observe that when researchers employ longitudinal designs (that is, studying married individuals or couples over time), researchers sometimes find that masculine traits like being assertive, independent, and willing to take a stand may be more important than feminine traits as relationships develop.[118]

In the field of psychology, masculine and feminine traits were originally thought to be on one spectrum. In other words, being more feminine meant being less masculine, and being more masculine meant being less feminine. The field of personality assessment has generally moved away from this single spectrum model. Masculinity and femininity are now placed on separate continuums. It is therefore possible, just as before, to be high in masculinity and low in femininity (or vice versa); however, it is also possible for an individual to be high on both masculine and feminine characteristics. In fact, for Lifestyle Poll participants, there is evidence of a strong showing of both types of traits. For example, when respondents reflected on their own personality characteristics, they described themselves as high in a number of both masculine and feminine traits. For example, the majority of respondents described themselves as independent, self-confident, active, affectionate, and emotional.

Further, results suggest that respondents may have grown into higher levels of several so-called masculine and feminine personality traits. I asked respondents to reflect on which traits (within a list of sex-typed traits) accurately described them as teenagers and then whether the same traits would describe them well at their present age. Respondents felt that they had grown more independent (from 60% in their teen years to 81% at the time of the study), self-confident (from 44% to 59%), and affectionate (from 44% to 61%). Interestingly, respondents also felt that they had grown to enjoy more feminine activities over time (from 25% to 39%) while reporting a relative loss of interest in masculine activities (from 35% to 25%). Other non sex-typed characteristics such as being traditional (23% to 21%) and pleasant (64% to 67%) were not perceived to have changed much at all. Thus, participants may be tapping into both masculine and feminine traits to support their happy marriages. Negotiating to a state of compromise was by far the most commonly reported outcome in marital disagreements. Respondents reported that when they have a marital problem, they negotiate to compromise 68% of the time on average, respectfully agree to disagree 16.8% of the time, and give in (in a one-sided manner) 15.4% of the time. Respondents are not only effective negotiators, powerful and willing to assert themselves, but are also an affectionate group of people; the large majority (80.2%) reported that they kiss their husbands every day, and an additional 13.7% reported that they kiss their husbands almost every day.

Ultimately, instead of suggesting that either feminine or masculine traits offer more benefits to the longevity and satisfaction of marriages, I believe it makes more sense to propose that the best of both sets of traits, regardless of how they are sex-typed in the literature, most benefit a marriage. So-called "masculine" traits such as being assertive, being willing to take a stand, and addressing problems with an eye to solutions will directly advance the growth of two individuals and the marital partnership. It is also beneficial for both partners—not just the female partner—to do the more traditionally "feminine" relationship work of being attuned to emotions, being compassionate, and being affectionate (to protect the marriage at the level of *G*). As I have pointed out previously, it takes work and energy to address problems, come to mutually satisfactory compromises, and participate in an ongoing stream of negotiation. Those individuals—whether male or female—who can pull from the widest possible range of behaviors, tenaciously striving to grow into people who can negotiate with heart, are most likely to sustain exceptional marriages.

Clearly, then, these marriages are not the type that can be set on the cruise control of permanently fixed traditional gender roles. These partnerships are not your father's (and mother's) Oldsmobile, but rather are more like hybrid crossovers that prioritize maneuverability and adventure above all else. In marriages that are *not* equal, there is a much greater chance that a couple will stay stuck in an unsatisfying arrangement since there is relatively greater rigidity to role distributions. Some couples lock into something that ultimately doesn't work well for one or both partners and they continue in the same pattern, lacking the agility to step back and say, "This isn't working for us," and then renegotiate how they manage their life together. On the other end of the spectrum, it seems to me that the *intentionality* invested in actively demonstrating love, respect, and support for new freedoms is a key distinguishing characteristic of a marriage of equals.

Intentional Love

What is intentional love? It is the conscious expression of love in ways that meet your partner's deepest needs. One of the most helpful models I've come across for learning to love your partner in an intentional way is Gary Chapman's book *The Five Languages of Love*.[119] With elegant simplicity, Chapman points out that our preferences for how we most feel loved often vary greatly between individuals. If you've read the book, I would add a couple elements to his analysis, which I hope will be helpful. The first modification I would make is to add a further dimension to the love language of "physical affection," splitting it into two independent parts. To clarify, Chapman proposes that there are a total of five love languages, which he refers to as words of affirmation, acts of service, gifts, quality time, and physical affection. Words of affirmation refers to when we praise our partners verbally or in writing, saying things that let them know how much we appreciate them, respect them, and love them, or how attractive we find them. Acts of service refers to showing love by serving our partners in some way—for example, by preparing a delicious dinner, getting the cars gassed up for the week, or pairing up their clean socks. Gifts do not necessarily have to be expensive—as I understand it, the essence of this love language is to give tangible objects that show our partners that we know who they are and were thinking of them when they were not present. So, buying your partner a double-pump chai latte with an extra sprinkle of cinnamon would definitely be an example of an act of love in the gifts category. Chapman's fourth love language, quality time, refers to giving our partners our focused attention, free from other distractions, in order to listen deeply to them and learn more about them. This may involve helping them understand their own experiences better or debrief a horrible day at work as I've previously mentioned.

Finally, in Chapman's theory, physical affection includes everything from holding hands to having sex. I would split physical affection into two categories, to emphasize the fact that many partners crave one or the other mode of love and that both are fully legitimate love languages—that is, some people desire lots of nonsexual physical affection but may not have a strong desire for sexual intimacy, and others strongly equate sexual connection with love. I think there has been too much tendency to view the latter as a uniquely male-driven need. The common stereotype that men always want sex more than women is not true for many couples I've seen in my clinical practice. Sex therapist Michele Weiner Davis, who wrote a book entitled *The Sex-Starved Marriage*,[120] has said, "If you've been thinking that low sexual desire is only 'a woman's thing,' think again. Many sex experts believe that low sexual desire in men is America's best-kept secret."[121] Several women who participated in the Lifestyle Poll indicated that this observation matched their experience. For example, I asked the divorced participants if they would let me know what they felt had led to their divorce, and sexual problems were a common reason. One participant said, "Sex was a huge problem and was one of the major reasons my marriage ended. Ultimately, we were sexually incompatible (ex had no sex drive whatsoever). Regardless of what anyone says, sex matters. Lack of sex results in decreased intimacy, trust, and physical affection. Sex is tied to more than just sex." So, by splitting Chapman's category of physical affection into nonsexual physical affection and sexual connection, I am hoping to emphasize that I view sex as a very legitimate need for many wives as well as for many husbands.

In Chapman's view, many marriages fail because people are not aware of how they can meet their partners' deepest needs for love. He outlines a few behavioral principles (highlighted in the text for easier identification) that provide insight into how people get set on autopilot in how they love each other. <u>First, he points out that we often repeat patterns we learned in our family of origin</u>. This is a well-established tendency, generally referred to as "social learning" or "modeling" in the field of psychology. If, for example, your parents were in the habit of referring to each other constantly with various terms of endearment, you are more likely to repeat this behavior in your marriage. Chapman also points out that <u>we often crave forms of love we did not get in our early years</u>. So, if we were raised by parents who did not provide much verbal praise, we might be strongly attracted to partners who provide a lot of praise. As I've stated before, family of origin experiences often result in repetition of previous patterns or in intentional rebellion against them. A third principle is a variation of the "Golden Rule" that doesn't always work out as well as the Golden Rule should: <u>We do unto others as we would have done unto us</u> (even when the form of love we offer misses the mark for the other person). In some cases, we might keep writing our partners love notes because this is what we would want from them. This isn't necessarily a selfish act; in fact, in my clinical experience, it's often as unconscious as speaking in our native language (and then feeling increasingly frustrated when other people do not respond in kind).

An additional principle that I would add is that we base our expressions of love on what we see in the media. The media has such a potentially powerful shaping effect that I decided to lead off with an effort to shed some light on the manipulations inherent in the script for how to fall in love, at least according to ABC. Finally, a further principle I would add, also an addition to Chapman's theory, is that we offer whatever causes us the least anxiety to offer. In some cases, it's not that we don't know what our partners would like to receive; rather, we may know what they want but continue to show love in ways that are easier for us to provide. If we are uncomfortable saying, "I love you," writing notes to express our affection, or making regular sexual connection a priority, we make nice meals and buy them little gifts. I see this pattern *frequently* in my sessions with couples. And when I do, I have to find a way to ask whether loving someone in the way that feels most comfortable to us (once we realize we're doing this) is actually love at all.

If you would like to love your partner more intentionally, the first thing to do is to find out whether your understanding of how he or she most wants to be loved is on target. I haven't included a multitude of self-assessments or exercises in this book, with the hope that the few I've included (the personal values inventory, the mini safety quiz, and the following love languages exercise) will stand out as especially helpful ones. The following is an exercise for getting a better understanding of how to love your partner more intentionally. Over the course of a lifetime, because you will both go through many changes, each of you can expect your preferred way of receiving love to change. For this reason, it's probably smart to view this exercise not as a way to lock in your understanding of each other, but as something to revisit every few years to see if there have been any changes.

Crossover Learning Exercise for Couples[122]

Consider the six possible ways of experiencing love – words of affirmation, acts of service, gifts, quality time, non-sexual physical affection, and sexual connection.

How do you think your partner would rank the ways he or she prefers to experience love? How does your partner actually rank the ways he or she prefers to experience love?

(in rank order—from most to least preferred-for you to complete)
1.
2.
3.
4.
5.
6.

(in rank order—from most to least preferred- for your partner to complete)
1.
2.
3.
4.
5.
6.

How does your partner think you would rank the ways you prefer to experience love? How do you actually rank the ways you prefer to experience love?

(in rank order—for your partner to complete)
1.
2.
3.
4.
5.
6.

(in rank order—for you to complete)
1.
2.
3.
4.
5.
6.

After listing your own ranking and your predictions of each other's preferred love languages, compare notes and ask yourselves the following questions.

Questions for Individual Reflection

- Am I surprised by any elements of my love language preferences?
- What things in my life have shaped me to feel most loved in these ways?
- In which ways do I most frequently express my love for my partner?
- Are there ways of expressing love that I'm avoiding (and, if so, what is this about)?

Questions for Couple Reflection

- How do our understandings of each other's love language preferences fit or not fit with our actual preferences for ways of experiencing love?
- Which of the five principles of auto-pilot loving [underlined previously in the text for ease of identification] have come into play in how we have been showing love to each other?
- What are three specific regular practices that we can each initiate to express our love for each other, taking each other's primary love language(s) into consideration?

Intentional Respect

A marriage of equals is attuned to intentional respect as well as intentional love. There are continual efforts to recognize imbalances of power and then to renegotiate and shift power in order to maintain a respectful balance. As such, a marriage of equals offers frequent checks against one partner having too much power over the other in a way that preserves and strengthens the core of equal respect in the marriage. Healthy self-esteem and openness to influence allows equally-matched partners to share power, to admit wrongs, and change course as needed. For example, consider this interaction between two equally powerful spouses who were working for different departments in the same company:

> Partner A: I'm really worried about this new policy statement put out by the company—do you think it's going to lead to anything I should worry about?

> Partner B: There are a lot of things to worry about in the world, but I don't think this is one of them.

Partner A: Whoa—that sounded condescending!

Partner B: You're right, sorry. I see that—I did just sound like a pompous ass—I just came from a staff meeting in which my boss praised me in front of the entire staff and my head was temporarily swollen. What I meant to say is that my read on the situation is that this isn't going to lead to anything bad for you and I hope you won't worry about it.

Despite my critique of the gender-based assumptions and sexist elements of the book *Love and Respect*, I would heartily recommend a read of this book if your goal is to learn how to be more intentionally respectful in your marriage. That is, in my view, if one were to remove the gender-specific language, the book offers very sound guidance in how to be intentionally respectful in your marriage. Given my earlier critique, not surprisingly, I would suggest some linguistic alterations to the set of handy acronyms and gender-specific "decoding keys" for translating the messages that wives and husbands receive through their so-called "pink and blue hearing aids." For example, husbands are urged to keep the acronym COUPLE in mind to prompt them to provide their wives with "closeness," "openness," "understanding," "peacemaking," "loyalty," and "esteem." The acronym CHAIRS is then offered to prompt wives to respect their husbands' "conquest" (that is, appreciate his desire to work and achieve), "hierarchy" (appreciate his desire to protect and provide), "authority," "insight," "relationship," and "sexuality" (appreciate his desire for sexual intimacy)." It seems to me that these are all good things, and I'm quite sure that most husbands and wives would benefit from receiving *both* COUPLE and CHAIRS. Let's focus on CHAIRS, particularly on the idea of conquest, which Eggerichs defines as a husband's desire to "go out and conquer the challenges of his world—to work and achieve."[123] For me, and for most of the female respondents I polled, the need for conquest is also very strong. In fact, the advice Eggerichs gives about appreciating the need for conquest pairs well with the concept of respecting your spouse in a marriage of equals. To briefly quote one specific example of responding to the "need for conquest" from *Love and Respect:* Your ~~husband~~ spouse will feel you appreciate his (or her) desire to work and achieve when...

- You tell him (or her) verbally and in writing that you value his (or her) work efforts.

- You express your faith in him (or her) related to his (or her) chosen field.

- You listen to his (or her) work (or family) stories as closely as you expect him (or her) to listen to your accounts of what happens in the family (or in any domain in which you invest your energy).

- You see yourself as his (or her) helpmate and counterpart and talk with him (or her) about this whenever possible.

- You allow him (or her) to dream as you did when you were courting.

- You don't dishonor or subtly criticize his (or her) work "in the field" to get him (or her) to show more love "in the family." [*sic.* I'm not sure why "in the field" and "in the family" are in quotes here.][124]

So, if you want to learn more about intentionally respecting your partner, I would refer you to *Love and Respect* (with the general recommendation that you make some alterations in the gender-based language).

Intentional Support of New Freedoms

I have previously likened a marriage of equals to a hybrid crossover vehicle that prioritizes maneuverability and adventure above all else. When I was a young woman looking at the types of marriage represented among my friends' parents, I didn't know if I would ever be able to establish a truly satisfying marriage. On a few occasions, I remember thinking, *If that is what marriage is like, I might be better off without a husband.* (To be fair, I may have been influenced by the high rate of divorce among the parents of several classmates in high school.) I had a strong independent streak (apparently like 81% of the Lifestyle Poll respondents, who describe themselves as "independent") and have always craved what I think of as *Walden Pond interludes*—that is, lengths of time when I can meet life on my own terms, often in solitude, and sometimes in various new social settings. At various times in my life, I have strongly identified with Henry Thoreau, who once said, "To be in company, even with the best, is soon wearisome and dissipating. I love to be alone. I never found the companion that was so companionable as solitude."[125] At the same time, I was very romantic and desired a kind of love and partnership that might be enjoyed in a type of marriage I dreamed of but did not often see among the examples I observed as a young woman. Of course, being independent and craving solitary time does not mean that one does not also highly value meaningful attachments. In fact, the three most common self-identified personality traits for women in the Lifestyle Poll sample were "intelligent," "friendly," and "independent."

I was ultimately fortunate enough to find a man who is strong enough to allow me to be who I am, and for the length of our relationship (15 years as of this writing), I've enjoyed freedoms I never thought would be possible when I was younger. My husband and I find expression of love in both our attachment to, and detachment from, each other. For instance, we have intentionally incorporated Walden Pond interludes as a regular rhythm of our life together. The support of my need for moments of complete autonomy is one of the most precious gifts my husband gives me within the context of our marriage. As author May Sarton reflected, "Perhaps the greatest gift we can give to another human being is detachment. Attachment, even that which imagines it is selfless, always lays some burden on the other person. How to learn to love in such a light, airy way that there is no burden?"[126] To illustrate the life-giving quality of these gifts of solitude, I'd like to briefly tell you about a few of our Walden Pond interludes. When I finished my Ph.D., I took a two-week walking tour through the hill towns of Tuscany to unwind from graduate school and prepare for the next chapter in my life. Most of the touring companies I contacted had a policy that every female must be accompanied by at least one other person, but eventually I found a representative in one company who was able to be persuaded that I would not be a liability, as I am a fully capable adult who can make intelligent decisions. This touring company moved my luggage from inn to inn, leaving me free to walk from town to town with only a day pack filled with a few thick slices of bread, a wedge of good pecorino cheese, a bottle of water, some maps, and a journal. I had no cell phone and was glad of it. For that two-week period, I lived entirely at my own whim, off the grid, pursuing whatever interesting adventures I might discover along the way. After a few days of unwinding, my mind began to explode with new ideas and insights. I wrote more than 100 pages in my journal, and to this day, I am still renewed when I remember this golden solitary interlude in my life.

A few years later, when I was feeling somewhat burned out, I pursued another Walden Pond interlude, this time a week in a cabin in the backwoods of a small town in North Carolina. Once again, my senses came alive during this trip, as I faced both new and anxiety-provoking situations. For instance, on the night of my arrival, I followed my GPS to a location in the wrong county, travelling several miles in a car without four-wheel drive up a one-lane, unpaved, slippery, snow-covered road with a sheer drop off to my left side, only to find myself blocked by a locked gate to someone's remote mountain lair. When I came to the locked gate and realized that my GPS must have led me far astray of my destination, I had to resist the urge to panic. There was no one else to depend on but myself and my maker. I had to stay calm and back slowly down the hill in the pitch dark of night with the driver's side door open to light the way so that I wouldn't miscalculate and pitch off the sheer cliff to my left. Experiences like this one have strengthened my ability to remain calm and address a number of anxiety-provoking situations without panicking (for example, I call on these abilities often when helping severely traumatized combat veterans readjust to life after deployment). During the same week in North Carolina, I also created some wonderful memories of hiking alone through the local mountains, interacting with the locals, and forming my own impressions of the costs and benefits (as I see it, anyway) of their way of life. In the midst of both the harrowing and pleasurable events of this trip, I noticed that somehow, my senses seem sharper when I'm alone.

Instead of the short-lived pursuit of each other during the cocaine-rush phase of our relationship, my husband and I have been pursuing each other for the past 15 years all over the United States. The desire to mutually support each other's goals and dreams has led to adventures in establishing ourselves in three time zones and a total of five states. About 12 years into our relationship, our job situations required my husband and me to stagger our relocation across the country by five months. With the help of my husband's parents, who have been an incredible source of support, I made the long drive first, towing a large trailer of the things I would need to establish myself for the next five months. I was responsible for getting some roots established, learning the ropes of my new job, negotiating the purchase of a house we wanted to buy, and completing a number of construction projects that would need to be done before we could move our things into our new home. My husband was responsible for closing the sale of our previous house and for packing, storing, and transferring the rest of our things. He had primary authority over what we would sell and what we would keep, and I had the primary responsibility to get our new life established so that when he arrived in the 26-foot moving truck with the rest of our things, our new house (a foreclosed property that needed a considerable amount of work) would be fully ready for occupation.

There were some very challenging times while we were apart, with each of us managing what felt like overwhelming responsibilities at times. Throughout this period, however, the partnership we had formed was a tremendous asset in making this a successful transition. During this extended Walden Pond interlude requiring us both to meet several waves of challenges alone, I took a trip within a trip and walked up the coast of our new home state of California. Again, there were moments of clarifying terror (as when I thought I encountered a baby mountain lion—possibly with its mother in the near vicinity—that my photos later revealed was a bobcat). As always, there were also moments of pure exhilaration and renewal, in a way that is *different* from the renewal I experience on adventures with my husband (which are most often a guaranteed good time for both of us).

My husband has also benefited from intentionally pursuing his own Walden Pond interludes. The year after I did my Tuscany walking tour, he attended a four-week research institute in Greece. He came home with stories of new friends and wild adventures. A few years later, he took a week in Hawaii, the first part of which was spent attending a professional conference. After the conference, other friends of his stayed on in the hotel while he pulled our two-person tent and sleeping bag out of his suitcase and headed off to stay on the beach for a few days. He told me about one particular night when it had rained heavily, which was not typical for that part of Hawaii at that time of year. He said, "It was raining, I was alone, and my sleeping bag was cold and wet. Everything was muddy, but I felt happy because I knew that I could figure it out and that I would remember the feeling of sleeping in the mud many years later." His night in the rain was fully met in the spirit of Thoreau or Sarton, as it was a "moment of open time, with no obligations except towards the inner world and what is going on there."[127] For my husband as well as myself, then, these experiences of meeting life on our own terms, moments of elemental reconstitution, are invigorating and clarifying and of great value. Once, when we had a conversation about why this is, he said, "I think it's kind of like when you first arrive at college. You remember everything so well because it comes down to you and you only…you have to figure it all out on your own, and this sharpens your senses."

In our partnership, we believe that finding each other should not be a reason to stop growing individually. We believe that moments of self-reliance are critical and that sustaining friendships with people who are friends of our marriage is a vital part of a successful marriage. As author Joan Anderson put it, "Every marriage needs community relief. How could one partner, no matter how remarkable, be everything to the other? It's ludicrous to believe so."[128] We question the notion that "two become one" means that we should stop having our individual identities, that we should show up everywhere as a unit, decline to go on outings when one of us can't go, and merge all of our personal space. (I wonder whether the relatively recent trend toward having "man caves" and "woman caves" is on some level a rejection of the traditional marital merge). And we are not alone in questioning these traditional assumptions or in seeking the benefits of Walden Pond interludes. In the Lifestyle Poll, I asked the question "How do you feel about spending time alone?" For the women in this sample, the most frequent response was "I really enjoy being alone and I frequently seek out time alone." The second most frequent response was "Being alone doesn't bother me—but I don't actively seek it out." Less than 20% of the respondents answered either "I would prefer not to be alone for too long" or "I don't like being alone—I strongly prefer to be with other people most of the time." I also posed the following hypothetical situation: "If you won an all-expense-paid trip for one to tour your favorite country in another continent for two months and the stipulation was that you had to go alone, and there were no practical constraints to accepting this, how would you respond?" Slightly less than 40% reported that they would be very excited to travel alone for two months. Another 47% said they would go despite their preference to travel with at least one other person. Less than 14% said they would not accept the offer to travel unaccompanied for two months. Respondents elaborated on the personal importance of such travel experiences in the open-ended portion of the poll. For example:

- I love to travel, and travel whenever I can, as cheaply as I can. Living and teaching in Mongolia helped me to put materialism in perspective—money is not equated with happiness. I love meeting people from different countries, and mixing with the locals when I do travel. I'm the type of person who talks to the people on the train or at the table next to mine in the cafe. Most of the time, people are surprised that I'm American—I break stereotypes all the time!

- My travels continually open my eyes to other perspectives. think they have made me more tolerant and curious, which I see as good things. They make me see people as us and not them.

- I think that my travels have exposed me to the way others live and have prevented me from taking anything I have or am able to do for granted. I have learned to be more flexible and to adapt more easily to all types of circumstances. Traveling with friends has significantly helped me get along better with others, and traveling by myself has made me braver and more adventurous.

- My travels have made me more aware of how small I am in the world, made me appreciate diversity. A recent trip to the Middle East made me rethink all of my positions on the Islamic world in a really fundamental way.

- Travelling has given me a sense that there is a purpose to life that is greater than myself. It has helped me to be less selfish.

- Travelling has given me perspective on life. My adventures abroad have made me more sensitive about cultural differences. They have made me a more interesting person, more compassionate. They have given me more wisdom and a ton of happy memories.

When asked how they would respond if their husband were offered an opportunity to "go out of the country to a place so remote that he would be totally out of contact for six weeks to learn a skill with several people of both genders," only 6% reported that they would make efforts to prevent their husbands from accepting such an opportunity. About half (50.8%) reported that they would give their husband a full and unqualified blessing to travel in this way, and an additional 44% said they would go along with the plan but would not be fully OK with it for one reason or another. Along the same lines, a greater portion of the married respondents reported that they share "some of their husband's hobbies" (53.9%) rather than sharing "most of their husband's hobbies" (33.2%), suggesting that individuation in pursuing activities and interests may be a consistent value in a marriage of equals.

To begin to summarize this portrayal of a marriage of equals, I'd like to return to a point I made in Chapter 2. As I have previously cautioned, when you find yourself saying (or even privately thinking) things like "We just met, but it feels like we've known each other forever" or "I think I just met my soul mate," inevitably, the truth is one of three things:

1. It could be the real deal, the kind of love that is invigorating, freeing, and sustainable for the rest of your life.

2. You and your new love are enjoying the *folie a deux* that you are soul mates who are destined to be together (which turns out to be a heartbreaking mirage).

3. What you are feeling may in fact be the echoes of former trauma in your life (which often morphs into the living nightmare of an abusive relationship).

In thinking about these outcomes, I propose thinking of a new relationship as the joining of two piles of sand into one tall pinnacle of hard-packed sand. As a relationship develops, the sands of time reveal its quality. In all cases, cracks will appear when the relationship is stressed, which will occur with the passage of sufficient time. In the case of the two false loves, however, cracks will become chasms as time erodes the foundation, and partners will "fall out of love" or will devolve into disrespectful, abusive patterns. In the case of the *folie a deux*, the relationship will quickly begin to crumble and blow away before the eyes of the people who had once felt they had met "the One." When the selection of a partner is based on that person's similarity to someone who caused a past trauma, time may etch the partnership into something monstrous, carving away at what first appeared to be love, leaving one or both in the bondage of a living nightmare.

In the category of real love, there are traditional and nontraditional unions, both of which can be successful and mutually satisfying. In the case of a traditional husband-as-head-of-the-household type of union, the sand is set in a certain way and hardens thereafter with relatively little change to its composition or appearance (which may still be beautiful to behold nonetheless). In the case of a marriage of equals, when both partners are open to influence, there is a sculptural process of growth. Like Michelangelo, who removed everything in the block of marble that did not conform to the thing of beauty he was driven to create, partners in growth-promoting marriages will work to remove whatever obstructs love, respect, and the freedom to fulfill potential. A marriage of equals will shift and change in response to the needs of the individuals and the unique aspects of their character and dreams. This is not a passive process—it is entirely active and intentional. It is not the easy path. The process of "iron sharpening iron"[129] hurts at times. It requires persistent strength of character to allow each other to grind out cavities and chip away at various character flaws. It takes significant energy to hold on to each other when stress hits, and an overriding commitment to hold on to what is good and life-giving in the bond when you don't feel close for a stretch of time. It requires each of you to understand that change is unavoidable and to trust that your partner will continue to show both love and respect through the various seasons of life.

If you don't connect to the sand analogy, consider the idea of theme songs. I would suggest that the theme song of the cocaine-induced pairing could be "Hooked on a Feeling":

> I'm... hooked on a feelin'/High on believin'/That you're in love with me/Lips as sweet as candy/The taste stays on my mind/Girl, you keep me thirsty/For another cup of wine/...I got it bad for you, girl/But I don't need a cure/I'll just stay addicted/and hope I can endure![130]

In my opinion, the lyrical refrain of Mumford and Sons' "Sigh No More" captures the essence of a marriage of equals, a love that is simultaneously modern in the form it takes in a truly equal marriage, and as ancient as the ancient of days:

> Love, it will not betray you/Dismay or enslave you/It will set you free/Be more like the man [or woman] you were made to be/There is a design, an alignment, a cry/Of my heart to see/The beauty of love as it was made to be.[131]

To conclude by reflecting on previous chapters, I would ask the question, "Is there something better than the thrill of the cocaine-rush phase of a relationship?" I would say *yes*, in a successful marriage of equals, successively deeper levels of love and respect take the place of unrealistic fantasies. Put another way, the essence of a marriage of equals is love and friendship paired with a sense of *freedom*. As you move through the testing phase of a relationship, the intentional investment of both love and respect produces an expansive freedom for you to live into your full potential and provides you and your partner with a wonderful form of support for doing so.

What kind of marriage would you create if you were assured of both your partner's commitment to you and of his or her commitment to supporting you equally in living into your full potential?

Chapter 6

The Testing Phase: Confronting the Usual Suspects in a Marriage of Equals

In the testing phase of relationships, arguments about money, sex, co-parenting, and chore sharing are four of the most common problems in many marriages, and this was no different for women who responded to the Lifestyle Poll. This chapter will focus on each of these areas to describe the form they take in the Lifestyle Poll marriages and to suggest principles for effectively navigating these areas with the goal of preserving a marriage of equals.

Financial Affairs

Research findings suggest a U-shaped association between level of socioeconomic status and divorce rates.[132] In other words, as previously mentioned, people with very low and very high incomes have the highest divorce rates. The Lifestyle Poll respondents were most often raised in families from the lowest-risk category, as they were mostly from upper-middle (44%) and middle-class (37%) homes. Respondents generally perceived themselves as upwardly mobile relative to their families of origin, as most (65%) felt that their financial situations were better than those of their mothers at the same age. An additional 15% felt that their financial positions were about the same, and the remaining 20% felt that their situations were worse than their mothers' were at the same age. Despite being too young to be anywhere near their full earning potential in most cases, in 2008, respondents reported extremely high household income levels relative to the population at large (see Figure 5.1). The majority (about 80%) reported that they were able to afford their lifestyles without going into debt. Most respondents (83%) had less than $5,000 in household credit card debt, and 70% had less than $1000 in personal credit card debt. Nearly half (45%) owned their homes. It's worth repeating that this data was collected in 2008, before the widespread financial collapse of the US economy and the current era of high unemployment and underemployment. I have no information about how respondents have weathered the changes in the global economy since 2008.

There is also some evidence that respondents are both financially knowledgeable and well engaged in the management of their finances. For example, most (72%) knew what the "S & P" refers to, and 59% reported that they could explain the difference between an IRA and a 401K without consulting outside sources. Respondents were investing in savings accounts (80%), 401K plans (64%), IRAs (55%), mutual funds (55%), stocks (43%), bonds (24%), and CDs (21%). The majority (70%) were actively investing in retirement accounts of some type. The majority (70%) also reported that they had financial buffers of at least three months in the case of some financial crisis such as a sudden layoff or loss of an income-earning spouse.

Within the married portion of the sample, working wives reported that they were making significant contributions to the financial health of their families. Half (50%) strongly agreed and another 17% somewhat agreed that their income was as vital to the well-being of their families as their husbands' incomes. More than half (54%) felt it was certain (22%) or probable (32%) that they could live as well as they did at the time of the survey if they were to lose their husbands to death or divorce. An additional 28% felt that this was possible but unlikely, and the remaining 18% felt that their standard of living would certainly decline if they were to lose their husbands. The large majority of mothers (82%) continued to work outside the home for an income. Most frequently, household bills were split 50/50 (44% of cases) or husbands paid for more of the expenses (39% of cases), yet for nearly one-fifth of the married sample (17% of cases), wives paid for more of the household expenses than their husbands. Married respondents perceived that they generally share responsibility equally with their husbands for managing the household finances and reported that they were slightly more likely than their husbands to submit payments for monthly bills. Slightly more than half (55%) had just one shared joint account, while the other 45% maintained separate accounts. One-third of the sample (33%) had a three-pot system—that is, both partners had their own accounts, and the couple had a joint spending account.

Given this picture of financial health, how then do we make sense of respondents' perception that "lack of money" has been the biggest obstacle in attaining the lifestyle they would seek? Further, given the unprecedented financial parity in these marriages, how might we make sense of the report that frequent "arguments about finances" was the third most highly ranked marital problem? The answers to these questions are not simple, and surely there are multiple factors at play. Based on my perspective and readings on this topic, a few general notions come to mind. First, stress about financial health is widespread these days for nearly every sector of the population, regardless of gender, with the potential exception of those in the wealthiest 5% or 10% of Americans who own and control more than 75% of the resources. With a small number of exceptions, I would not characterize the women in the Lifestyle Poll (or their husbands) as being a part of this upper 5%–10%, at least at this point in their lives. As Miriam Peskowitz, author of *The Truth Behind the Mommy Wars*,[133] explains, "Generation X-ers are haunted by financial insecurity." Finance and business editor Jill Fraser asserts that "long term financial stability has disappeared, within a business world in which layoffs and other cuts have been as rampant during periods of economic prosperity as during turndowns."[134] Tamara Draut, the director of the Economic Opportunity Program at Demos, a financial think tank, assessed the national situation in 2005 and characterized the economic climate (before the crash of the US economy!) as a "dog-eat-dog economy that rewards only a handful of players and leaves everybody else with scraps."[135] When I reflect on these analyses, I am reminded of the famous "rat utopia" studies of NIMH researcher John Calhoun in the mid-19th century.[136] Calhoun initially created an environment with ample space and plenty of access to the elements of the good life (as a rat would construct *la dolce vita*, anyway). Over time, as the rats bred freely with each other, the environment became overcrowded and resources were increasingly difficult to access predictably. The rat utopia morphed into a living nightmare for those in the once-harmonious colony. Insecure and threatened in this primal way, the rats became aggressive, organizing themselves into gangs that roved around attacking the more vulnerable members of the group.

In one sense, it might seem silly to compare the rat's nightmarish environment to the situation of citizens living in a country where most of society continues to enjoy a much higher standard of living than most people across the world. Yet, in another sense, although we do enjoy a higher standard of living in many ways, we also feel more vulnerable to a sudden and unpredictable change in our quality of life relative to people in many other countries. We live in an age when it's much more likely that we will "get poor quick" than that we will ever "get rich quick." That is, we live in a country where even the wealthiest families are at risk of becoming bankrupt, for example, because of the unchecked cost of medical procedures. Many families today are one serious health condition (or one baby) away from perilous levels of financial strain. Those in all levels of corporate America can be fired or let go of at will. Like the fattened chiefs of some ancient tribal colonies who were the first to be sacrificed, those nearer the top may actually be at greater risk of losing their positions and struggling for many years without a job because of their higher salaries.

The past few years have shown us how easy it is to lose one's job, home, and position in society. Previous social contracts between employee and employer and between individuals and lending institutions have been replaced by a "might makes right" mentality on the part of whoever is the "bigger dog" (almost always the company or lending institution). Companies are not required or even pressured in any consistent way to do right by customers or employees. When companies merge, middle managers, fearful of their own job security, can easily be compelled to lay off multiple employees. Such layoffs are often facilitated by the lack of an existing relationship between those who come in to restructure a company and those who have been employed in that company. Restructuring consultants will often trot out the tried-and-true line "it's just business...it's not personal," and truthfully, there is no way it could be personal, given the lack of a relationship. The individuals doing the restructuring are somewhat like the "teachers" in Stanley Milgram's classic study on obedience to authority who administered supposedly lethal shocks to a cardiac-compromised "learner"[137] from another room. It's basically an ideal formula for corporations to move people around on the chessboard (or take them off the board completely, in many cases) without any regard to the impact they are having on the employees and their families. As Richard Florida puts it in *The Rise of the Creative Class*, "There is no corporation or other large institution that will take care of us...we are truly on our own."[138] In America today, it seems that if you don't own a hospital or a health insurance company (or have assets to match those who wield such influence), you exist in a chronic state of potentially high financial vulnerability. I would argue that "standard of living" should not be equated to how many square feet of living space one can buy, what quality of school you can access for one's children, or how many weeks of vacation you can afford to take, without also considering how quickly and easily you can suddenly and unpredictably lose all of these things.

Further, it seems that women consistently have greater financial vulnerabilities relative to men. A large insurance company, Allianz Insurance, discovered a widespread fear within a sample of 1,925 women they studied: the fear of losing everything and ending up on the streets.[139] Despite the fact that 48% of the sample had an annual income of more than $100,000, almost half of the respondents (46%) were troubled by a "tremendous fear of becoming a bag lady." When I heard about this study, I began to wonder whether these findings might be replicated in my target sample—would a significant number of female graduates of top universities, who are highly successful to all outward appearances, also be plagued by this level of personal, financial, and professional insecurity? Although I posed many blunt questions in the Lifestyle Poll, I stopped short of asking participants if they had a fear of ending up as "bag ladies" (Allianz Insurance's term, not mine). However, I did include a couple of questions that were a variation on the imposter syndrome, a phenomenon that was first described by psychologists Pauline Clance and Suzanne Imes.[140] Specifically, I asked participants to indicate their agreement with the statements, "I often think that if people really knew me, they would not feel that I'm as successful as I appear to be" and "I have doubts that I can maintain the level of professional success I have accomplished in the past." For the first statement, 33% of respondents agreed (8% strongly agreed). For the second statement, 33% agreed (9% strongly agreed). What was particularly interesting, and should be noted about these responses, was the number of respondents who skipped these questions entirely. These questions were two of the very limited number of questions in the poll for which a noticeably large portion (165 women, about 13% of the total number of participants) skipped entirely. Respondents freely shared sensitive data in a number of areas, including their incomes, fears of divorce, physical and mental health conditions, and personal reasons for having sought therapy, yet many elected to skip the questions assessing feelings of being an imposter. From my perspective, the tendency to skip this question may be a form of data to consider in making sense of these results. Although it is impossible to draw any firm conclusions, it appears that the findings of the Allianz study were at least partially replicated in the Lifestyle Poll sample, given that at least one-third of those who responded (and possibly more) endorsed significant feelings of anxiety about their ability to maintain the place they have achieved in their professions.

Why might women be especially vulnerable to financial worries? As many, many writers have mentioned, women are often paid less for the same work. Advancement opportunities continue to be relatively limited for females in comparison to their male peers. Women who wish to become mothers (the vast majority of Lifestyle Poll respondents) have a particular set of vulnerabilities. Economist and author Sylvia Ann Hewlett argues that better access to education and higher-paying jobs "has not translated into better choices on the family front—indeed, when it comes to children, [high-achieving women's] options seem to be a good deal worse than before."[141] Along the same lines, author Miriam Peskowitz writes, "More women than men bear the economic brunt of job sacrifice that comes with parenting, and we're left more vulnerable as a result."[142] Daniel Brook, author of *The Trap: Selling out to Stay Afloat in Winner-Take-All America*,[143] explores the thorny complications that face modern couples with children: "First the husband quits the job he loves in order to start a family. Then the wife quits her job because the cost of child care means it no longer makes economic sense for her to work. All of a sudden, a progressive couple...is forced back into 1950s gender roles, with the husband an unfulfilled breadwinner and the wife an unfulfilled stay-at-home mom."[144]

Within my personal network of friends and contacts, the typical mindset I've observed is a keen awareness of the limited number of years one has to ascend in one's profession while free from the constraints of parenting responsibilities. In my circle of friends, there is often great pressure for women to complete at least one graduate degree and become professionally established before children enter the picture. Husbands often feel incredible pressure to obtain salaries high enough to absorb the future loss of their wives' full-time income and the high expense of child care support. Working women who want to have children have a different set of anxieties. First, to the degree that those who choose to become parents cut back on their paid work hours or take lower-paying jobs with more flextime, there may be the need for ongoing discussions about how to retain a financial buffer despite new expenses in case of some unforeseen issue (e.g., loss of a job or development of a costly health problem). From a psychological perspective, there may be a need to address increased feelings of financial dependence on the part of the partner who cuts back on working outside the home. Maintaining a feeling of equal power may become more difficult to the degree that an individual's sense of power and "freedom to choose to stay in the marriage" was partially based on advancing in his or her field, earning an income, or maintaining some sense of financial independence. A loss of such power has the potential to radically shift the relationship from that of two people staying committed to each other because both "want to," to a commitment based on the financial dependence of one partner. Such feelings should be assessed, and if present, they should be actively discussed and addressed in the couple's strategic planning. The goal would be to minimize unwanted feelings of dependence and to maintain a healthy level of equality in each partner's relative sense of financial security.

Sexual Tension (the kind you don't want)

"Arguments about sex" was one of the top three sources of strain in the Lifestyle Poll marriages, along with chore sharing tension and financial arguments. Most of the married respondents reported that they have sex 1 or 2 times per week (44.9%), but a third (32.3%) of the sample reported having sex once or twice a month. On the ends of the spectrum, 9.8% reported having sex 3 or more times a week, and 12.5% said they have sex less than once a month. When I asked participants how they feel about their libido, 43.3% reported that they are satisfied with their general level of sexual desire. When there is dissatisfaction with their level of sex drive, however, the tendency for Lifestyle Poll respondents was to feel that it's too low. Specifically, 56.2% said that it's too low, whereas less than 1% said that it's too high. The data on husbands makes an interesting comparison. Most participants (66.7%) were satisfied with their husbands' levels of sexual desire. When wives were dissatisfied with their husbands' sex drives, the tendency was to perceive it as too high (24.4%). In 9.1% of cases, however, participants expressed their husbands' libidos were too low. Therefore, although this information generally supports findings of other studies suggesting that husbands may have a higher desire for sex than wives do, a notable portion of the sample felt that their husbands' sex drives were lower than they would prefer.

Several good books focus much more specifically on sexuality in marriage. Three that I would recommend are *Passionate Marriage*[145] and *Intimacy and Desire*[146] both by Dr. David Schnarch and *The Sex-Starved Marriage: Boosting Your Marriage Libido: A Couple's Guide*[147] by Michelle Weiner-Davis. Given that I do not know the specific nature of the sexual problems of Lifestyle Poll respondents, I will confine my comments to a general perspective on sex in long-term relationships. First, as

I have said before, I believe that sexual connection is an entirely legitimate need in a marriage—one that should not be shamed, minimized, or overlooked. For this reason, in Chapter 5, I expanded Gary Chapman's conceptualization of love languages to include sexual connection. Couples who ignore sexual problems in their marriage do so at their own peril.

One of the early readers of my book draft, a psychologist I respect, recommended that I read *Intimacy and Desire* by David Schnarch. I took his advice and found it to be quite simply the best book I've read on the topic of healthy sexuality in long-term committed relationships. Schnarch argues very persuasively that levels of sex drive are never equal between two partners – there will always be one partner whose desire for sex is greater. It is possible that partners may switch off in terms of whoever is driving the sexual relationship at different points in time. However, as a general trend, my clinical experience fits with Schnarchs' observation; baseline levels of sexual desire between long-term partners are usually discrepant (just as lots of other individual differences surface when people partner for life). Further, low libido is not always a female problem, as a lower-than-desired sex drive affects some portion of males. Because of prevailing notions that men have a higher desire for sex than women, relatively lower sexual desire in men is particularly likely to be under-reported and inadequately addressed. In fact, Schnarch reports that males are the lower desire partner in half the couples he sees in his clinical practice.

Moreover, Schnarch proposes that sexual problems are unavoidable and completely *normal* as couples make the transition from what I refer to as the cocaine-rush phase to the testing phase of a relationship. Citing Helen Fisher's research, he maintains that once our brains make the shift from cocaine-like chemical explosions to a flood of hormones associated with long-term attachment,[148] it is impossible to re-capture the same type of sexual thrill we felt during the initial phase of a relationship. As Schnarch puts it, "your brain function shifts from infatuation and romantic love to long-term attachment, where your sexual desire drowns in pools of vasopressin or oxytocin."[149] At this point in the relationship, sexual desire needs to come from a new source, a source much deeper than wearing sexy new underwear. Schnarch highlights the centrality of personal growth as the primary vehicle for sexual enrichment. That is, sexual desire problems create opportunities to forge a more solid sense of self which develops as a function of "confronting yourself, challenging yourself to do what's right, and earning your own self-respect."[150] I could not agree more with this statement. A strong sense of self then allows us to have the courage to openly convey the full range of our erotic self to our partner. This ability to hold onto ourselves while moving with intentional desire towards our partner is the basis of a deep well of (often mind-blowing) intimate sexual connection. For anyone interested in revitalizing or expanding sexual connection in a long-term relationship, any book authored by David Schnarch qualifies as highly recommended reading in my opinion.

Threats to Sexual Fidelity in Marriage

In addition to asking about the frequency of sexual connection, I also asked Lifestyle Poll respondents to rank the biggest threats to their sexual exclusivity, for their husbands and for themselves. Wives rated attractive co-workers of the opposite sex as the biggest threat to their husbands' ability to stay faithful, followed by their husbands' use of internet pornography and by his single friends of the same sex who are still living "the single life" (and who might presumably expose him to some tempting situations). Interestingly, in reflecting on their own vulnerabilities to infidelity, the picture for wives was somewhat different. Specifically, wives ranked their ex-lovers and old flames as the biggest perceived threat, followed by attractive co-workers and then by longtime friends of the opposite sex.

Some existing research validates the potential risk of the threats perceived by Lifestyle Poll respondents to be most problematic for marital fidelity. The late Dr. Shirley Glass, a well-respected marital affairs expert, conducted a study of 350 couples in her clinical practice and found that 62% of the unfaithful husbands and 46% of the unfaithful wives had had an affair with someone they had met at work. Moreover, more than half of these husbands (55%) and half of the wives (50%) who had had affairs at their workplaces had not had previous affairs.[151] Glass also cites the unpublished doctoral dissertation of Debbie Layton-Tholl, who found that 27% of the respondents in her infidelity study met their affair partners on the internet.[152] Clearly, the internet can be fertile ground for the development of affairs, given the level of secrecy, anonymity, and lack of accountability for online communications. A third high risk area is old flames, which can easily be reignited. Glass explains that when former lovers meet again, "they look into each other's eyes and see each other as they once were: younger, more beautiful, and full of life. Their passion quickly takes root in them again. They know each other and being together feels like coming home."[153] I would imagine that old flames that reunite have intoxicating (and positively biased) memories of their first shared cocaine-rush of new love and that the long absence before the moment of reconnection boosts the anticipatory expectation of a second cocaine-rush with each other.

For a spouse who had assumed monogamy, the discovery of an affair ranks at the top of the list in the categories of violated expectations and attachment traumas. Glass's concept of "walls and windows" helps shed light on how affairs—whether sexual or emotional—are destructive to the foundations of a marriage. She explains that in a healthy marriage, there is a window between the spouses, who share with each other the intimate details of their deepest thoughts and feelings. To some degree, there is a necessary (and healthy) wall around the marriage such that those outside the marriage are not privy to the same level of intimate knowledge as the partners within the marriage. When one partner has an affair, this reverses the direction of the walls and windows. The secretive rupture of the marital bond effectively walls the betrayed partner out and opens a new window between the two new lovers. One of the most damaging psychological aspects of affairs is the destruction of a former assumption that there was no other person who knows your spouse as intimately as you do.

Affairs are devastating for anyone, but I wonder whether they might be especially traumatic for those whose relationship was constructed as an equal partnership between two individuals with a strong physical, emotional, *and* mental connection. Related to this possibility, I asked Lifestyle Poll respondents to provide information about which of a set of behaviors on their spouses' part would be unacceptable to them. In terms of what was unacceptable to this group of wives, it was very interesting to note that the idea of one's husband having cybersex with another woman was virtually as unacceptable (88.1%) as the idea of one's husband having an actual sexual relationship with another woman (89.8%). These types of affairs—whether virtual or in the flesh—were also judged to be more unacceptable than any other type of potentially unfaithful behavior. Second to these in unacceptability was the idea of one's husband having a deep emotional relationship with a female co-worker. The fact that 70.2% of participants stated that they would find this unacceptable converges with these wives' sense that attractive co-workers in their husbands' work settings are the biggest perceived threat to their husbands' fidelity. Viewed as a set, these reports from wives seem to illustrate the high importance that is placed on the mental and emotional bond, as well as the sexual bond, for the wives in this sample.

The walls and windows model proposed by Glass is also helpful in conceptualizing the process of correcting and repairing ruptures of trust with couples in the clinical setting. In the general process that allows couples to survive an affair, the couple first needs to engage in radical honesty with each other. Typically, the hurt partner talks about how the offense has ruptured his or her trust, and the spouse who had the affair shares what actually happened *in as much detail as the hurt partner wants to know*—that is, the offended partner, not the partner who has been unfaithful, determines the level of detail to be shared. Although this information is always painful to hear, as a rule, free-floating anxiety exists in proportion to what we don't know, and a hurt partner will often fill in the blanks with the worst possible scenarios. In fact, thinking patterns in the aftermath of an affair are the opposite of the ways we think during the cocaine-rush phase of a relationship. That is, early in a relationship, when the world feels full of hope and possibility, we optimistically fill in the blanks with the best possible scenarios (if our partner is unreachable, it is probably because he is working hard to advance world peace), but later on, when we are really invested in a relationship and we become aware of an affair, we tend to fill in the blanks with the absolute worst-case scenarios. Most often, what really happened is not as bad as our self-torturing visions of the level of intimacy shared by our unfaithful spouse and his or her affair partner. Even if it is, we can get adjusted to known truths—even horrible ones—but many individuals can't even begin to adjust when they don't know the parameters of the offense. Exactly how much knowledge is necessary to begin to adjust to a "known truth" varies between individuals. Some hurting partners have some general questions to ask, and others really do need to know all the details before they can begin to heal. When the formerly unfaithful spouse honors the request to share as many details about the affair as his or her partner asks to know, this begins to correct the loss of intimacy created by the affair and begins to restructure the walls and windows to their former positions.

When telling the hurt partner about the affair, the partner who was unfaithful must take responsibility for his or her decision to stray from the marriage. There can be no denial or minimization on the part of the one who engaged in the hurtful behavior. After all, if she or he denies, minimizes, or presents what happened as justifiable in any way, doesn't that mean it could happen again? The one who had the affair must show that he or she realizes how much and in what ways the infidelity has wounded his or her spouse. It is often very healing to the hurting partner when the offending partner discloses feelings of shame and guilt and talks about how he or she now views the affair in consideration of how the spouse has been wounded. The one who had the affair must then show that he or she is working to restructure the walls and windows in the marriage. The unfaithful partner must also be willing to cut off all contact with the affair partner and, if this is not possible, must be cooperative with any reasonable restrictions the spouse feels are necessary to maintain appropriately protective boundaries. For example, it may not be possible to avoid all future encounters if the affair partner was a co-worker, but the couple might agree to no texts, e-mails, calls, or one-on-one contact at all with the affair partner. The goal at this point in the process is to facilitate the formation of a collaborative plan to rebuild the wall that existed and thereby rebuild some trust. As I have said previously, the growth of trust is a function of the alignment between what someone says he or she will do and what the person actually does. When both partners are actively involved in the plan to rebuild trust, there are opportunities to observe the alignment between what has been agreed upon and what occurs. Without such opportunities for observation, trust is much harder to re-establish.

After these steps have been successfully negotiated and the wounded partner feels sufficiently safe, it is also important that the couple discuss any factors that may have contributed to either spouse's vulnerability to having an affair in the first place. There isn't always a specific reason for a spouse to cheat. Too many factors are involved for a simplistic explanation for why people are unfaithful. There are, however, often some common factors, such as unresolved traumas, or unmet needs in one or both partners in the marriage, that may increase the susceptibility to temptation. Peggy Vaughan, infidelity expert and author of *The Monogamy Myth: A Personal Handbook for Recovering from Affairs,* writes the following:

> What will NOT prevent affairs [is] "being in love," promising to be faithful, threats or ultimatums, religious commandments or parental injunctions, having more children, getting caught, repeating the marriage vows, spicing up your sex life, trying to be "perfect," and trying to meet your partner's needs.... What is most likely to prevent affairs [is] being aware that no one is immune from having an affair, discussing and agreeing on your commitment to monogamy, regularly renewing your commitment, engaging in open, honest communication about everything that

impacts your relationship, and acknowledging that the issue of monogamy is never settled once and for all.[154]

One of the dominant themes in Peggy Vaughan's work is the importance of honest and open discussions about everything that may affect the marriage. Having been influenced by her insights, in the Lifestyle Poll, I asked the question "In your marriage, how do you handle attractions to other people?" I was surprised to note that only a little more than one-third (36.4%) talk openly about attractions to other people with each other. The most frequent response (for 63.8% of the married sample) was that they avoid discussing attractions with each other. Furthermore, in the previously mentioned list of unacceptable behaviors in marriage, more than a third (37.3%) of the respondents actually said that it was *unacceptable* for their husbands to talk about attractions they have to others. Peggy Vaughan suggests that avoidance of discussing attractions to others may make a marriage more vulnerable to affairs. Approaching this topic may be difficult, but Vaughan contends that doing so "is far more likely [to] lead to a closer relationship because of the comfort involved in feeling that you will be told the truth about anything that comes up."[155]

Chore Sharing

In the early 1900s, author and philosopher May Sarton commented, "Whatever college does not do, it does create a climate where work is demanded and where nearly every student finds him- or herself at the demand with powers he did not know he had. Then quite suddenly a young woman, if she marries, has to diverge completely from this way of life, while her husband simply goes on towards the goals set in college. She is expected to cope not with ideas, but with cooking food, washing dishes, doing laundry, and if she insists on keeping a job, she needs both a lot of energy and the ability to organize her time."[156] To the present time, researchers continue to note that most of the time, whether in a research or clinical context, married women report that they do the vast majority of the household chores. In the book *Mistakes Were Made (but Not By Me)*[157] (published in 2007), psychologists Carol Tavris and Elliot Aronson summarize research on perceptions of chore-splitting in marriages. They explain, "When researchers ask married participants what percentage of the housework they do, the wives say, 'Are you kidding? I do almost everything, at least 90 percent.'"[158] To be fair, these estimates are at least partly explained by the fact that we are more aware of our own pain than our partners' pain. We are intently aware of the painful boredom of washing the same dishes every day, like Sisyphus pushing the same boulder up the hill over and over, but are much less aware of our partners' boredom when he or she does some equally unrewarding task while we're off doing other things. Nonetheless, strain in relation to household chores may be especially high for high-achieving women. Author Sylvia Ann Hewlett, who examined the top 10% of wage-earning women in a national sample in 2001, reported that "40% of high achieving wives feel that their husbands create more work for them around the house than they contribute."[159]

In the Lifestyle Poll results, I found a possible indication of a dramatic shift in these findings. That is, in stark contrast to these well-established norms, married respondents in my sample estimated that they are doing "about 62% of the chores," which can be practically translated as "slightly more than half of the chores." When I created the Lifestyle Poll, I built in cross-checks by asking for related data in multiple forms. So, for example, when I asked about marital satisfaction, I also asked about other related areas like willingness to marry one's spouse again, perceptions of equal or unequal benefit in the marriage, levels of affection (e.g., how often they kiss their husbands), fears in the previous three years that the marriage might have been in trouble, and regrets about having married their spouses. In the case of marital satisfaction, although there was evidence of frank responding in the acknowledgment of fears that their marriage might have been in trouble in the past three years for nearly 60% of the respondents, every other piece of data consistently pointed to a high level of marital satisfaction. In assessing satisfaction with chore sharing arrangements, I asked participants not only to indicate what percent of the chores they feel they do, but also to rank the biggest problems in their marriages, to provide a subjective rating of how equally distributed they feel their chore sharing arrangements is, and to check off within a checklist of chores those chores for which they have primary responsibility 75% or more of the time. The results are very intriguing.

As mentioned previously, respondents initially estimated that they do slightly more than half of the chores ("about 62%," specifically). Despite global perceptions of fairly well-distributed chores, however, respondents also cite tension about how chores are shared as their *number one marital complaint*. This is the case even though 43% of the respondents reported that they pay for housekeeping help. Most respondents with housekeepers—66%—have access to this kind of help only once or twice a month, however, leaving couples to negotiate a number of repetitive and unrewarding chores without outside help. When I listed 15 of the most common household chores (Figure 6.1) and asked respondents to check off which tasks were "their primary responsibility 75% or more of the time," they indicated that they are more likely than their husbands to assume primary responsibility for doing the laundry, cooking, changing sheets/towels, shopping for groceries, washing dishes, scrubbing floors, vacuuming, paying bills, cleaning bathrooms, and buying and wrapping gifts for social events. They reported that their husbands are more likely to assume primary responsibility for mowing the lawn, other yard care, and taking out the garbage. Two chores—managing financial investments and caring for family pets—are seen as quite equally distributed.

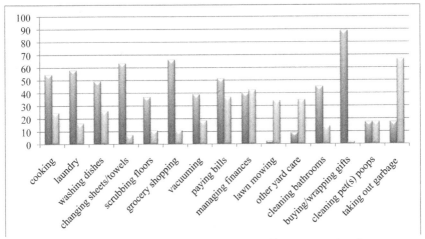

Figure 6.1. Perceptions of "Primary Responding" Duty for Common Household Chores

In Figure 6.1, dark bars represent chores that Lifestyle Poll respondents feel that they take responsibility for "at least 75% of the time" and light bars represent chores that the partners of Lifestyle Poll respondents feel they take responsibility for 75% of the time. As shown in Figure 6.1, consistent with many other research studies that suggest women bear the brunt of household labor, my respondents perceived that they are much more likely to assume primary responsibility for high-frequency tasks (e.g., cooking, washing the dishes). In contrast, they report that their husbands are more likely to assume primary responsibility for relatively low-frequency tasks (e.g., mowing the lawn, taking out the trash). I estimate that most people mow their lawn and tend to their yard work about once a week on average during a relatively short season (spring, summer, and into fall depending on where you live) and that taking out the garbage is most likely a once-a-week deal for most families. There were a few chores that I didn't think to include, such as car maintenance, which I would expect might fall disproportionately on husbands, and social planning and event hosting arrangements, which I would expect might fall disproportionately on wives. I should have asked about performing household maintenance tasks—that was a miss on my part, and I'm willing to bet that husbands do more of this type of work on average. Even if they do, however, the frequency of engagement in these kinds of tasks would probably not be the same as for cooking meals or washing dishes, which are typically daily requirements for household management. So, ultimately, no matter how you slice it, consistent with many other research studies, if these estimates are accurate, the extra work that the women in my sample are probably doing adds up to anywhere between 10 to 30 hours of additional housework each month relative to their husbands.

After presenting the checklist of chores, I then asked a question to assess whether participants feel under, over, or equally benefitted in the area of chore sharing. The response to this question is particularly interesting when compared to a parallel question about "getting an equal deal" in the marriage overall. In the marriage-overall question, the vast majority of participants (71%) felt that they are "getting an equal deal." With respect to how chores were split up, after reflecting on a number of specific tasks they felt primarily responsible for, however, only 34% agreed that they were "getting an equal deal." In the marriage-overall question, 17% percent felt that their husbands were over-benefited (12% felt that they themselves were over-benefitted), while in the area of chore sharing, a full 50% felt that their husbands were over-benefitted (16% felt that they themselves were over-benefitted).

Admittedly, this data is based on respondents' perceptions and not on tested reality, but the interesting thing is the discrepancy in how they view the fairness of chore sharing allocation overall after reflecting on a number of specific chores, in comparison to their initial report that they do "slightly more than half" of the chores. The apparent discrepancy between the two reports, provided within a 10–15 minute time frame, may reflect a lack of awareness or the subconscious influence of the psychological discomfort (what psychologists call "cognitive dissonance") that accompanies the recognition that significant inequities exist. That is, it seems that the question that assessed respondents' global perception of what percent of chores they do may have tapped what they *wish* would be happening and what is emotionally palatable to believe (given their preference for an egalitarian marriage), whereas the second question may have tapped what may be somewhat closer to the truth (although perhaps not the full truth) of the situation.

If I had to construct the gist of the "truth" from the chore sharing data, I would suspect that husbands are doing more than wives are aware of and that they are doing much more to contribute to the household chores than most men of the previous generation. Because of their clear contributions over and above what the fathers of the wives would likely have done in their own marriages, the Lifestyle Poll respondents, who love their husbands and see their relationships as much more equal than those of their parents', maintain an unexamined global perception that they are doing "just slightly more" work at home. Despite this global perception, however, tension about unequal distributions of chores continues to operate in an insidiously corrosive manner in their marriages. When I challenged the wives to really nail down how much responsibility they bear for specific chores, they realized on a more conscious level that they actually feel much more responsible than their husbands for a majority of the chores most of the time. As they came to a fresh awareness of the physical and *mental* burden imposed by this headship of domestic affairs, their perceptions of fairness shifted noticeably in the final question about the fairness in how chores are allocated.

As we try to understand why chores are so often a sore spot in relationships, it is helpful to be aware that in some cases, a chore may not be just a chore. Certain chores, such as cooking meals or taking care of the family vehicles, have cultural traditions or may be particularly important to an individual's sense of self or family. Sometimes, a less-than-fair chore sharing arrangement is a consequence of our own family heritage. Often, we assume roles learned from our own families and have unspoken expectations about the division of household chores. Sometimes, we take on chores by default because our partners seem to assume it is our role, and then a form of inertia, continuing to do what has always been done, may play a role in failing to discuss this common source of conflict and resentment.

Reluctance to stir the pot or risk a confrontation, or a mistaken belief that our partners may be inflexible, sometimes leads us to avoid discussing how chores are shared; however, failing to discuss an unsatisfying chore arrangement is clearly a big problem in relationships (even when we might be motivated to believe that it is not a serious problem). Avoiding this conversation could be likened to avoiding a sinkhole in your backyard. In case you've never heard of a sinkhole, here is a quick rundown. Sinkholes are formed when tiny rivers of water seep through the subsoil layers over many years until the substrata bears a striking resemblance to an ant farm.[160] The state of Florida, which is basically a large sandbar, is especially prone to sinkholes. Floridian newspapers regularly run stories about unlucky individuals who require rescue efforts when the ground beneath them suddenly collapses. A marriage built on an unbalanced and unexamined chore sharing arrangement is like a house built over a sinkhole. My respondents' discrepant reports about chore sharing as a source of tension and their apparent process of heightened awareness on deeper reflection illustrate that this may be a conversation worth having, even when you might think things are fairly well distributed. When couples approach this topic, they often find that after some period of adjustment, they can greatly improve their quality of life if they become more *intentional* in sorting out how chores are distributed.

As I have said previously, one hallmark of a true marriage of equals is the ability to renegotiate roles and responsibilities to guard against perceived imbalances of power; nonetheless, successfully negotiating chores in a relationship can be particularly challenging and requires respectful communication, flexibility, assertiveness, empathy, and willingness to make compromises (in other words, a number of both "masculine" and "feminine" social skills). Although some negotiated division of labor is usually efficient, the healthiest relationships demonstrate flexibility and a willingness to pitch in, switch roles, or help each other out in a spirit of sharing. Flexibility is a must, because life will occasionally, if not frequently, throw us curveballs that will make it difficult to follow Plan A. Flexibility is also needed because of fluctuations in work schedules and the need to accommodate the skills, strengths, and weaknesses of each partner. Seasonal adjustments may be necessary as well. Some chores, like mowing the lawn, are seasonal. Other chores, such as stocking the house with food and doing the laundry, are necessary all year. Because chore sharing is such a common source of tension in relationships, I offer the following suggestions as ideas for working toward a more satisfying arrangement. Some of these ideas may be worth trying in a reasonably healthy relationship. In other cases, though, the battle over chores is a marker of more serious difficulties, and the use of judgment would mean working with a professional counselor before attempting to make any significant changes.

As an initial intervention, it may make sense to simply run the financial figures and see if doing something such as hiring a part-time housekeeper, ordering out on occasion, or having a high school student mow the lawn makes sense. Sacrificing a bit of cash to pay someone else to take care of routine but time-consuming chores may be the fastest way to improve your quality of life and prevent the buildup of resentment in your marriage. Given that most people don't live like the Vanderbilt family, however, even if you can hire some part-time help, there will still be many responsibilities to negotiate. To proceed respectfully in a marriage of equals, it is important to create an open process when you are negotiating anything. So, in this case, if you are dissatisfied with how you and your spouse are dividing the chores, the first thing you need to do is to let your partner know that you'd like to take a look at this area of your marriage. It is generally helpful to ground the discussion in shared values—for example, the desire to love each other well, to avoid the buildup of resentment that would drive a wedge between you, and to partner as true equals. Even if you have years of pent-up frustration, it is important to avoid going into primitively reactive Mojo mode. For example, instead of saying something like "I am so sick of picking up after you. When we got married, I never signed up to be your personal maid," you might try "I've been feeling overwhelmed by all the chores after work and on the weekends...maybe you have been, too. Let's talk about making some changes so we can have more time for fun when we're not working." This will help keep your partner from becoming defensive, because the emphasis is on generating changes that will benefit both of you. As in most productive discussions, avoid placing blame or assassinating the character of your partner (or that of their parents, relatives, or ancestors who may have set a bad example or spoiled them rotten as children). Let your partner know that as a first step, you want to get some good information on how you are dividing your responsibilities in order to get an accurate understanding of how chores are affecting both of you.

Make sure your partner understands that you assume that he or she is surely doing many helpful tasks you are not aware of. In a marriage of equals, if you avoid any manipulation and suggest a respectful, fair process, your partner will generally approach this request with curiosity rather than view this initiative as threatening to a situation that may over-benefit them. To figure out how much time each of you is actually investing in chores, you can modify a basic time-management chart. Each of you would chart the name of each task you do and the amount of time you devote to that task. Based on this, you will both get a sense of how much time each chore takes. If there are a lot of chores, or if they vary from week to week, you may need to get two or three weeks of information before you have a fair sense of how responsibilities are divided. Of course, one potential outcome of this exercise is that you might discover that chores are more equally distributed than you thought and reallocation isn't necessary. In this case, you may develop a new appreciation for the many ways that your partner is contributing to the life you share and this new realization should effectively curb any further resentment.

When sufficient time has passed, sit down together and take a look at the information you've gathered. Don't neglect some discussion of the meaning of chores for each of you and individual preferences for orderliness, which can vary significantly between partners. For example, consider the case of a husband who lives according to the principle "a place for everything and everything in its place." He might say, "When everything is in order, I am most efficient and can best achieve a state of flow." A wife married to such a man might chafe against his need for orderliness and might say, "When I get home, I want to relax. I feel happiest in a space that isn't too orderly—I get inspired to create in a space that looks and feels lived in, a place where interesting combinations of designs surprise the eye." Even with such different approaches, creative compromise is still possible. In my clinical practice, I helped one such couple come to a workable and mutually satisfying compromise. First, the couple created a transitional space near the front door with cubbyholes and a storage bench where both could deposit their things either in various cubby holes in a more orderly way or in a more relaxed way, by simply dumping things into the storage bench. This ritual of leaving most items from the day in the mudroom bench eliminated most of the messy trails that had previously been a source of frequent irritation for this order-loving husband. The partners also freely gave each other permission to pick up any personal items left around the house and to put them in a particular place in the mudroom bench (so the other would know to check there first for any missing items). It was also important for each to have some individual space so each had a little individual real estate in their home—the husband designed a well-organized "man cave" in a rectangular section of the basement, and his wife fashioned an artist's retreat under the uniquely shaped attic of their old Victorian home. Both could decorate and enjoy their individual spaces as they felt most comfortable, and neither had any say about the design or appearance of the other's private space. If guests were over, each had the right to simply close the door to his or her private space if desired. With their needs for order (or creative disorder) met in their personal retreats, it was easy for the couple to agree that the common space would be maintained by both and would generally be kept free of clutter so both could feel comfortable inviting guests to share that space at any time. In the case of this couple, the *intentional* allocation of some personal space in their home helped each retain a healthy sense of individuality that then contributed to a more harmonious use of the space they enjoyed together.

When you sit down together with your chore-related time sample, take a look at the time required to complete various chores and how demanding or unpleasant each task is judged to be. You may be pleasantly surprised to find that you and your partner have natural preferences for different chores (that may or may not run along traditional gender divisions), which you can factor into a potential redistribution of chores. For example, if you enjoy vacuuming the house, feeling a sense of satisfaction as you create those little parallel lines across your carpeting, you might get a similar feeling from mowing the lawn. Likewise, if balancing the pool chemicals intrigues one of you, the chemistry involved in gourmet cooking may tap the same skill set. If you can both view chores as activities requiring various skill sets, you will have greater flexibility in redistributing chores along the lines of individual inclinations. As a next step, you might try to match up the chores in two columns, distributing them according to how much time each requires and how boring or distasteful each is. After you line up all the chores in two matched columns, each of you can pick one column. For some couples, a 50/50 split may not be fair, such as when one of you is working full-time and the other is working part-time and you do not have children. In this case, the difference in work schedules and demands should be taken into consideration. Perhaps doing 30% of the chores may be the fairest split for the partner who works full-time in this scenario. It is generally not a good idea to allocate chores on the basis of salary comparisons, because regardless of occupations, the key to a respectful marriage is one in which partners are seen as having equal worth. The goal is for both partners to have about the same amount of free time to relax, pursue hobbies, and enjoy each other.

To implement your re-distribution of chores, you may find it helpful to post a checklist on your refrigerator so that each of you can check things off as chores are completed. This may help reduce bickering because it will be clear if each person is getting his or her chores done, and if all goes well, such a list will provide a sense that progress is being made. (Of course, it may also increase bickering if one partner is not on board with using this system or is noticeably lagging in completing chores.) Sometimes this visual aid also serves as a reality check by increasing awareness that some things still need to be done. Keeping a visible checklist posted in your common space may help with planning or adjusting for the rest of the week and may provide some concrete information about whether the current plan is realistic. Posting a list of chores also facilitates trading chores (for example, "I see you have not gotten to X. I'll do that, if you do Y"). To break the monotony of doing the same set of chores every week, you can also try switching the columns of chores every few months or so. If you've balanced them equally in the first place, both lists should be comparably burdensome.

I'm aware that some readers might think, *Ugh...checklists...I'd never want to do all that, and my partner would never go for it.* The use of increased structure (like checklists of chores), is meant to be a temporary tool to help each of you change existing habits. Re-distributing chores is like changing any habit. Most couples are successfully able to incorporate new habits and can stop using the checklists after some amount of time. The goal is not to micro-manage each other's time. Generally, it takes three or four months for people to develop any new habit, so this would be the target time for using a checklist to develop a better internal awareness of chores that need to be done. If you lack mutual buy-in to the idea of using checklists, then don't use them, because in this scenario, this would put one of you on the fast track to recasting yourself as a member of a "Chore Sergeant" (and then a Chore Sergeant becomes a Major Pain). In this case, see if you can come up with some other way to keep changes on the radar and assess how successfully they are being implemented.

Still, if this sounds too complicated, you might consider just using time as a factor to split chores. You might want to set aside a specified time each week to work side-by-side in completing the chores (e.g., Wednesday evening and first thing Saturday morning) before doing something you both enjoy. Psychologists refer to the strategy of requiring a non-preferred task to be done before a preferred task as the "Premack Principle." The classic example is requiring children to eat their broccoli before they can have dessert. This increases the likelihood that the non-preferred behavior will be completed. For example, watching a favorite TV show (a pleasant activity) might be a good reward for cleaning the bathrooms (an unpleasant activity). If you are working as a team, you might try rewarding yourselves by going out for a lunch date after you have put in three hours doing chores each Saturday morning between 9 a.m. and 12 p.m. Another thing to try might be setting aside a specific 15–30-minute period to do "speed chores" each night. If you want, you can make it a game in which the first one to complete his or her fair share of the chores earns a five-minute massage from the other person.

Let's say that you have a partner who vetoes the idea of making changes with any kind of structure. A less desirable strategy than openly renegotiating and trying various splits of chores can be considered if one partner is uncooperative. This alternative involves natural consequences. That is, the partner who is lagging in sharing the chores may become more willing to take on the chores that have unpleasant natural consequences associated with them if they are not completed. For a couple in which the wife felt that she was bearing an unfair amount of the kitchen work, life became easier when the husband was designated the chef of the home. She bought him a set of Alton Brown DVDs, and he was surprised to see how easily he could learn to create some amazing meals. He connected with the chemistry of cooking illustrated by Alton Brown and, thanks to the masculinization of culinary arts, correctly perceived that others admire the skills of a talented chef. His hunger pangs, paired with his desire to apply his new skills, kept him motivated to cook the meals, and his wife promised to wash any dishes he might create while whipping up his incredible dinners. It turned out that he was a better cook than his wife had been, and his wife, happy to be relieved of something she saw as a burden, was happy to take on the chore of washing the dishes after dinner. As a second example, a partner for whom a clean house is important may become motivated to take out the trash if it is left to overflow. Be warned, however, that this strategy of natural consequences may be best left to those who approach life with a sense of humor.

If both of you have a good sense of humor, you may find some playful ways to come up with reminders about chores that need to be completed. One creative wife used her sense of humor when she found several dead cockroaches near the kitchen sink because of some food waste that had been left by her husband. For most of the first year of their marriage, she had been relaying a persistent concern that food waste would draw bugs into their kitchen. One day, after a weekend away, she returned to find these gruesome little stiffs lying on their backs with their legs straight up in the air. She slid their bodies onto a party invitation and penned the following note: "Thanks for a great time last night, guys. You have the perfect party house—we're going to tell all our friends, because I'm sure they'd like to make this kind of place a regular hangout spot!" She then placed the note (and the cockroach corpses) on her husband's bureau. This humorous handling of the situation got through to her husband in a way that more than a year of expressing her concerns had not. Another example that comes to mind is of a wife that forgot to clean the cat's litter box for several days. This was her designated responsibility, and her clever husband left the following note for her one morning: "Help!! I'm up to my knees in my own poop!"

When going with this natural consequences approach, remember that escalation into a war in which each partner is avoiding chores to get the other to do them is not the aim. In fact, escalation into such a war may mean that there are more serious problems that need to be discussed with a professional counselor. If you have tried the suggestions I've offered and continue to find yourself resentfully stuck in a dissatisfying chore sharing arrangement, a deeper issue such as a masked power struggle may be at play. In such cases, talking with a licensed psychologist who is experienced in marital and family issues may help you discuss the obstacles to reaching a compromise, explore expectations and needs, and assist you in negotiating a more workable arrangement.

When Equals Become Parents

As UCLA marital researcher Dr. Tom Bradbury once remarked (tongue firmly in cheek), "A good marriage is a risk factor for having children." After reading the research literature on the effect of children on marital satisfaction, one might begin to wonder whether the transition to parenthood marks the end of the happiest chapter in a marriage. Multiple studies point to a consistent association between having children and a significant decline in marital satisfaction, particularly for wives.[161] We might graph these findings as shown in Figure 6.2.

Do kids really kill a good marriage? I asked the (mostly young) mothers who responded to the Lifestyle Poll how the addition of children has affected their marriages. A sizable portion (73.9%) of the sample did acknowledge significant declines in sexual satisfaction after they had become mothers; slightly less than half (47.4%) agreed with the statement "Our sex life is somewhat worse," and an additional quarter of the sample

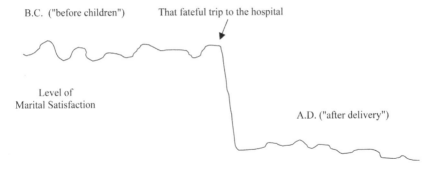

Figure 6.2. Theorized Effects of Children on Marital Satisfaction (possibility #1)

(26.5%) agreed with the statement "Our sex life is much worse than before we had children." In terms of the marriage overall, however, less than one-quarter (22.9%) agreed with the statement "our relationship has become more distant since having children." The majority (50.2%) agreed with the statement, "We have become closer since having children," and an additional 26.9% reported that having children has not led to any loss or gain in marital intimacy. Most of the time then (in 77.7% of cases), for Lifestyle Poll participants, despite acknowledging a negative effect on their sex lives, the consensus was that marital intimacy has not been lost and has in fact grown deeper with the addition of children.

Let's take a critical look at how most of the existing "parental transition" research has been done. The design of many of these studies is to take cross-sectional snapshots of marital satisfaction at "critical" time periods during the transition to parenthood, typically during the final weeks or months of pregnancy and/or in the first few months following birth. To lay aside all of the fancy analyses in favor of common sense, imagine that you are an expectant parent. You and your partner are planning for the arrival of your child, and your emotions run high with some mix of excitement and anxiety. As you plan together, you conspire happily about your future and dream about what your baby will be like and how you will create and enjoy an expanded sense of family that includes your child. If a researcher were to ask you how close you feel to your spouse within this context, how would you be likely to respond? Now imagine that you are a new parent. Your life has been thrown into a blender. You are suddenly knocked down to the very bottom of Abraham Maslow's hierarchy of needs,[162] to the basic survival levels of functioning. Because human babies are altricial—that is, born completely helpless and defenseless—your daily life refocuses entirely on the most basic needs vital to physiological survival and safety (yours and your child's). Any previous routine you may have had is gone, and day blends into night. You are bleary eyed and chronically exhausted, a slave to the feeding and sleeping schedule of your baby. Your focus and energy (and those of your spouse) are intensely centered on your new child, and you are both expending massive amounts of energy to attend to the constant (and often unclear) needs of your baby. You are highly attuned to your newborn, completely focused, hyper-vigilant about any signs that something might be "off" or to any early indication of potentially life-threatening health problems. In this context, if a researcher asked you how satisfied you are feeling with your marriage or how close you feel to your spouse, how would you be likely to respond?

Some researchers have suggested that lower levels of marital satisfaction after children are born may represent a return to pre-pregnancy levels of satisfaction.[163] If this is true, then, marital satisfaction would follow the pattern depicted in Figure 6.3.

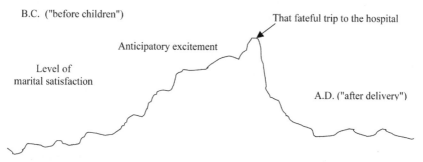

Figure 6.3. Theorized Effects of Children on Marital Satisfaction (possibility #2)

Two of the most respected researchers in this area, Drs. Philip and Carolyn Cowan, married parents themselves, have extensively studied the transition to parenthood and concluded, "We believe that children are getting an unfair share of the blame for their parents' distress....We are convinced that the seeds of new parents' individual and marital problems are sown long before their first baby arrives."[164]

Although a strong marriage is likely to weather the stress of this transition,[165] having a family may be especially hard for those in a marriage of equals. Researchers have consistently found that the transition to parenthood often brings a seismic shift in roles. Couples that were once equals often find that practical considerations compel a move to more traditional chore sharing arrangements,[166] and wives end up shouldering a far greater burden of the chores than they did before having children.[167] Not surprisingly, this shift to a more traditional division of labor and the increased burden of Sisyphean chores is associated with declines in marital satisfaction[168] and increased risk for depression in new mothers.[169] As May Sarton, author and philosopher, has put it, "The wife has suffered an earthquake and the husband has not. His goals have not been radically changed; his mode of being has not been radically changed."[170]

I know less about the experience of new fathers, as my practice, teaching, and research in this area have been primarily focused on women's development, so the following sections will be generally directed toward illuminating the experience of new mothers. Where I do have some basis for insight, however, I will attempt to describe elements of the parenting dynamic from a new father's perspective. I do not think that mothers are to blame for the problems and stresses they face, but I will try to point out common patterns that heighten the possibility of continued inequality and marital dissatisfaction for both partners in the parenting phase. Based on many, many conversations with new mothers, in both clinical and nonclinical contexts, and on the open-ended responses of mothers I have studied, here is my sense of why this transition is especially rocky for those who have enjoyed a marriage of equals before having children.

Split Worlds: The Trauma and Ecstasy of Giving Birth

In a marriage of equals, there is a strong element of collegiality. Partners see each other as co-adventurers. Those within a marriage of equals are prone to brainstorm together, bounce ideas off each other, and debrief outcomes of stressful situations with each other. Relative to more traditional couples, they are also more likely to plan meals together, shop and cook together, and fold each other's laundry. Most often, both partners are engaged in paid work, and they can and will mutually relate to experiences in each other's workplace settings that would make for ripe material for a show like *The Office*. There is an overriding sense of respect and teamwork in a successful marriage of equals, and the worlds of the partners often overlap in ways that the worlds of partners in more traditional marriages do not. The arrival of children seems to change this dynamic very suddenly and sometimes permanently, often to the great dissatisfaction of one or both partners.

Having a child is both a trauma and a peak life experience, simultaneously. When a woman gives birth, her body suffers a physical trauma that requires a lengthy period of withdrawal from her previous routine and life as she knew it. In most cases, even if she is not breast feeding, she is completely tied down by a baby's need to feed every few hours. She suddenly inhabits a completely new world in which her daily experience is far removed from everything she has known in the past. Time gets fuzzy, and she experiences extremes of emotion—both highs and lows—when contemplating the awesome responsibility that she faces for the next 18 (or more) years. The idea that this transition is in fact a trauma may be a helpful concept given that new mothers often report that they are frequently alone with their feelings and lonely in a way that they have never felt before. A central element of a trauma is living through an experience that defies easy explanation, something that one feels no one else can really understand without having lived through something very similar. Combat veterans frequently say, "You can't really know what it feels like unless you have been there" in a way that reminds me of how new mothers try to express their subjective realities in this post-birth transitional phase. Those who have not personally lived through either of these experiences—combat or giving birth—often attempt to intrude on the experiences as though it were their right to do so, apparently seeing war and new birth as human universals.

Violations of boundaries by outside observers such as touching a pregnant woman's stomach or asking a combat veteran, "So, did you kill anyone?" occur with striking frequency in the case of both pregnant women and combat veterans. Perhaps it's because we feel we can lay claim to perceived universal experiences such as the forces of life and death, *eros* and *thanatos*. Unfortunately, these boundary violations only heighten the sense of separation for the recipient and generally achieve nothing by way of understanding what it *really* feels like to be in the fray of either new life or death (both of which are violent in their own way). New mothers often talk about having to actively resist the tendency to become depressed in their sense of isolation, an isolation that seems to be as much mental as it is physical. They often feel more extremes of hope, triumph, joy, love, panic, sadness, helplessness, and hopelessness than they have ever felt before. It may be that the experiences of new mothers defy explanation in any words, and that they simply cannot convey to those around them (including their partners) how profoundly their worlds have altered. New mothers may also be inclined to self-protectively limit discussion of how terrified they have felt at times or how their sense of competence has been challenged as they take on this new role. As one new mother put it, "there is such pressure on women to be perfect moms that they often won't talk about their true feelings for fear of being perceived as a poor mom." Either way, new barriers in communication seem to accompany the transition to motherhood for many women.

Giving birth is potentially traumatic, but it also mirrors the experience of falling in love for many new parents.* In fact, many people in healthy monogamous marriages fall in love again and again with new people throughout their lives (that is, with each of their children). New mothers experience a raging waterfall of many of the same pleasure-inducing chemicals that are released when two people fall in love.[171] As in the case of falling in love and snorting crack cocaine, there is "the most intense sense of being alive" in the presence of one's newborn. This out-of-body bliss generated by massive surges of oxytocin, norepinephrine, and dopamine helps bond us to our vulnerable little charges. The stimulatory effect of this rush of chemicals helps to offset the physical exhaustion that we feel when our sleep cycles are continually disrupted by the care of infants. Mothers often say, "I don't know how you do it, but when you hear your baby crying, no matter how exhausted you are, you get the energy to go to them at night." Those falling in love will endure sleep deprivation to be awake all hours of the night with their beloved for a limited time when compared to parents of young children, who will endure the same for several years in many cases. As with the traumatic element of new birth, in many cases, new mothers experience the bliss and stimulatory effects of this new love to a greater degree relative to new fathers. Fathers have increased levels of some of these bonding chemicals, but nowhere near the levels that mothers have. For mothers in particular, between moments of sheer panic, there is a cascading sense of joy, vitality, and connectedness that is the "other greatest natural high." In fact, new mothers consistently maintain that the experience of falling in love with a child is even more powerful than the experience of falling in love with

---

*Of course, mothers don't always feel delighted with their children and motherhood also brings a variety of powerful negative emotions such as guilt, loss, and fears of incompetence. In fact, a sizable portion of new mothers (13% according to one multi-study analysis) develop a serious mental health condition, post-partum depression, during the transition to parenthood. (O'Hara, M., and Swain, A. (1996). "Rates and Risk of Postpartum Depression: A Meta-Analysis." International Review of Psychiatry, 8, 37-54).

a future spouse. Research seems to support this contention; as the title of one article summarizes: "Pup Suckling Is More Rewarding Than Cocaine."[172] (I suppose they needed to test this theory with dogs, because an institutional review board would be unlikely to approve a study that involved giving human mothers a choice between pressing a button for access to either their hungry babies or lines of cocaine).

In light of this possibility, it's interesting to compare Lifestyle Poll participants' responses to questions about any marital and parental regrets. When asked, "Do you ever wish you had not married your husband?" 65% of the Lifestyle Poll sample answered "no, *never.*" About 24% reported that they "rarely" have regrets of this kind and a small, but noticeable, portion (about 11%) said that they occasionally or frequently had regrets about marrying their husbands. Later in the poll, I asked a parallel question about regrets related to having children ("Please indicate your agreement with the following statement: 'If I had it to do over again, I would not have any children'"). Fully *96.1% of respondents strongly disagreed* with this statement and <u>*not one single mother*</u> *strongly agreed* with this statement (about 2% *somewhat agreed* and another 2% *somewhat disagreed*). Recall that during the cocaine-rush phase of a new romantic relationship, our partners can do no wrong in our eyes, yet after some time has elapsed, we eventually withdraw this protective shroud and begin to see them as flawed (sometimes very deeply flawed). The interesting thing about becoming a parent is that a similar loving cocoon of positive thought biases often gets extended *forever* to children, who can do no wrong in their parents' eyes. In the clinical setting, it is interesting to witness this apparently everlasting love blindness, to note the tendency for parents to love (and ally with) destructive and disrespectful children more than with supportive spouses.

Along the same lines, when we begin to date someone we're excited about, we focus on them and attempt to pull them into every other part of our lives, including all of our conversations with our friends. We talk about who we are falling in love with because it feels good to us and makes us feel connected to the object of our affection when they are not in our presence. Again, though, as in the case of willingness to endure sleep deprivation to stare deep into their eyes, this is usually a temporary thing. That is, after some period of time, we generally stop referencing our partners in every conversation ("Oh, you ordered mashed potatoes? Tim likes mashed potatoes, too!"). However, in the case of children, parents continue to feel "mini brain bursts" of pleasure when viewing their children throughout their children's entire life development ("That's *my* son!"). Recall my earlier argument that one of the markers of falling in love with a potential spouse is the thought, "Our story would make a great movie script." For parents, the very common parallel thought is "My child is the smartest, most adorable child, ever!" This thought helps explain why many parents are inclined to "go viral" on You-tube with clips of their babies' discoveries of their ability to shriek, to giggle, to pass gas, etc. Hara Marano, editor of *Psychology Today* magazine and author of *A Nation of Wimps: The High Cost of Invasive Parenting,* says, "The cultivation of preciousness of one's offspring seems to breed in parents the conviction that everyone else in the culture, or at least the neighborhood, is as interested in and delighted by children, specifically *their* children, as they are."[173] I think ultimately these videos and detailed reports from parents can ultimately be translated as, "Isn't this just absolutely amazing! I am living in the presence of a daily miracle!" In the midst of this widespread and often permanent behavioral pattern, however, there seems to be a striking lack of insight that others may not find all the details we want to share about our own children quite so fascinating as we do ourselves. It's a kind of long-term blind spot that is interesting to consider in relation to the more time-limited blind spot about constant references to our new love partners.

Happily, in most cases, fathers and some close family members and friends have a large capacity to welcome these reports and to respond to them with equal joy. Although this kind of talk can help bond new parents together, shifting the vast majority of communication to conversations about the baby can narrow the range of life experiences that are discussed between partners who used to discuss their experiences on multiple planes of existence. In these ways, then, the trauma and ecstasy of giving birth may create a subjective gap in experience that is particularly challenging to bridge for partners who once enjoyed significant overlap in the nature of their personal life experiences.

Potential for Violated Expectations and Attachment Wounds

During the transition to parenthood, a marriage of equals also seems especially vulnerable to violated expectations. If the status quo before birth was a chore sharing arrangement that felt more equal than that of a traditional couple, the shift in roles makes the post-birth situation ripe for violated expectations. Violated expectations in the post-birth phase have been studied by multiple researchers and are consistently associated with decreased marital satisfaction following birth. Lawrence, Rothman, Cobb, Rothman, and Bradbury found that parents who were more satisfied with their marriages prior to starting a family experienced *greater* declines in satisfaction across the transition to parenthood when compared to parents with lower levels of pre-pregnancy satisfaction.[174] Hackel and Ruble followed new parents for four months after giving birth and concluded that violated expectations concerning the division of household and child care responsibilities were linked to declines in marital satisfaction, particularly for wives who were doing more than they expected to do.[175] In a study of working-class, dual-earner relationships, violated expectations in the division of child care were a stronger predictor of women's depression and anxiety symptoms than were actual divisions of child care or housework.[176] Cowan and Cowan found that the larger the discrepancy between wives' expectations and husbands' levels of actual involvement in looking after the baby, the more relationally dissatisfied the wives were likely to be.[177]

For the Lifestyle Poll mothers (277 mothers in total), one third (32.9%) endorsed the statement "My husband helps with 50% or more of the childcare responsibilities," but the larger majority (53.1%) felt "My husband helps a lot, but I still do most of the work." An additional 14% of the sample felt that their husbands "could help a lot more" or "don't really get involved at all most of the time." When I asked the more specific question "When your child is ill, who picks him/her up from school/daycare and attends to him or her most of the time?" nearly half the sample (47.8%) said "I do," whereas only 3.6% said "My husband does." (Others get help from outside sources or decide on a case by case basis). Consistent with many other studies, then, wives appear to be taking the bigger hit when it comes to child care responsibilities and this discrepancy is likely to impact their marital satisfaction.

In the clinical context, I have noticed that in some cases, the scale of violated expectations for some wives approaches the level of an "attachment trauma." In her book *Emotionally Focused Therapy for Trauma Survivors*,[178] Dr. Sue Johnson provides a very helpful description of an attachment trauma as "a specific incident in which one partner is inaccessible and unresponsive in the face of the other partner's urgent need for the kind of support and caring expected of attachment figures…*a potential prototypical bonding scenario that turns into the nightmare of finding oneself alone when one is most helpless and desperate* [which is] then continually used as a touchstone as to the dependability of the other partner."[179] New mothers I have spoken with in both non-clinical and clinical contexts frequently raise questions about how much they will be able to depend on their husbands, and many relay specific experiences of feeling completely helpless and alone in the face of overwhelming responsibilities. The quality and intensity of these feelings of helplessness and vulnerability are often reported to be unlike anything they've ever experienced in the past. Added to this, the temporary loss of connection with their partners due to "split worlds," in combination with a seismic shift toward the very traditional roles they formerly resisted, can sometimes set off a state similar to what Sue Johnson identifies as a "primal panic." In such a state, individuals will typically do one of a few things—they may become demanding and clingy, withdrawn and detached, or may alternate between the two states of being—none of which will ultimately tend to draw their spouse into a closer connection.

I would guess that at some point, all new mothers reach moments when they feel completely helpless, terrified, or vulnerable. Most of the time, the pattern I see is that when a wife reaches these very low points, she will make a concerted effort to appeal to her husband, and she will do so with great intensity and frequency initially, sometimes in full Mojo mode. If these efforts meet with a helpful response from her husband, no attachment wounds are formed and the marital bond is further strengthened. If, after repeated attempts to clearly and urgently communicate, a husband fails to understand the depths of his wife's needs or is not responsive for any other reason, attachment wounds may be inflicted. After some period of time, the fight goes out of the wife and she begins to withdraw, usually into the world of her children. In cases like these, a wife speaks about her marriage with resigned disappointment and tends to say things like "He hasn't been there when I really needed him, so I learned that I can't depend on him. It's going to fall on me, and this isn't what I expected or wanted." In my opinion, these statements mark the critical turning point of marriages that are likely to be dead on arrival when children have been launched. As such, violated expectations and unmet needs can be a significant problem for those in a marriage of equals.

Profound and Disorienting Shifts in Sense of Identity

For my doctoral dissertation, I completed a meta-analysis of ten different types of stress on marital satisfaction across 133 studies that could be statistically combined. Compared to 9 other possible types of life stressors, being unemployed had the biggest negative effect on marital satisfaction, even more than dealing with the serious chronic illness of a spouse or a child. I think this is because undesired unemployment disrupts every other domain in a person's life and cuts to the core of a person's very identity. When high-achieving women become mothers, they may or may not quit (or be squeezed out of) their jobs. Some may choose to prioritize the parenting role, especially while their children are young, but such a choice often has negative consequences if and when a mother later decides to return to full-time work. As I've mentioned previously, the vast majority of mothers (82%) who responded to the Lifestyle Poll continued to work outside the home in a paid capacity. There is wide agreement (84.7% of the sample), however, with the statement, "I have cut back on my career involvement in order to meet the needs of my family." Recall that in a different question, we saw an ideal of equal responsibility for a husband to attend to the needs of his family as a priority when work and family needs conflict. Specifically, I asked participants to indicate their level of agreement with the statement, "In case of conflicting demands, a professional woman's responsibility is to her family." About one third of the sample (34%) strongly agreed with this statement, and an additional 43% somewhat agreed with this statement. When I asked the same question, substituting the word "man's" for "woman's," nearly the same proportion of respondents agreed (34% strongly agreed and 47% somewhat agreed), so the message I read from these responses is a rejection of the double standard that wives should take a bigger hit than husbands when their families need them. In reality, however, wives are taking a bigger career hit than husbands. Eighty-five percent of mothers had cut back on their work schedules, and the average number of hours spent at work for mothers in the sample was 35, which is less than a full-time commitment. When their children are sick, it is the mothers who are cast in the role of the primary responder. So, even if these mothers are not giving up their jobs entirely, they are frequently shunted into a different category within the work setting—that of part-timers. In this scenario, husbands are not the oppressor. In fact, many men wish that they had the relatively wider range of options that women have. In many cases, the structure of husbands' jobs or expectations placed on men in the workforce prevents them from doing anything less than full-time work.

Other authors (for example, Miriam Peskowitz and Sylvia Ann Hewlett) have written thoughtful analyses on the implications of being on the "mommy track." Some of these implications include much greater financial dependence and vulnerability, loss of ability to advance in one's chosen field, loss of job security, the potential for being viewed by colleagues as not fully committed (and, really, who can blame a person for having divided loyalties when he or she is cast as the primary responder when a child is ill?) Of all the implications, however, the one I would most like to emphasize is the profound loss of place that mothers report when they shift away from their former roles and positions in organizations. My sense is that the highly successful "alpha" women who comprise a good portion of the Lifestyle Poll sample have a particularly tough time with the transition to parenthood whenever they are compelled to scale back on positions they have worked very, very hard to achieve and maintain prior to starting families.

Exhaustion on Two Levels

In the Lifestyle Poll sample, of all the challenges of being a new mother, the most frequent challenge reported was exhaustion. The physical exhaustion inherent in parenting, especially in the earliest days of a baby's life, is obvious and well documented (but, of course one doesn't really know what it feels like unless one has lived it). A friend of mine who had a set of twins once said, "I've had days where I've been so exhausted that I can't even walk up the stairs—I've had to crawl up to my bed on my hands and knees." This comment made an impression on me because this particular individual was a very stoic, hearty person, not at all prone to over-exaggeration. The unpredictable feeding schedule of a very young infant is like being on the most taxing of work schedules, the rotating shift schedule. Mothers I've spoken with talk about the disorientation that comes from loss of routine as the first few weeks or months after birth feel like one long day without a full night of sleep.

Sleep deprivation has been shown to have a strong positive association with depressive symptoms. According to one study, the critical factors associated with a depressed mood state are the total amount of sleep obtained in each 24-hour period and the frequency of nighttime sleep interruption, for which daytime napping cannot adequately compensate.[180] Much has been made of the negative effects of sleep deprivation. Lack of sleep impairs clarity of thought and judgment. Based on the results of sleep-deprivation studies, we are warned that drowsy driving is like drunk driving.[181] For this reason, public-service postings urge motorists to "pull over and take a nap" because sleep deprivation causes one out of every five accidents on the road (a total of 250,000 accidents per year).[182] Lack of sleep has been linked to mood disorders and even to psychosis—that is, loss of touch with reality.[183] In my clinical experience, loss of touch with reality is not uncommon for those who are sleep deprived. For instance, a substantial portion of the PTSD*-diagnosed veterans whom I treat experience a variant of psychosis, the experience of visual hallucinations of enemy combatants that occur in fully wakeful states. With notable frequency, veterans report that while fully awake in the middle of the day, they see enemy combatants run past out of the corners of their eyes or that during the night, they get a feeling that an intruder is in the house, wake up and check the rooms of their home, and then see an enemy lurking in the corner of a room, watching and ready to strike. These reports increase with predictable frequency whenever sleep patterns are especially disturbed, which is also quite common for veterans diagnosed with PTSD.

In Veterans Affairs hospitals, we don't ask about this kind of hallucinatory experience in the most commonly used brief measures of PTSD, but these experiences surface so often with my patients that I've now added the following question to my standard PTSD assessment: "Do you ever see enemy combatants that appear real even though your mind knows what you are seeing is not really there?" I've actually informally tracked the response to this question about psychotic features in veterans with PTSD. In a sample of 36 combat veterans on my clinical caseload, half report that they have this experience. Asking this question and letting veterans know that this experience is quite common for those who have been in combat is extremely therapeutic. Invariably, patients say, "I had no idea that other people might be dealing with this... I thought I was going crazy." The point I'm making is that sleep disturbance is a huge contributing factor in many negative emotional and mental health outcomes, to the degree that some loss of touch with reality may even be fairly normative for individuals suffering from extreme sleep deprivation. For new parents, and mothers in particular, extreme sleep deprivation is practically a given.

Arguably, there may be something even more draining than the physical exhaustion of the parenthood transition—the mental exhaustion. As soon as a baby is born, there is a massive increase in the number of needs that must be tracked and attended to. Wives commonly report that they feel primarily responsible for predicting and addressing the needs of themselves, their children, and sometimes their husbands as well. As roles shift toward a more traditional arrangement, wives end up doing the mental work of figuring out what each member in the family needs and providing

---

*PTSD means "Post Traumatic Stress Disorder"

for it. This planning and organizing role is often all consuming and causes profound fragmentation in the life of the mother. For example, on top of planning for her own needs, a new mother might be thinking about the ongoing evolution of her baby's feeding and sleeping schedules, the appointments she needs to keep with the baby's doctor, how to get the best products for her baby's health (and figure out how to avoid dangerous ones), the specific array of activities for stimulating the baby that are suitable to his or her developmental level, the supplies in short stock that she needs to pick up for the baby (and often for the household in general), the passage of various milestones, and the need to update scrapbooks and keepsake albums, etc.

Having empathy and consideration for others' needs is one thing. It's another thing entirely to have a streaming ticker tape in your brain of the needs of two or more other people, and a variety of urgent mental pop-ups that require additional energy to attend to. I haven't studied this in any formal way, so I can only hypothesize here, but I have often wondered whether "mommy brain" might be largely a function of the multiple tracks of thought related to this kind of mental work (it surely must also be partly a result of sleep deprivation as well). Think of the brain like a computer. One that has many programs running on it at the same time is likely to be much less efficient than one with only one or two programs running at the same time. Sudden realizations about something the baby needs are like pop-up ads on a computer, and it makes sense to me that having too many pop-ups and background programs on the brain's computer directly contributes to mental fatigue, a general downward shift in mental efficiency, and specific difficulties concentrating and remembering important things.

It's impossible to address a problem when you have no awareness of it, and in my experience, many mothers aren't always aware of the important distinction between physical labor and mental labor. They often just report that they are "totally drained." Some primary caregivers are able to successfully engage their partners in contributing more to the physical labor necessary for raising a child, but until both parents become aware of the *mental* burden that is often held by the "primary responder," there is no way to re-structure some of this unequal responsibility, and resentment in the marriage will continue to remain high. Consistent with the perspective of Cowan and Cowan,[184] I would argue that the seeds of this unequal mental burden are sown well before children enter the picture. I'll present a specific idea about how to change this pattern later in this chapter.

Loss of Control and Predictability May Lead to Perfectionist Strivings

Loss of control and predictability and all of the previously mentioned transitional challenges (new financial vulnerabilities, the split-world effect, profound shifts in identity, loss of place, violated expectations, new attachment wounds, and physical and mental exhaustion) create a perfect storm that propels primary caregivers (usually mothers) to hold on to as much control as they can. I would imagine that the high-achieving women who responded to the Lifestyle Poll come into parenthood within a context of highly developed competence in many previous life roles. If they get married, they aim to marry people who respect them and appreciate their well-developed areas of competence. The transition to parenting brings a very steep learning curve. New parents are thrust into the unknown and are often left to figure out much of this learning curve on their own, with the help of some good books but relatively little *applied* transfer of knowledge. Uncomfortable feelings of incompetence, self doubt, and guilt seem to come with the territory after the arrival of children. These feelings add to the strain of the transition, especially if they are not addressed in emotionally honest conversations between the partners in the marriage.

Although both parents experience peak levels of anxiety while trying to figure out how to meet a string of new challenges, I think it's fair to suggest that mothers may experience this disproportionately for a few reasons. First, they are usually the ones in most frequent close contact with helpless newborns. Biology and social expectations work together to put mothers in the role of the primary responder, and as a result, mothers carry an extra burden of perceived responsibility for their children's outcomes relative to fathers. Second, mothers' loss of place when they cut back on their career activities creates a pull toward approaching parenting rather like a job. The more ambitious members of the workforce are constantly looking for ways to improve their performance and exert increased control over outcomes. Whether male or female, alpha (by which I mean a strong willed person with many leadership qualities) individuals have typically experienced a high level of perceived control in other domains of their lives and naturally assume that the same strategy of controlling outcomes will work in the parenting domain. High-achieving women in particular are likely to apply the strategies that have helped them succeed elsewhere to their roles as mothers. In the book *A Nation of Wimps: The High Cost of Invasive* Parenting, author Hara Marano points to the research of developmental psychologist Dr. Suniya Luthar, who argues that professionalizing the parenting relationship underwrites perfectionist strivings and results in kids who become the projects of professional moms, especially those who have dropped out of the workforce and have all their energy to focus on their kids[185] (for any fellow *Lord of the Rings* fans, I wonder if it would feel like growing up under the eye of Sauron to have such a parent?).

Alpha working women become alpha moms, making Olympian efforts to put their children ahead of all the other children, to shape their offspring into once-and-future kings and queens. Leadership ability has always been prized to some degree, but never more so than in recent generations. In previous generations, children were shaped to be well-respected contributors to society. Today, parents want their children to be the top one percent-ers, the leaders of generations to come. I share some of Hara Marano's concern about children who are raised in the art of being the king (or queen): When parents make children feel like the center of the universe, give them endless choices, and teach them that they don't need to answer to anyone, children are set up for massive violations of expectations later in life. Even the most successful people generally need to submit to someone's authority for a season of their lives, and children raised in the art of being kings and queens are ill-equipped to tolerate this reality.

In addition to wanting control because they have often achieved control, parents want control because so much feels so out of control these days. As Daniel Brook explains, "It may be counterintuitive, but talented young people actually have less control over their lives in a society in which they can get rich quick because, in such a society, the consequences of not getting rich quick become much more serious."[186] Not surprisingly, parents these days are especially fearful and seem to be ever vigilant that their children are "tracking" in the right direction and getting exposed to stimulating people and abundant opportunities to develop (and display) their talents. Our age is one of great anxiety for new parents. The economy has collapsed, we seem to be engaged in endless war, and while some achieve incredible levels of prosperity, others suffer constant feelings of financial insecurity. Parents worry about the bad things that could happen to their children, or the good things that may not happen unless they work at perfecting their parenting approach and take full advantage of any opportunity offered to them. In this schema, every moment of every day is a potentially teachable moment, and many parents have fears that if they miss these teachable moments, they will jeopardize the futures of their children. The perception of parenting as a high-stakes endeavor, coupled with a loss of control and predictability, prompts parents to re-assert control in an attempt to get a handle on the situation and bring increased order and structure to what feels so chaotic.

The problem is that with parenting, there is no way to achieve anything near perfect control of outcomes. Parents frequently say things like "nothing teaches you that you are *NOT* in control so much as raising a child." Parents certainly have a good deal of influence on their children, but there are simply too many factors at play—the temperament of a child, social and cultural contexts, influences of other children and other caregivers, the omnipresent forces of the media, and so on—to feel that one has a high level of control. In many cases, it doesn't stop parents from aiming for near total control, though. As Johnson points out, when people feel insecure, they "become anxious, angry, or controlling."[187]

Will kids really become the future bag ladies and gentlemen of America if we don't constantly pump them full of stimulating experiences? People in many other countries don't seem to believe this will happen. Two of our best friends (a couple) are from Australia. Before they started a family, they mentioned that they found it odd that American parents devote so much time and attention to their children, to the exclusion of many of the activities (and friendships) they had before children arrived. They found it strange when I told them I have come to expect friends with children to completely drop out of the picture socially for many months, if not forever. As these friends went through their own pregnancy and transition to parenthood, it soon became clear to us how different their attitude was compared the attitude of many American parents. In their case, the process of being pregnant and going through this time of transition occurred in the context of continued social connection with family members and friends. They told us that in Australia, it is not normal to be so focused on children that most of one's energy is diverted to this central cause for many years. They also explained that parenting outcomes don't play quite such a central role in the self-esteem of Australian parents. Kids are a joy, and certainly, parents love and invest in them, but parents continue to enjoy active mental lives outside the world of their children. Parents are likely to send their children to stay with relatives while they take summer vacations without them. Thanks to family-friendly government policies, parents receive government subsidies when they start families, and people don't worry that they could lose everything because of one serious health problem in the family unless they amass an obscene amount of money.

In contrast to Australia, as Daniel Brook explains, "America is the only developed country where an individual has to choose between the career she desires and the health care and education her family needs."[188] As a federal employee, I was surprised to learn that although plenty of political lip service is paid to "family values" and "the need to support families," the federal government provides absolutely no paid maternity leave to its employees. Even California, with its severe budgetary issues, offers partially paid leave to new mothers while they recover during the weeks following birth. Partial paid leave on the birth of a child is a benefit that is not available to federal workers who are stationed in California, despite the fact that we pay California taxes. As a result, even before deciding whether we might attempt to start a family, I have had to stockpile my leave for the past several years, taking very, very few vacations and dragging myself to work when I'm sick so that I will have time to recover from delivering a child. This has meant a choice between engaging in good self-care (e.g., taking breaks for my own health and to prevent exhaustion and burnout) and having enough time to recover and bond with our child without putting our financial stability at risk. Given that my job largely involves helping combat-traumatized veterans recover from the horrors of war, it has been no small sacrifice to work for three straight years without taking a reasonable amount of time off to rest and refresh myself. My husband, meanwhile, has not been faced with this harsh choice. It's not his fault that federal policies are so family *un*friendly and that I have suffered a much higher cost in this regard. However, this is a good example of how our government's lack of any real support for families sets up disparities in freedom and flexibility for working wives and creates relative differences in the quality of life for wives, in comparison to their husbands. Clearly, then, the extent and quality of the support that Australians receive, from individual friends and family and from their government, radically alters the parenting experience, allowing parents to spend more time enjoying their children without being constrained by the limitations and obstacles faced by even the most fortunate couples in America.

Strategies for Reducing Parenting Conflicts

In addition to urging strategic advocacy for improvements in structural supports for families (and equally supportive policies for individuals who choose to remain child-free to take short-term sabbaticals to pursue personally meaningful endeavors), I also have some specific suggestions for ways to navigate this time of transition within a marriage of equals.

First, when you talk to your spouse about the possibility of having children, unless you are both strongly in favor of having children or strongly opposed to having children, consider discarding the question "Do we want to have children or not?" Framed in this way, this sweeping question begs a yes–or–no, all-or-nothing response. I have a theory that feelings about having children are analogous to Alfred Kinsey's spectrum of sexual orientation. Around 1950, Kinsey and colleagues[189] presented research findings that changed the prevailing model of sexual identity. Prior to Kinsey and colleague's reformulation of the model, it was thought that people were either straight or gay. In the Kinsey study, a substantial portion of research subjects endorsed degrees of homo- and heterosexual identities. On this basis, Kinsey and colleagues proposed a seven-point spectrum of sexual orientation, with gay and heterosexual orientations at the two poles and bisexuality as the spectral midpoint. My goal is not to critique or authenticate this model, but to note that the Kinsey-esque notion of a continuum fits well with what I have observed when couples talk about having children. That is, some people will say things like "I've always known I wanted to be a parent" or "I could never imagine having children, and I've never wanted them" in a way that feels strikingly similar to the way that people will say, "I've never been at all attracted to anyone of my gender" or "I've always known that I was gay." I specifically asked Lifestyle Poll participants about any feelings of ambivalence in relation to having children and received some very interesting responses that seem to support my theory. As you can see, some of the respondents were strongly oriented to having children:

- No ambivalence—I'm very excited to have children!

- I definitely want children.

- I would love to have a child. Mostly to have the bond of true love versus love that can come and go with a flighty lover.

- Can't wait to have children!

- I can't identify—I've always wanted a family.

At the other end of the spectrum were statements such as these:

- I have never wanted children; from my earliest memories, I knew I did not want them.

- I have no real feelings about children. I have no maternal instinct to speak of. The idea of me having children means as much to me as the idea of me growing wings and flying about the room.

- I am not ambivalent—I have always identified as adamantly child-free. Under no circumstances will I ever consider having children.

- I don't want children. It isn't the calling for me like it obviously is for most people.

- I have never wanted to have children for as long as I can remember. I was never ambivalent; from the first time I seriously considered it, I knew I didn't want to be a parent.

- I am completely secure in my decision to never have or care for children. I would rather provide an example to others or use my own life to accomplish what my parents, who rate their children as their most important contribution to the world, never had the time to do. I am not an important person, but I plan to make a difference during my life, what I have or will do, instead of putting that responsibility onto an unborn person who would have their own hopes and dreams and shouldn't have to be burdened with mine.

A third variant of responses is illustrated by comments such as these:

- I'm a fence-sitter. I'm not too sure I want children, but at the same time, I want that option. I would classify my ideal life plan as full-time career and maybe parenthood.

- I see myself eventually having children, but I am hesitant to give up my single life.

- I can identify with this. I do want children; I am the one pushing for them in my relationship, but I'm not sure that I want them now. Children would be both a joy and a burden, and it's a big step that I'm nervous about taking.

- For most of my life, I have not wanted children because I was too afraid of the responsibility and changes that would occur in my life. Recently, I have become lukewarm to the idea because I know I could handle it in my life. But at 40, I don't think having a child is a wise choice for me. My husband and I are just too set in our ways. And he doesn't want kids, anyway.

I think of the individuals like those who made the first set of responses as reproductively sure ("repro-sure" for short) and those like the individuals who made the second set of response as non reproductively sure ("non-repro-sure" for short), while I think of those in the third group as somewhere in the middle of the spectrum, or "repro-curious." Based on conversations I have heard between married couples, in both research and clinical settings, and in discussions between friends, I suspect some level of repro-curiosity among many of those who are considering starting a family. To label this as "repro-curious" is not just to assign cute terminology. What is helpful about this concept is that it moves us away from binary choices and begins to suggest new questions such as, "Under what conditions would we want to start a family?" or "What supports and systems need to be in place before we would feel sufficiently comfortable attempting to start a family?" Asking questions like these gives partners in a marriage of equals the necessary flexibility to approach the discussion from multiple angles and perspectives.

One of the most commonly-stated arguments about starting a family is "There is no good time to start a family." I agree that starting a family will always entail some degree of stress and transition, no matter how prepared we may feel before a child arrives; however, I do not agree that all timing is equally favorable to starting a family. There are huge factors in the equation whose presence or absence will radically change the nature of the experience: individual identity formation, access to extended family support, relationship stability and shared ability to meet other types of challenges, responsibility sharing patterns *prior* to having children, quality health insurance, access to good medical care, the degree of each partner's career establishment, and geographic and financial stability, to name a few. Though not exhaustive, I would offer the following set of questions to stimulate the kinds of conversations that would be wise to have as you consider starting a family:

Sources of support

- If we were to have children, what level of support might we have for childcare assistance?

- Are members of our families willing to get involved with caring for our children, and to what degree are they willing to help us during the months or years following childbirth?

- Do we have friends we can depend on for some support who want to be involved in helping us raise our child to some extent?

- Will we need to put our child in daycare? How do we feel about having our child in daycare? Are there any quality day care centers near where we live? What do they cost, and how would we afford this?

- Are there other affordable options we might consider for childcare support?

- How do we feel about hiring babysitters to watch our child? (This may change once you have children, but it is still good to get a read on where you sit with this prior to having children.)

- Do we have good health insurance and/or access to quality medical care?

- How much parental leave will each of us be able to take in the period just after birth?

Expectations

- What shifts will each of us need to make in our career activities to support a family?

- To what degree will one or both of us be expected to cut back on our career commitments if we have a family? How does each of us feel about this? Do we have a general plan for when one or both of us may be able to turn more attention back to career goals (if applicable)?

- What might be the financial implications if one or both of us cut back on our career activities? How will our finances need to be restructured to ensure that we have enough to pay our bills and enough so that each of us feels an equal level of financial security? (Agreements about financials buffers are especially important if one or both of you decrease your commitment to a paid position.)

- Will one of us be expected to be the primary responder, or will we hold this responsibility equally? How will this arrangement work from a practical sense? For example, when our child is sick, how will we decide who picks him/her up and takes care of him/her? Will we both be equally responsible for taking our child to medical appointments, buying supplies for our family, and changing diapers?

- How equal and balanced is our current chore sharing arrangement? (In my opinion, this question is so critical that it warrants some focused attention later in this chapter.) How would we allocate chores after children are born, given the addition of significant childcare needs, to minimize resentment and pursue equality in our respective quality of life?

Readiness

- Does either of us have serious reservations about how children may change the things we enjoy most about our current lifestyle? Do the benefits of pursuing this path together seem to outweigh the costs? (The latter question may be hard to answer because we are well aware of the benefits of current freedoms, but unable to assess the impact of losing much of this freedom while gaining an unknown quantity of joy we may find in having a child.)

- How well do we handle uncertain, and very stressful, situations together? Are we able to plan and organize well, and be flexible whenever there is need?

- How well do we negotiate changes and transitions together? In what ways might we need to become a better team before considering starting a family?

- How do we weigh biological considerations in this decision, given well-established declines in fertility and increased risk for pregnancies for women throughout the 30s and early 40s?

- Are we able to argue about heated topics without disrespecting each other?
- What is the current level of resentment (if any) over non-resolved issues in our marriage?
- Does either of us feel that the sacrifices of having a child at this time would create future obstacles that would be exceptionally difficult to overcome (e.g., having a child before one of us completes a degree that he/she wants to finish before starting a family)?

If a couple were to have a series of discussions on questions like these, I imagine they could come away with a much better defined agreement about whether and when they are open to possibly having children. Below are some hypothetical outcomes to conversations like this:

> Couple 1: We are working well as a team, and we agree that chores are split up evenly. After we have kids, I'm willing to take on these additional chores you are doing now to account for the fact that you will be the primary responder when our child has needs during working hours. Also, your parents have offered to give us some support in raising our children, so let's come up with a plan to relocate closer to them within the next two years so we can get some additional help.

> Couple 2: Neither of us is willing to lose the freedoms we enjoy now. It seems like you would like to have children somewhat more than I would, but you are also unsure. Let's continue to talk about this, because clearly, we aren't ready to make a decision right now.

> Couple 3: We both want to raise children, but, right now, neither of our positions provides adequate maternity or paternity leave. You've put a lot of time into getting your degree, so let's wait a year until you finish your degree, and then let's see if at least one of us can line up a job that will provide better health coverage and family benefits. This means that we'd probably

start trying when we are 33 or 34 years old. If we can't conceive within five years, let's talk about adoption as a possibility.

Couple 4: Kids are good for some people, but when we talk about all that it would mean for us, they don't seem right for us. Some of the most remarkable people in history have made a similar decision to invest their time and energy in other things. Since we are going to be child-free, let's talk about the interesting ways our lives may unfold and the things we'd like to pursue.

Couple 5: There is still a lot we need to figure out. We are still fighting about chores, and when we fight, I feel scared about our future together. Let's go see a marital counselor to see if we can figure this out before we consider starting a family.

In any family planning discussions, make sure to address a number of topics that may be overlooked. For example, make sure to fully discuss the emotional aspects of starting a family. Talk about the personal meaning of any shifts you may need to make in your professional lives and any related feelings of vulnerability and loss of power that may come with these changes. In the Lifestyle Poll, I asked participants to indicate their level of agreement with the statement "It is impossible in our present society to combine a career, in the fullest sense of the term (uninterrupted, full-time work with a high degree of commitment and desire for success) with the demands of a family." More participants agreed than disagreed. A total of 18.4% strongly agreed, 41.6% somewhat agreed, 27.6% somewhat disagreed, and 12.4% strongly disagreed. This suggests that these women (and probably their husbands as well) have some sense that serious tradeoffs are part of the family deal. In your discussions with your spouse, it is important to be open about these perceived tradeoffs and to come up with a plan for how you might reduce the strain of them. Of course, you can't plan everything out, but this isn't the point. The point is to spend significant time discussing your expectations, and making it a habit to engage in open discussion and respectful negotiation of concerns in order to maximize satisfaction with the parenting experience for both partners. And, in parallel to the process of selecting a spouse in the first place, it is smart to count the cost before making a binding decision that will change the rest of your life.

Second, it is important that each spouse is aware of the strong biological drives that kick in during this transition. Specifically attend to the disproportionate way in which biology influences mothers in comparison to fathers. Very, very few people regret having children, but the "falling in love" aspect is arguably stronger for wives than for husbands because of the chemical properties of childbearing, delivery, and early nurturance activities. As I've previously mentioned, wives may feel vulnerable in particular ways that husbands do not. Ultimately, biology, culture, and social modeling increase the probability that wives may disengage from their husbands and turn in to the world of their babies. In Chapter 2, I argued that it is important to be aware of and swim against the tide of emotions and hormones to wisely choose a mate. In a similar way, during the transition to parenthood, it is especially important for parents to swim against any tide that would bond one parent or the other to the child in a way that leaves the other on the outside. Otherwise, people get squeezed in ways that strain the marriage and endanger the long-term viability of the new family. Wives may get squeezed out from previous areas of competence and from their formerly more equal status in marriage, and husbands may get squeezed out of the intense bonding experience between mother and child.

Third, you would be wise to attend not only to emotional considerations, but also to very practical aspects of starting a family. Research shows us that pragmatic arrangements are important. Cowan and Cowan of UC Berkeley found that fathers who were more involved in childcare had lower parenting stress and lower levels of depression. Their wives were more satisfied with the marriage and felt that the family was more cohesive.[190] Shared involvement in childcare conveyed direct benefits to children, especially daughters. Specifically, the Cowans discovered that fathers' engagement with their preschool-aged daughters is directly associated with how the fathers' relationships with their wives play out in the first few years of raising a family.[191] As such, in your strategic planning process, make sure to address difficult areas such as chore sharing and new feelings of financial dependence.

Since I believe that existing inequities in chore sharing allocations directly lead to even greater inequities in parenting responsibilities, I want to focus further attention on this topic. I haven't tested this in any formal way, but I have a theory about how to prevent an all-too-common parental phenomenon I think of as "diaper-bag rage." The cap-off-the-toothpaste moment that sets many a new parent into a state of primal rage is the unreplenished diaper bag. Although this does not reach the level of an attachment trauma, the presence of piercing rage is probably not great for a marriage. I've heard variants of the following story many, many times in clinical sessions, most often from new mothers:

> We have a diaper bag with pockets for everything you need when you are out. When I use an item, I replace it, but somehow, my husband doesn't ever do this. How could he not think to do this? He just leaves it on the counter when he gets back from taking the baby out! So, I'm in the park the other day, and the baby starts puking, and I look in the bag, and there are no *@&*$#$ (politely translated as "doggone") burp cloths! I'm out in public, covered in baby puke and I had to pull out a clean diaper and press my baby's face into the crotch of a diaper! I would NEVER put my husband in that position—why is he so thoughtless?!

Here is my theory: If we trace the stream of diaper-bag rage upriver, we will almost always find that the rageful partner acceded to the role of the supply sergeant for the household long ago. In domestic terms, a "supply sergeant" is the person whose job it is to realize when the house is nearly out of toilet paper and to restock all kinds of items that the couple needs. Matthew Killingsworth, a doctoral candidate at Harvard University, and his mentor Dan Gilbert, best-selling author of *Stumbling on Happiness*,[192] published an article on the use of experience sampling to assess happiness during different states of mind. Experience sampling means using technology (it used to be beepers, but now researchers use cell phone texting) to contact people at various times throughout the day to collect information about what they are doing and how they feel about it at that exact moment. What they discovered is that "a wandering mind is an unhappy mind." As they explain, "The ability to think about what is *not* happening is a cognitive achievement that comes with an emotional cost."[193]

Imagine the implication of this finding for the supply sergeants among us whose minds run to a constant stream of thoughts such as "I have to call the plumber again tomorrow," "The car insurance needs to be paid tomorrow," or "We're out of toilet paper again. If I don't get more today, I'll have to stock the bathrooms with leaves from the backyard." As I noted previously, people will often point to discrepancies in allocations of specific chores and completely overlook the mental cost of trying to track the needs of themselves and their partners (and everyone else in their family when children enter the picture). As I have suggested previously, the impossible challenge of remembering the needs of several people at all times of the day and night may even be the root cause of what some people call mommy brain. A distracted brain is not only an unhappy brain, but is also an inefficient brain. Perhaps the brains of the family supply sergeants are like computers with a number of programs (and a few viruses) running simultaneously on them at all times. With so many bits and bytes of information floating around, everything slows down and becomes much less efficient.

What can be done about this? My husband and I have long had a system to prevent one of us from bearing this mental burden in an uneven way. We started with a small chalkboard in the hall, on which we would note groceries and household supplies needing to be replenished. We began adding to this list a number of items that need attention in the near future (bills coming due, for example) and began to see the potential of the idea. We needed more room, so we actually painted a 6' x 8' foot hallway wall with chalkboard paint and are using this as our shared mental-planning headquarters. Some of the categories on the board are "things we need" (groceries and household supplies), "events this week," "home projects to do," "people to see soon," "calls to return," "bills coming due," "places to eat out," "local things to check out," and "weekend getaways." This system has allowed us to fully co-manage the unfolding of our life together (and when we have a child in the next few months, you can bet there will be a few more categories added to the board—perhaps "things the baby needs," "childcare coverage to arrange," and "baby's upcoming appointments").

If you identify with the role of household supply sergeant, is there any hope of reversing this pattern once it is in place? Yes, in many cases there is, depending on a few things. First, you have to have a partner who really does feel that people are equally valuable, regardless of gender. This core value is the basis for launching all kinds of necessary discussions about how responsibilities in the home may need to be periodically reviewed and re-balanced. Second, if you are the supply sergeant, you must be willing to let go of control. Yes, control. I have found that frequently, at the bottom of maintaining this pattern is a supply sergeant's admission that, on some levels, she or he enjoys providing in this way or likes emulating Kelly Ripa in those ridiculous dishwasher commercials ("Now you can be even more amazing"). A related motivation that comes up quite often is that running the details of the household staves off some form of chronic anxiety. This is really just control in a different frock. Once this pattern is in place, when a child enters the picture, the use of control as a way of coping with anxiety is increasingly likely to occur. Although the conscious motivation of the controlling spouse is not to control, but to reduce his or her own anxiety, this behavior is inconsistent with sustaining a marriage of equals. Although there are exceptions, in my experience, wives are more susceptible to this behavior than husbands. A wife may complain that she "does everything," but when I challenge her (in a clinical capacity) to do less so her partner can step up, she will often say something like, "No, it's less painful for me to do it myself because I know that it will get done and he won't do it right." The inconvenient truth is that in many cases, wives socialize their husbands into a sense of entitlement, incompetency, or both.

Sometimes we do this because child-rearing has become our primary job and we're bent on being the CEO, CFO, and COO all at once. If we define our role this way, then any attempt on our mate's part to restructure elements of how we do business can feel like an unwelcome incursion into what we've defined as our territory. I feel compelled to challenge this thinking very directly in the spirit of demonstrating how to sustain a marriage of equals. How is it that the husbands of highly accomplished women, men who were initially selected as well matched in their cognitive abilities, come to be perceived by their wives as something in the spectrum of "nebbish" to "dead weight" to "additional idiot child?" Is thinking ahead and predicting what is needed to pave the course of a life well lived a uniquely female competence? Is nurturing a uniquely female competence? What does one mean by doing something "the right way"? If a husband is squeezed out of equal authority and responsibility in the parenting role, how will this affect his self-confidence as a father? What message does this send about perceived competence on his part? What does this say about how much he is *really* trusted when it comes to the important things in life?

If you want to engage in some upriver prevention by equalizing the mental burden of running your household before you have children, you might begin by identifying the current pattern truthfully, as in "I don't exactly know why or when, but long ago, I seem to have volunteered myself for the role of supply sergeant in our house. I recognize now that in some ways, I was holding on to a form of control that keeps us unequal as co-leaders of this house. I want to back off holding on to so much control and give you the

The Testing Phase

respect of running our house as a fully equal partner. I have an idea. What if we were to make a list of the essentials on a chalkboard—stuff we need on a weekly basis—and agree that whoever checks off more of the things that need to be picked up by the end of the week gets to pass on picking up everything on the list? So, that person "wins" in the area of doing some mental work for the family and his or her partner has to go get all the stuff. If you were to set up this challenge, then whether you end up checking off more items on the list or going and getting everything on the list, both of you are guaranteed to have the needs of your household on your radar in some way. The response cost of having to go get everything on the list is also likely to be a significant motivator in prompting a less mindful partner to become more mindful about the status of your supplies. If your partner agrees to this plan, in fairly short order, it should begin to shift the consciousness of how you run your home as a couple and you'll have a very good chance of avoiding the possibility of finding yourself in public, covered in baby sputum and cursing your partner from afar.

Ultimately, if you are the one who is doing the lion's share of the chores and are feeling resentful as a result, there are two logical courses to consider if your goal is to stay happily married: (1) you can recalibrate the level of your resentment based on the insight that assuming most of the control at home is a *choice* you are making, or (2) you can take a leap of faith and invest some anxiety in making changes. To be specific, you might say something like "I haven't trusted you as I should have. I'm sorry. I have been too controlling, and I've realized that I've been doing this to try to cope with my anxiety about raising [child's name]. I would like to trust you more, and I want to return to working as a team as we did before [child's name] was born. Will you help me let go of some of this control? What would you like to take a lead on that I'm doing now?" If your spouse can't think of something, then you might make a suggestion, such as "It would really help if you would plan and shop for our meals this week. I'll be your sous chef—how does that sound to you?" Remember that if you are trying to let go of control, you must be willing to follow your spouse's lead, to respect that he has have an equally valid way of operating as a parent. Asking your partner to step up in new ways means additional work for him, but in the long run, the benefits of re-establishing a more equal partnership will pay off in boosting both mutual marital satisfaction and mutual satisfaction with parenting.

To end on a positive note, I'd like to share an example of a couple in our circle of friends who have worked out the mental burden of running their household in a beautiful way. I was having a conversation with the wife, who is a woman I respect greatly, and she mentioned that her husband (who is also a high-achieving, career-oriented individual) was home making cupcakes with one of their sons. She said, "He asked Antonio how school is going and what is coming up at school, and Antonio said that he needs to have cupcakes for a school party on Friday. So Julian stopped at the supermarket on the way home, helped Antonio get all the ingredients, and is now baking up a batch of cupcakes with Antonio." When I heard this story, it was very telling, and quite influential in helping me to appreciate the benefits of sharing the mental burden related to organizing the needs of a household. To me, this brief conversation provided a rich example of a dad who is fully tuned in to his children's needs, operating at the top of his game as an equal partner who shares equal responsibility for gathering this kind of information, and planning ahead for what his children will need. Fathers like these demonstrate that this type of sensibility is *not* a uniquely female ability, and their children are sure to benefit from their full engagement in the physical and mental aspects of raising them.

Chapter 7

Tested Romanticism

The aim of this final chapter is to zoom out and take a bird's eye view of the life span of the most stable and satisfying marriages. To briefly review earlier material, let's return to the earlier model of a long-term marriage as unfolding across just three phases. That is, all love relationships kick off with a cocaine-rush phase, some relationships survive and even thrive through a prolonged testing phase, and highly successful relationships may achieve a state of what I refer to as tested romanticism. During the cocaine-rush phase, the main developmental challenges are to override the desire to rush into a foolish commitment, assess your relationship's actual potential over a sufficient length of time, and establish healthy ways of relating to each other. It also seems wise to shed the false hope of happening upon a soul mate in favor of identifying someone of character who is open to influence and capable of creating a lifelong partnership. The transition from the cocaine-rush phase into the testing phase is marked by the end of illusions of mutual perfection.

The testing phase is by far the longest phase of a marriage. It is also where the work of a marriage primarily occurs. During the cocaine-rush phase, biology aligns with desire to compel effortless investment of energy in the relationship. It is during the testing phase that the marital bond competes with the emergence of other calls on our time and energy. In the testing phase, the main developmental tasks are to negotiate challenges and transitions while treating each other with love *and* respect, and to proactively invest energy in maintaining your bond when career goals or love of children could supplant marital connection. A number of major life transitions also typically occur during the testing phase of marriage as individuals forge careers, set down geographic roots, and, in some cases, become parents. As a result, each couple passes through several tunnels of chaos—for example, when making a major relocation, adding children to their family, losing a job, changing a career, or sending a child to college. Within each tunnel of chaos, the previous rules and assumptions of the partnership get shaken up and potentially realigned. Successful couples are able to stay connected within the chaos, protect their relationship at the level of G, and adapt to new roles to meet the demands of new stressors. There is nothing quite like these tunnels of chaos to throw the soul mate ideal into question, yet it is in the very process of navigating these tunnels of chaos that two people actually begin to become soul mates.

The research literature presents strong and consistent support for these first two phases of relationships in my model (the cocaine-rush phase and the testing phase). For example, studies consistently demonstrate that marital satisfaction is highest at the very start of a relationship (i.e., during the cocaine-rush phase) and then drops shortly thereafter (i.e., during the testing phase).[194] The idea that it's all downhill from the wedding day onward is a depressing thought to consider, and I'm confident that this is not the reality in the case of many couples. Specifically, as in the analysis of how children really affect marital satisfaction, it is important to think critically about the timing and context for collecting this information. As Umberson and colleagues point out, "much of the best recent research on marital quality starts with newlywed couples and follows them over time."[195] When marriage is seen as the launch of a relationship, however, the richness of one couple's long and thoughtful courtship is equated with the impulsive vow exchange of two individuals who barely know each other and lack the emotional maturity to sustain a healthy marriage. Any study that records marital satisfaction at the time of marriage includes some portion of couples that have shared a thoughtful courtship; however, because many couples rush into marriage in a relatively short period of time, what researchers are often measuring at the time of the wedding is the euphoria of unrealistic fantasies during the cocaine-rush phase. The inclusion of a number of marrying couples who are "on cloud nine" with very little actual knowledge of who they are marrying would greatly inflate the average ratings of satisfaction for all marrying couples. If a researcher were then to compare these artificially high ratings of marital satisfaction to later reports of marital satisfaction once the cocaine-rush has subsided from the peak of untested bliss, there would be nowhere to go but down. In fact, when some researchers suggest that feelings of love and closeness peak at the time of marriage, and then decline thereafter, I would question whether they are actually assessing love in the first place. I'd propose that what they are actually capturing are the effects of cocaine-rush fantasies. Also, remember that researchers are averaging outcomes across couples, so the findings they report may not be meaningful at all for some couples. I would theorize that couples who marry impulsively after short courtships would almost universally experience a huge drop in satisfaction within the first year or two of marriage, whereas couples who have already transitioned from the cocaine-rush phase into the testing phase during a long and thoughtful courtship would probably experience a much smaller drop in satisfaction (or none at all) relative to what research would suggest.

Relative to the testing phase, there is also solid consensus in the research that life-cycle stressors are reliably linked to declines in marital satisfaction during the early years of a marriage.[196] By far, most of the research on family transitions has focused on the transition to parenthood, which I've already covered in the previous chapter. To briefly summarize my previous writing on this area, although new types of stressors emerge during the child-rearing years, this is normal, and strong marriages are likely to weather the stress of this transition.[197] In fact, many couples find that raising children brings a new level of marital intimacy and forges a stronger bond. Recall that 77.7% of the Lifestyle Poll respondents felt that marital intimacy had not been lost and had in fact grown *deeper* in most cases with the addition of children. So, again, I would point out that steep declines in marital satisfaction during the testing phase of a marriage are not universal, or bound to occur in all cases.

My theory is that, following the testing phase, successful couples eventually arrive at a state of what I call "tested romanticism." As I propose the term, tested romanticism refers to the highly satisfying union of two people who have developed a genius for loving each other well and whose risk of divorce is virtually non-existent. At the relational level, a couple in the tested romanticism phase fulfills the promise of what a marriage can be—a safe and supportive home base that allows each partner to flourish. At this stage of marriage, the bond of mutual love and respect is often highly visible to others, and the couple frequently becomes naturally generous toward others out of the abundance of their love and joy. Others may witness a state of harmonious interdependence that puts real meaning to the wedding day ideal that, in marriage, two become one. In fact, the two-becoming-one dimension of marriages in the tested romanticism phase helps explain what researchers refer to as "the widowhood effect," which is the tendency for those in very bonded marriages to die in close succession. This is not merely romantic fantasy portrayed by writers like Nicolas

Sparks in *The Notebook*.[198] Several research studies have shown that when one partner in a long-term marriage dies, the survival of the remaining spouse is often short-lived.[199]

Another key hallmark of a relationship in the tested romanticism stage is evidence of growth at the highest levels of individual and relational potential. The security and steady investment of mutual love and respect create the perfect conditions for both partners to develop their individual potential. In these marriages, one often sees two individuals who have become distinctly successful in life pursuits they find meaningful. As psychiatrist Peter Kramer puts it, "A true marriage requires, as a precondition, the achievement of some hidden potential—call it adulthood—that can emerge in the course of negotiating a relationship."[200]

There are some thought-provoking parallels between the tested romanticism phase and the initial cocaine-rush phase of a relationship. As in the cocaine-rush phase, the drive to separate in the tested-romanticism phase is almost non-existent; in both cases, there are strong drives to be together, and divorce is quite unthinkable. There is also an exceptionally high level of marital satisfaction, feelings of closeness, and what some call romanticism[201] (which inspired the term "tested romanticism"). Also, as in the cocaine-rush phase of love, the relationship feels more effortless again—feelings of love seem to flow naturally for those who are long and happily married. As during the cocaine-rush phase, couples in the later stages of happy marriages are also quite affectionate, even during conflict discussions.[202] There is one huge difference between these two relationship phases, however: Feelings of love during the cocaine-rush phase were based on untested hopes, whereas feelings of love during the tested romanticism phase are based on a lifetime of mutual support, love, and respect.

In the final stages of marriage, some couples reach a deeper, more satisfying level of love than anything that anyone encounters in the cocaine-rush phase of a relationship. In one sense, to make a comparison between the experiences of love at these two relationship stages is like comparing apples and oranges. I would argue that love of a deep and meaningful kind is only possible when based on real knowledge. If being loved is based on being known for who you are (at the level of s) and cherished despite your flaws (at the level of G), then the feelings one has during the cocaine-rush phase can't be love. These feelings would be some combination of other pleasurable things like hope and attraction, and illusions of the soul-mate variety. What feels a lot like love in the cocaine-rush phase does not compare to the love that couples may enjoy in the tested romanticism phase of marriage. If you doubt that this is true, consider the difference between the giddy feelings of being in love with someone you've known for a short time and the feelings of love you would have for someone who has been your journeying partner for the past 60 years of your life—the person who has been by your side through thick and thin, who has believed in you and invested in you. If this is difficult to picture, then, as an analogy, imagine the way it would feel to move into your dream home, full of excitement and thrilling plans for the future (in parallel to the cocaine-rush phase of a relationship). Now, imagine the feelings of love and attachment you would have about the same home after making every square inch of the home suited to your personal tastes and filling it with layer upon layer of joyful memories over the course of a full and rich life (in parallel to the tested romanticism phase). The feelings you would have in either case cannot be compared as equals, but I would guess that most of us would cry harder if the home full of memories caught fire.

When I looked to the research for validation of my idea of the tested romanticism phase of love, I discovered a muddle of contradictory findings. Research on marital satisfaction at different points of the lifespan appears to have first gained traction in the 1960s. In one of the earliest studies on this topic, Deutscher surveyed 33 urban middle-class couples to find out how they were adjusting to the launch of their children (what he calls the post-parental phase). Deutscher concluded that, far from being a time of crisis, "the post-parental phase is a 'good' time" associated with "freedom from financial responsibilities, freedom to be mobile (geographically), freedom from housework and other chores, and finally, freedom to be one's self for the first time since the children came along."[203] What a welcome message this surely would have been for any family in the teenage phase of child rearing! I think of this thesis as the "pot of gold at the end of something much less pleasant than a rainbow." Over the next thirty years, researchers continued to present consistent evidence that those in long term marriages experience increasingly high levels of satisfaction in the later years of the relationship. A multitude of research studies[204] appear to reliably demonstrate that initial declines in marital satisfaction (which often coincide with family transitions) are temporary, followed by an increase in the later years of the relationship (often after the successful launch of children). Consistent with these findings, studies of the general population show a marked decrease in divorce rates with increasing age and marital duration.[205] Studies that fail to support the pot-of-gold theory[206] were few and far between. The vast majority of these studies were based on single snapshots in time, and some were based on comparisons of different age groups at various phases of the family life cycle. However, two studies that found evidence of a U-shaped curve in marital satisfaction involved collection of information over time: White and Edwards tracked a national sample over four years and picked up on a "modest post launch honeymoon"[207] for empty-nesters, and Gorchoff, John, and Helson tracked 123 women over an 18-year period and found that increased marital satisfaction in middle age was likewise related to the launch of children.[208] Gorchoff and colleagues theorized that increased marital satisfaction in the post-launch phase is a result of the couple having more time to focus on and enjoy each other during the later stages of marriage, an idea that seems quite logical.

Beginning in the 1990s, however, a handful of studies began to pose serious challenges to the pot-of-gold theory. Post-1990s researchers were quick to identify limitations in the cross-sectional design of the majority of earlier studies. Longitudinal studies, which involve collection of information over time, consistently regarded as the gold standard for study design, came into the picture and virtually upended the pot-of-gold theory. Using new methods that permitted analysis of change over time, some found evidence of stability across many years of marriage,[209] and others actually found a pattern of steady decline in satisfaction over the marital lifespan.[210] Some argued that results of earlier studies were caused by cohort effects—in other words, that different groups of people at different points in history would characteristically evaluate their marriages differently (no one pointed out the possibility that there could also be some cohort effects among the researchers themselves in terms of how they have philosophically tackled this question at different points in time). You can almost hear the pathos in the words of Norval Glenn, one of the most prominent investigators in this line of research. In 1990, he remarked, "A curvilinear relationship between family stage and some aspects of marital quality is about as close to being certain as anything ever is in the social sciences."[211] A mere eight years later, upon finding evidence to contradict the U-curve theory, he ominously intoned, "We must wait for the results of other studies, especially those with individual-longitudinal data, before we give the mid-term upturn thesis a decent burial."[212]

Within this body of research, additional sources of confusion further muddy the waters and limit consensus. For example, a frequent criticism in the literature is that results of these studies are likely to be positively skewed because long-term marriages include an artificially high number of high-quality marriages (because unhappy marriages that end in divorce would fall away from inclusion in these analyses). In other words, since the best marriages are usually the ones that last in the first place, then the happily married spouses in the later stages of these marriages would be a self-selected group. In contrast to this notion, I would point out that any pool of long-term marriages also includes a number of relationships that grind on despite chronic dissatisfaction for one or both partners. These marriages are stable but not very satisfying. Most of the time, in these marriages, the cost of leaving the marriage, whether financial, social, or otherwise, is perceived to outweigh the cost of staying within the less-than-satisfying arrangement. This type of long-term marriage certainly exists today but was probably even more common in past generations, when barriers to divorce were greater. A spouse who stays in such a marriage often considers the significant "spent cost" he or she has invested and will often voice the belief that breaking free of the marriage would result in a terminal loneliness to which the dissatisfying marriage is preferable. Clearly, this is not the outcome anyone shoots for and desires. In my experience as a clinical researcher, when granted anonymity or confidentiality, dissatisfied spouses are often quite pleased to report how terrible their marriages are or have been, so I would imagine that the reported marital satisfaction of those in marriages that grind on despite dissatisfaction would be quite low. When researchers look at whether people experience an increase in marital satisfaction during the later stages of marriage, they are usually computing averages. As such, there is the distinct possibility of lumping two sets of people with very different experiences of marriage into one group, rendering the results less helpful in understanding the true course of marriage for each discrepant set of individuals.

In addition, distortions in how we perceive and recall events, and limitations in our ability to predict future outcomes may influence research results. For example, Vaillant and Vaillant's 40-year longitudinal study permitted comparison of retrospective (that is, looking back in time) and prospective (looking at ratings from various data-collection points across time) perceptions of marital satisfaction. When couples were asked to retrospectively reflect on their levels of satisfaction, there was a weak U-shaped curve in satisfaction, with satisfaction levels at their lowest point about 20 years into the marriage. In other words, in this sample, there seemed to have been a shared feeling across couples that could be translated as "We were least satisfied with our marriage about 20 years into it, but our marriage has improved somewhat since that time." Vaillant and Vaillant are thoughtful in trying to understand the possible decline around year 20. They point out that this reported decline in satisfaction corresponds with the time when participants would have had adolescent children at home during the 1960s and 1970s, when children were "experimenting with anti-establishment rebellions."[213] When the researchers then looked at the prospective data (the ratings of marital satisfaction that were recorded at various time points as the marriage unfolded), however, they found that satisfaction levels remained relatively stable across time. On this basis, they questioned the existence of a U-shaped trend in marital satisfaction.

The discrepancy the researchers note in retrospective and prospective ratings of marital satisfaction has been repeated in other studies. For instance, Karney and Frye show that newlywed couples tend to perpetually adopt the belief that "things have been getting better lately."[214] This relationship-sustaining belief is a positive illusion bias that does not match the newlyweds' prospective reports of marital satisfaction at various points in time. From a broad read of the psychological literature, it seems that this type of thinking bias is quite normal, and highly adaptive. When we are faced with challenges, it is healthy to summon beliefs like "This too shall pass" and "Better times are on their way." Recall that in a good marriage, positive thinking biases are common. Happily married individuals are more likely to blame situational factors when stressed (as in, "We're fighting right now because we're both bone weary from staying up all night feeding our baby") and make internal attributions for successes (as in, "We made it through those exhausting night feedings because we love each other and our marriage is strong"). These marriage-sustaining thoughts echo the form and function of positive illusions in many other domains of functioning. For example, victorious wrestlers make more stable and personally controlled interpretations for their victories ("I won because I was the superior athlete"),[215] and teachers of students who win in a national essay contest attribute success to internal factors (their own teaching abilities), whereas teachers of losing students attribute losses to external factors ("the judges weren't fair").[216] These types of positive illusions and narrative interpretations are so common in non-depressed individuals that they have a name: the self-serving bias. Thus, the retrospective interpretation that "things are getting better lately" may be a way for all married couples, even those in strong relationships, to support their marriages during challenging times.

Ultimately, there is a tendency among researchers to put longitudinal designs on a pedestal without considering their limitations. For example, when researchers assert that prospective reports of satisfaction are more valid than retrospective reports, what they are really saying is that what people say at a particular slice of present time is a more valid truth than how they interpret their history. There are distortions of all kinds in both present and retrospective recall, however. For instance, there is never a uniform basis for judgment when people address global questions like "How satisfying is your marriage?" One man might think, *well, my partner doesn't treat me like she used to when we were dating* and on this basis, he might decide that the marriage is not very satisfying. Another person might evaluate her marriage as very dissatisfying in relation to the love she sees between Jack and Rose in the movie *Titanic* or some other source of Hollywood fantasy. A third person might think, *Given that we are under tremendous stress with the new baby, even though we fight way more often than we used to, since there are moments when we can laugh together, we're doing great.* Even when we use our own relationships as the basis for judgment, we can only compare our feelings against what we've known thus far, and memory is imperfect at best. The range of how happy, or unhappy, we may be in the future is unknown. Whether looking at the present, reflecting on the past, or anticipating the future, we see through a glass darkly. A happily married person could easily rate his marriage as extremely satisfying throughout the years and yet validly assert that he has became increasingly happier in the marriage and closer to his spouse than he had ever thought possible over the length of the marriage. This person's ratings of marital satisfaction would be consistently high, and a U-shaped curve would not materialize. So, whether we are judging the present or making interpretations of the past, we cannot avoid all kinds of distortions in how we evaluate our circumstances, and we cannot avoid inconsistencies in the way research participants approach such questions. Even the best research designs do not eliminate these problems.

    After I reviewed the literature, it seemed to me that the only conclusion that could safely be drawn is that marital satisfaction declines to some degree for most couples in the early stages of marriage, whereas experiences of those in long-term marriages are mixed. Some who study the later phases of marriage find increases in satisfaction, others find declines, and some find stability. I have been privileged to witness the close and joyful partnership of several couples who are in the tested romanticism phase, and I was initially disappointed that the research failed to reliably demonstrate evidence of this stage of marriage. Sometimes, when one is trying to make sense of seemingly contradictory results, it is helpful to convert the focus to a similar question in a different domain. So, instead of asking the question "Are those in long-term marriages generally very satisfied in their relationships?" I asked myself, "Are those in long-term academic research careers generally satisfied in their posts?" When I reframed the question in this way, the cause for mixed results became clearer. As a graduate student, I had ample opportunity to observe the paths of professional development of academic researchers at various points in their careers. In the early part of a career, the experience of being excited and then somewhat disillusioned seems to be fairly universal. Academic professors compete against incredible odds for research-funded, tenure-track university positions. When they are hired (often out of several hundred applicants), they have the potential to achieve the security of tenure (similar to the way a marriage offers the potential promise of security) within a university that is going to invest significant resources (lab space, funding for graduate students, and the like) so that academic researcher can study what he or she finds meaningful. This is part of the allure of the academic path—a life spent pursuing the study of things that one finds interesting. Young professors are full of hope and excitement about how their careers will unfold. Some may have visions of lecturing to masses of admiring students who are captivated by their wisdom and wit. The honeymoon phase for a new hire is often short-lived, however.

The first several years of the academic career (the "publish or perish" phase upon which tenure decisions are made) require very hard work and high levels of personal sacrifice of time and other pursuits. A recalibration of some initially unrealistic positive expectations would be normal in this phase of the career. Young professors may realize that they are living in a place they would never want to live, and working in a job with absolutely no support for "work-life balance." The expectation of strong university support is diminished as researchers jump through tangled webs of institutional hoops and find that large amounts of their time and energy may be shunted into activities they do not find meaningful, like sitting on various committees. As in the case of early-stage marriage, then, the typical experience probably follows the pattern of a peak in satisfaction, followed by a predictable decline. In contrast, the later-career experience of long-term academics varies considerably, depending on a number of factors. For example, the compatibility between the professor and his or her host university (similar to the compatibility between two spouses) would certainly affect long-term career satisfaction. The individual's own choices would also have a large impact on long-term job satisfaction. Some who achieve tenure fall into a mind-numbing pattern of teaching the same class(es) every year, sitting on the same committees, and investigating the same line of research over several decades with minor expansions in the scope of their research inquiries. Other career academics are highly innovative, and over the course of their careers, they become masters of their domain and highly respected members of the community within their respective universities. Thus, instead of asking a more global question like, "Are career academics highly satisfied with their jobs over the long term?" it might be wiser to ask a question like, "Under what conditions is an academic professor likely to achieve a high level of satisfaction over the course of his or her career?"

Going through this exercise helps illuminate the research on the life course of marriages. My original assertion (and consistent belief) is thus that *all* love relationships kick off with a cocaine-rush phase, *some* relationships survive and even thrive through a prolonged testing phase, and *highly successful relationships* may achieve a state of tested romanticism. In seeking evidence of tested romanticism in studies of long-term marriages, I was looking at what is *common* and expecting to see consistent evidence of what is *possible*, which are two very different things. In other words, my theory is that the initial period of some disillusionment from the cocaine-rush phase to the testing phase is fairly universal, but that the course of marriage over the lifetime varies greatly between couples. It may be helpful to classify all marriages into one of four broad categories: those that were never viable to begin with, those that are dead on arrival as soon as children are launched, those that grind on despite chronic dissatisfaction, and those that achieve a state of tested romanticism. Marriages in the first three categories would probably have the pattern of peaking and then steadily declining. Marriages in the fourth category could fit a U-shaped pattern in a way that mirrors the curve of relationship satisfaction during the transition to parenthood, which also begins with intense bonding and future-looking excitement, followed by the emergence of new relationship stressors, and, for successful couples, eventual stabilization and reconnection at increasingly deeper levels of attachment. Alternatively, these marriages may experience little decline relative to most, remaining generally stable and satisfying throughout their lifespan.

In my review of the literature, one particular study stood out because of some interesting parallels between the research sample and the sample of women who responded to the Lifestyle Poll. Specifically, Valliant and Valliant, who were mentioned earlier in this chapter, actively recruited Harvard students, 99% of whom were college graduates and 75% of whom later completed graduate degrees. With the exception of gender, there are several similarities with my research respondents: I actively targeted a Harvard sample, 98% of whom were college graduates, and 75% of whom either had or were actively pursuing graduate degrees. As in the case of my sample, the Vaillant and Vaillant sample represents "a narrow segment of society."[217] In their case, participants were actually prescreened as having "no mental or physical health problems" and were specifically selected by the Harvard College dean as "promising adults."[218] In other words, they were the very men that some morally twisted geneticist might selectively breed in order to create a "master class" of people.

Like Vaillant and Vaillant, I focused my recruitment efforts on Harvard College students. Whereas my recruitment efforts were launched through Harvard networks, however, no one was excluded from participation. Quite the opposite, participants were actively invited to forward the link to the poll to anyone they wanted to invite. Although the Lifestyle Poll respondents are also high-achieving planners with a level of education similar to the Vaillant and Vaillant sample, they are much more likely to be relatively normal individuals with common struggles and concerns. Along these lines, Lifestyle Poll participants reported a number of physical and mental health concerns such as depression, which was reported in 28% of the sample. Well over half (60%) of the Lifestyle Poll sample said that they had been in therapy to address mental health or other adjustment concerns at some point in their lives. Nonetheless, although my sample is relatively more representative of the population at large, given some of the overlap in the sample traits, I was curious to see whether Vaillant and Vaillant's participants reported a similarly high level of marital satisfaction. If I hadn't been actively looking for this information, I might have missed an important study limitation that the researchers did not highlight in their article that makes a huge impact in the interpretation of their findings. Specifically, their measure of marital satisfaction included these four specific questions:

1. Solutions to disagreements generally come: 1=easily, 2=moderately hard, 3=always difficult, 4=we go without a solution.
2. How stable do you think your marriage is? 1=quite stable, 2=some minor weaknesses, 3=moderate weaknesses, 4=major weaknesses, 5=not stable

3. Sexual adjustment is, on the whole: 1=very satisfying, 2=satisfying, 3=at times not as good as wished, 4=rather poor.
4. Separation or divorce has been considered: 1=never, 2=only casually, 3=seriously.

The scores on these items were summed to provide the global measure of marital satisfaction. The score of someone who is blissfully happy in his or her marriage and feels that the marriage is absolutely perfect would have a score of 4 (1+1+1+1). To really understand the results of the Vaillant and Vaillant study, it's helpful to translate these numbers into meaningful statements. Someone with a perfect score would essentially be saying, "We solve disagreements easily, our marriage is quite stable, our sex life is very satisfying, and we've never considered divorce, ever" (I wonder, would anyone *other than a newlywed still in the cocaine-rush phase of a relationship* ever score a 4?). On the other end of things, the score of someone who is miserably unhappy with his or her marriage could be as high as 16 (4+5+4+3). In other words, someone with the highest score on this scale would essentially be saying, "Our disagreements go unresolved, our marriage is not stable, our sex life is disappointing, and we have seriously considered divorce." The average ratings of the quality of marriage for husbands and wives in this sample *over the first 15 years* of marriage were 5 and 6, respectively. *After 31 years of marriage*, the average ratings for husbands and wives were 6 and 7, respectively.

Here is an example of how we could translate these scores based on the meaning of the items. A score of 5 could hypothetically be translated as saying, "Solutions to disagreements are generally easy to come by, we have never considered divorce, our marriage is quite stable, and our sexual relationship is satisfying." A score of 6 could hypothetically mean "Solutions to disagreements are moderately hard to come by, but our sex life is satisfying, our marriage is quite stable, and we've never considered divorce." A score of 7 could hypothetically mean "Solutions are not always easy to come by. Sometimes, negotiating is even moderately hard, so I'd say that our marriage has some minor weaknesses, but our sex life is still satisfying and we never think of divorce." In other words, both husbands and wives in this sample rated their marriages as near perfect to begin with and still near perfect after 31 years of marriage! With such a high rate of marital satisfaction in the first place, there is a significant ceiling effect. Marital satisfaction could have gone down, but it stayed almost the same across time. Because it didn't dip much at all in the first place, it would have been impossible to find any significant increase in satisfaction in the later years of these marriages because participants stayed so highly satisfied all along. Therefore, if there's no pot of gold at the end of these marriages, it is because these couples have been enriched all along by their successful partnerships.

To loop back to the original question, "Does marriage get better over time?", whether a U-shaped curve actually exists or is the result of retrospective biases, plenty of research suggests that the later stages of high-quality marriages are particularly sweet. If humans can develop finely honed skills in music, athletics, and language arts, wouldn't it be equally possible for them to become perfectly suited and *completely irreplaceable* to their spouses? A virtuoso develops perfect pitch and can instantly play complex musical patterns after listening to them just once. The best soccer players combine incredible footwork skills with a holistic awareness of the playing field; at the highest levels of play, soccer becomes a game of angles, similar to billiards. Someone who becomes fluent in a language "thinks" in that language—there is no effortful retrieval once the language becomes second nature. Along these lines, for a couple in the tested romanticism stage, effective and respectful negotiation of challenges has become habitual. Global attributions (what I've called G) have reached a stable, positive set point, and thoughts of separation or divorce are completely alien. The partnership has become so multifaceted and the compatibilities so intricately dovetailed that one's spouse could never be replaced by anyone else.

I suspect that happily married couples eventually pass a threshold into this last, most rewarding stage of marriage. My model is different from the pot-of-gold theory, which suggests that if a couple is patient and waits long enough, marriage will bring sweet rewards in time. In my opinion, marriages don't get better as a function of time alone but get better as a function of the spouses continuing to treat each other with love and respect despite the challenges life brings. The transition point into the stage of tested romanticism would be different for each couple, and some couples would arrive earlier than others. Perhaps this shift is the result of successful reconnection at a certain key transition point, such as the reconnection that follows the launching of adult children or the transition to retirement, but whenever the threshold is crossed, the remaining years of marriage are grounded in security and a rare and special form of earned intimacy. As I see it, during the tested romanticism phase, the developmental tasks would be to celebrate and make meaning of the life you have lived together, operating as sacred keepers of each other's history, and to become generative together to others. Life will continue to bring challenges, but the bond between you will be strong enough to meet these challenges.

Creating and sustaining a marriage that will reach the tested romanticism phase is arguably the best investment you can make earlier in life. Yet, this subject receives far less attention than making financial provisions for the post-retirement stages of life. The stakes of failing to think about *emotional* and *relational* provisions are very high for many people. When the waves of support and friendship recede as longtime friends move to retirement communities, downsized living arrangements, and locations closer to grandchildren, long-term married couples live increasingly in the shelter of each other. A couple who has successfully crossed the bridge into the tested romanticism phase of their marriage experiences the later years of life together as a joyous celebration of a beautiful union. In my opinion, the achievement of tested romanticism is the final reward for continually investing in a marriage of equals; being perfect for and irreplaceable to the person who has *become* your soul mate, and spending the generative years of life in a state of deeply intimate connection is the ultimate second marshmallow.

Appendix

Further Information about the Lifestyle Poll Project

The idea of launching the Lifestyle Poll project arose during one of many walks with my husband. In addition to my intrinsic interest in women's issues, when I was conceptualizing this project, I thought about the "tradition of remarkable women" at Harvard-Radcliffe and the many amazing women I have met in my life after Harvard. To test my theory that respect is equally critical for many women as for many men, I set out to profile the marriages of some of the smartest women I have known and their equally capable friends. Equipped with a budget of less than $500 for internet hosting and data collection, I had to get creative. I had been teaching a course in Personal Growth through the University of Florida for several consecutive semesters. Based on my strong interest in personal growth and my belief in the value of self-examination, I designed the Lifestyle Poll to operate simultaneously as a data collection tool and as a stimulus for the personal growth of my research participants. I assembled more than 200 questions and recruited participants primarily through unofficial networks of Harvard graduates. Word of the project spread organically, mostly through word of mouth and invitations between friends. My goal was to see if I could get 500 respondents within one year. In fewer than eight months, more than 1200 women had completed the poll.

Moreover, what I had once seen as an obstacle (the need to create a project that would stimulate strong intrinsic motivation because I could not pay anyone to participate) soon showed itself as an asset. In many traditional research studies, there is some inherent acknowledgment that people don't really want to participate in studies, that most people would rather be doing other things with their time. So, in most cases, participation is either made as painless as possible (e.g., a very brief online measure that promises to take "only 10 minutes" or a brief reader poll in a widely circulated magazine) or is induced through some *extrinsic* motivator (e.g., course credit, monetary reimbursement, entry into a raffle to win a big prize). In my opinion, making a measure shorter, and less painful, especially in the case of an anonymous online survey, would seem to produce a lot of "junk" data from people who are not invested in the research. Sweetening the pot with financial inducements may also affect the quality of one's data. In contrast, when people engage in behavior based on the type of *intrinsic* motivation that was a defining feature of the Lifestyle Poll project (that is, an opportunity to do some meaningful self-reflection), they are more likely to invest genuine effort. In this case, because my participants had no extrinsic motivation at all to participate, and the Lifestyle Poll was so long, the significant "response cost" of participation suggests that the data was entered thoughtfully, by respondents who were invested in the project due to intrinsic motivations. The unsolicited feedback shared by participants and the lengthy, thoughtful responses to the open-ended questions that were posted over and above the original set of more than 200 questions confirmed my sense of a high level of intrinsic motivation among the Lifestyle Poll participants.

Eight months into the project, in the summer of 2008, I got an offer I couldn't refuse—an opportunity to move back to my home state of California and accept the very meaningful job I now have at a Veterans Hospital. I put the writing process on hold while learning the ropes of my new position in the VA and sometimes wondered if I would ever get back to writing up the results of the Lifestyle Poll. At times, it felt overwhelming to turn back to this massive data set and begin the process of exploring the truths within it. Ultimately, the biggest force that has compelled me to return to my data and write it up is the investment made by the women who participated in the Lifestyle Poll project. It would not sit well with me to ask this of my respondents and then fail to find a way to make meaning of the stories they shared with me. This book is in large part an analysis of this data, in the context of my evolving understanding of successful marriages.

If you participated in the Lifestyle Poll, I wish to very sincerely express my gratitude. My work on this project has been one of my most rewarding professional experiences to date, and I am hopeful that your insights will greatly benefit others who are striving to fulfill the promise of a marriage of equals.

Demographic Characteristics of the Lifestyle Poll Sample

Ethnicity*
- Caucasian/White — 73.1%
- Asian — 10.5%
- Hispanic/Latina — 5.3%
- Of mixed ethnicity (per self-identification) — 5.1%
- African American/Black — 4.0%
- Indian — 1.7%
- Native American — 0.2%

Self-identified spiritual/religious beliefs
- Agnostic — 28.7%
- Protestant — 24.1%
- Catholic — 21.2%
- Jewish — 11.9%
- Atheist — 10.1%
- Buddhist — 2.1%
- Hindu — 1.3%
- Muslim — 0.7%
- Not reported — 15.0%

Age (years)
- Mean — 31.0 (S.D. = 3.6 yrs)

Annual pre-tax household income
- More than $100,000 — 47.7%
- $76,000 – $100,000 — 12.4%
- $51,000 - $75,000 — 15.1%
- Less than $50,000 — 24.9%

Self-identified level of SES in family of origin
- Wealthy — 3.6%
- Upper middle class — 43.6%
- Middle class — 37.1%
- Working class — 13.3%
- Poverty level — 2.5%

Marital status (percent married) — 48% (n = 607)

Self-identified sexual orientation
- Heterosexual — 93.2%
- Bisexual — 4.4%
- Homosexual — 2.1%
- Asexual — 0.4%

Average length of relationship (for married women) — 7.8 years (S.D. = 3.7 yrs)

Parenthood status (percent with children) — 22.8% (n = 288)
- Average number of children at time of poll — 1.5 (0.7)

*Unless otherwise indicated, the total number of participants = 1260

Further Recommended Reading
(Alphabetized within Subject Categories)

Assertiveness

Cloud, H. and Townsend, J. (1999). *Boundaries in Marriage.* Grand Rapids, MI: Zondervan Publishing House.

Davis, M, Eshelman, E.R., and McKay, M. (1995). *The Stress and Relaxation Handbook.* Oakland, CA: New Harbinger Publications, Inc.

Personality Assessment and Partner Selection

Bernstein, A.J. (2001). *Emotional Vampires: Dealing with People who Drain you Dry.* New York: McGraw-Hill.

Cloud, H. and Townsend, J. (1995). *Safe People: How to Find Relationships that are Good For You and Avoid Those That Aren't.* Grand Rapids, MI: Zondervan Press.

Halpern, H.M. (1982). *How to Break your Addiction to a Person.* New York, NY: McGraw Hill, Inc.

Van Epp, J. (2008). *How to Avoid Falling in Love with a Jerk: The Foolproof Way to Follow your Heart without Losing your Mind.* New York: McGraw-Hill.

General Relationship Topics

Chapman, G. (1992) *The Five Languages of Love: How to Express Heartfelt Commitment to your Mate.* Chicago, IL: Northfield Publishing.

Gottman, J. (1994). *Why Marriages Succeed or Fail...And How You Can Make Yours Last.* New York: Fireside Books.

Eggerichs, E. (2004). *Love and Respect: The Love She Most Desires; The Respect He Desperately Needs.* Nashville, TN: Thomas Nelson, Inc.

Johnson, S.M. (2008). *Hold me Tight: Seven Conversations for a Lifetime of Love.* New York: Little, Brown and Company.

Kramer, P.D. (1997). *Should you Leave?* New York, NY: Penguin Books.

Lerner, H. (1989). *The Dance of Intimacy.* New York: Harper and Row Publishers.

Sexual Intimacy

Glass, S. (2003) <u>Not</u> *"Just Friends": Protect your Relationship from Infidelity and Heal the Trauma of Betrayal.* New York, NY: The Free Press.

Schnarch, D. (2009). *Intimacy and Desire: Awaken the Passion in your Relationship.* New York, NY: Beaufort Books.

Schnarch, D. (2009 reprint). *Passionate Marriage: Keeping Love and Intimacy Alive in Committed Relationships.* New York, NY: W.W. Norton and Company.

Vaughan, P. (2003). *The Monogamy Myth: A Personal Handbook for Recovering from Affairs (3rd edition).* New York, NY: Newmarket Press.

Weiner Davis, M. (2003). *The Sex-Starved Marriage: A Couple's Guide to Boosting their Marriage Libido.* New York, NY: Simon and Schuster.

Parenting Topics

Cowan, C. P. & Cowan, P. A. (1992). *When Partners Become Parents: The Big Life Change for Couples.* New York, NY: Basic Books (a division of Harper Collins Publishers).

Hewlett, S.A. (2002). *Creating a Life: Professional Women and the Quest for Children.* New York: NY: Hyperion Books.

Louv, R. (2008). *The Last Child in the Woods: Saving our Children from Nature-Deficit Disorder.* Chapel Hill, NC: Algonquin Books.

Marano, H.E. (2008). *A Nation of Wimps: The High Cost of Invasive Parenting.* New York, NY: Random House, Inc.

Peskowitz, M. (2005). *The Truth Behind the Mommy Wars: Who Decides what makes a Good Mother?* Emeryville, CA: Seal Press.

Contemporary Concerns

Brook, D. (2007). *The Trap: Selling Out to Stay Afloat in Winner-Take-All America.* New York: NY: Henry Holt and Company.

Draut, T. (2005). *Strapped: Why America's 20- and 30-Somethings Can't Get Ahead.* New York: Anchor Books (A Division of Random House).

Florida, R. (2002). *The Rise of the Creative Class and how it's Transforming Work, Leisure, Community, and Everyday Life.* New York, NY: Basic Books.

Fraser, J.A. (2001). *White Collar Sweatshop: The Deterioration of Work and its Rewards in Corporate America.* New York, NY: W.W. Norton & Company.

Twenge, J. (2007). *Generation Me: Why Today's Young Americans Are More Confident, Assertive, Entitled—and More Miserable Than Ever Before.* New York, NY: Free Press.

Other

Goleman, D. (1995). *Emotional Intelligence: Why it Can Matter more than IQ.* New York, NY: Bantam Books.

Tavris, C. and Aronson, E. (2007). *Mistakes Were Made (but not by me): Why we Justify Foolish Beliefs, Bad Decisions, and Hurtful Acts.* Orlando, FL: Harcourt Books.

Notes

1. Dion, K.K. and Stein, S. (1978). "Physical attractiveness and interpersonal influence." Journal of Experimental Social Psychology, 14, 97-108.

2. Abbott, A.R. and Sebastian, R.J. (1981). "Physical attractiveness and expectations of success." Personality and Social Psychology Bulletin, 7, 481-486.

3. Etcoff, N. (2000). *Survival of the Prettiest: The Science of Beauty*. New York, NY: Anchor Books.

4. Fellowes, J. (2004). *Snobs*. New York, NY: St. Martin's Press, pp. 106-107.

5. Frank A. (1991). *Anne Frank: The Diary of a Young Girl*. Ed. O. Frank and M. Pressler; New York, NY: Alfred A. Knopf. English translation copyright held by Doubleday, a division of Random House Press, p. 137.

6. Ibid, p. 136.

7. Ibid, p. 32.

8. Ibid, pp. 34-35.

9. Ibid, p. 164.

10. Ibid, p. 199.

11 Pennebaker, J.W., Dyer, M.A., Caulkins, S.R., Litowitz, L., Ackreman, P.L., Anderson, D.B., & McGraw, K.M. (1979). "Don't the Girls Get Prettier at Closing Time: A Country and Western Application to Psychology." *Personality and Social Psychology Bulletin,* 5: 122-125, p. 125.

12 Ibid, pp. 122-125.

13 Johnco, C., Wheeler, L., and Taylor, A. (2010). "They do get Prettier at Closing Time: A Repeated Measures Study of the Closing-time Effect and Alcohol. *Social Influence,* 5: 261-271.

14 Seuss, D. (1971). *The Lorax.* New York, NY: Random House, Inc.

15 Meston, C.M. and Frohlich, P.F. (2003). "Love at First Fright: Partner Salience Moderates Roller-Coaster-Induced Excitation Transfer." *Archives of Sexual Behavior, 32*: 537-544.

16 Grayson, B. and Stein, M.I. (1981). "Attracting Assault: Victims' Nonverbal Cues." *Journal of Communication, 31,* 68-75.

17 Dr. Helen Fisher, as quoted during a segment of the Discovery Channel show "The Science of Sex Appeal" (aired in February 2009). Selected clips may be posted at the following web address: <http://dsc.discovery.com/videos/science-of-sex-appeal/>

18 Williams, K., and Brooks, G. (1990). "New Way to Fly." (Performed by Garth Brooks). From the Album *No Fences.* Nashville, TN: Capital Nashville.

19 James, M. (1968). "Hooked on a Feeling." (Originally performed by B. J. Thomas.) From the album *On my Way.* [Recorded by Scepter Records].

20 Fisher, H. (2000). "Lust, Attraction, Attachment: Biology and Evolution of the Three Primary Emotion Systems for Mating, Reproduction, and Parenting." *Journal of Sex Education and Therapy, 25,* 96-104.

[21] "In Search of the Big Bang: What is Crack Cocaine?" Accessed February 10, 2011. <http://www.cocaine.org/>

[22] Bartels, A. & Zeki, S. (2000). "The neural basis of romantic love." *Neuro Report, 11*, 1-6.

Glausiusz, J. "The Chemistry of Obsession: Treating Obsessive-Compulsive Disorder of the Brain." Accessed January 5, 2011. <http://www.ocdhope.com/ocd-chemistry.php>

[23] Murray, S., Holmes, J.G., and Griffin, D. W. (1996). "The Benefits of Positive Illusions: Idealization and the Construction of Satisfaction in Close Relationships." *Journal of Personality and Social Psychology, 1*, 79-98, p.79.

[24] Beach. S.R. and Tesser, A. (1988). "Love in Marriage: A Cognitive Account." In *The Psychology of Love.* ed. R. Sternberg and M. Barnes. New Haven, CT: Yale University Press, pp. 330-355.

[25] Sarton, M. (1975). *Crucial Conversations.* New York: W.W. Norton and Company, p. 112.

[26] Knee, C. R. (1998). "Implicit theories of relationships: Assessment and prediction of romantic relationship initiation, coping, and longevity." *Journal of Personality and Social Psychology, 74*, 360-370.

[27] Ibid, p. 365.

[28] Silverstein, S. (1976). *The Missing Piece.* New York, NY: Harper Collins.

[29] Peele, S. with A. Brodsky. (1975) *Love and Addiction.* New York, NY: Taplinger Publishing Company, p. 70.

[30] Macrae, F. "Your Third Marriage? It May be the Death of You, According to New Research." (posted August 13, 2010). Accessed January 22, 2011. <http://www.dailymail.co.uk/news/article-1302632/Your-marriage-death-according-new-research.html>

31 Alvarez, L., and Jaffe, K. (2004). "Narcissism Guides Mate Selection: Humans Mate Assortatively, as Revealed by Facial Resemblance, Following an Algorithm of 'Self Seeking Like.'" *Evolutionary Psychology, 2*, 177-194.

Bleske-Rechek, A., Remiker, M.W., and Baker, J.P. (2009). "Similar from the Start: Assortment in Young Adult Dating Couples and its link to Relationship Stability Over Time." *Individual Differences Research, 7*, 142-158.

Buss, D.M. (1985). "Human Mate Selection." *American Scientist, 73*, 47-51.

Gonzaga, G.C., Carter, S., and Galen, B.J. (2010). "Assortative Mating, Convergence, and Satisfaction in Married Couples." *Personal Relationships, 17*, 634-644.

Neimeyer, G.J. (1984). "Cognitive Complexity and Marital Satisfaction." *Journal of Social and Clinical Psychology, 2*, 256-263.

Van Straaten, I., Engels, R., Finkenauer, C., and Holland, R.W. (2009). "Meeting your Match: How Attractiveness Similarity Affects Approach Behavior in Mixed-Sex Dyads." *Personality and Social Psychology Bulletin, 35*, 685-697.

32 Fisher, H. (2009). *Why Him? Why Her? How to Find and Keep Lasting Love*. New York, NY: Henry Holt and Company.

The Socionist (blog). "Helen Fisher's Types: Explorer, Builder, Director, Negotiator." (posted April 1, 2009). Accessed February 17, 2011. <http://socionist.blogspot.com/2009/04/helen-fishers-types-explorer-builder.html>

Fisher, H. "The Nature of Love." (posted March 28, 2007). Accessed February 17, 2011. <http://helenfisher.typepad.com/>

33 Fisher, H. "What's your Love Type?" (posted November 12, 2007). Accessed February 17, 2011. <http://articles.cnn.com/2007-11-12/living/o.love.types_1_personality-types-negotiators-traits?_s=PM:LIVING>

34 Fisher, H. as quoted in the Discovery Channel Documentary "The Science of Sex Appeal" (aired in February 2009).

35 De Becker, G. (1997). *The Gift of Fear and Other Survival Signals that Protect us from Violence.* New York, NY: Dell Publishing (a division of Random House, Inc.), p. 65.

36 Author unknown. Accessed March 4, 2011. <http://www.itp.edu/resources/crc/pdf/values.pdf> (available in the public domain).

37 Peele, S. with A. Brodsky. (1975). *Love and Addiction.* New York, NY: Taplinger Publishing Company, p. 70.

38 Fein, E. and Schneider, S. (1995). *The Rules: Time Tested Secrets for Capturing the Heart of Mr. Right.* New York, NY: Warner Books, Inc., p. 24.

39 Ibid, p. 49.

40 Ciotola, K. "Gator Bites Off Arm of Kanapaha Exec." (posted September 24, 2002). Accessed February 22, 2011. <http://www.igorilla. com/gorilla/animal/2002/aligator_kanapaha.html>

41 Cloud, H. and Townsend, J. (1999). *Boundaries in Marriage.* Grand Rapids, MI: Zondervan Publishing House.

42 Davis, M, Eshelman, E.R., and McKay, M. (1995). *The Stress and Relaxation Handbook.* Oakland, CA: New Harbinger Publications, Inc.

43 Ibid, p. 190

44 Neff, L. and Karney, B. (2005). "To Know You is to Love You: The Implications of Global Adoration and Specific Accuracy for Marital Relationships." *Journal of Personality and Social Psychology, 88,* 480-497.

Neff, L. and Karney, B. (2002). "Judgments of a Relationship Partner: Specific Accuracy but Global Enhancement." *Journal of Personality, 70*, 1079-1112.

[45] The term "primitive panic," a state which is set off when the attachment bond is perceived to be insecure, is described in Dr. Sue Johnson's work:

Johnson, S. (2008). *Hold me Tight: Seven Conversations for a Lifetime of Love.* New York, NY: Little, Brown and Company.

[46] Jones, E.E., and Harris, V.A. (1967). "The Attribution of Attitudes." *Journal of Experimental Social Psychology, 3*, 1-24.

[47] Miller, D.T., and Ross, M. (1975). "Self-Serving Biases in the Attribution of Causality: Fact or Fiction?" *Psychological Bulletin, 82*, 213-225.

[48] Neff, L. and Karney, B. (2002). "Judgments of a Relationship Partner: Specific Accuracy but Global Enhancement." *Journal of Personality, 70*, 1079-1112.

[49] Mischel, W., Shoda, Y., and Rodriguez, M. (1989). "Delay of Gratification in Children." *Science, 244*, 933-938.

[50] Lerner, H. (1989). *The Dance of Intimacy.* New York: Harper and Row Publishers, p. 221.

[51] Rubin, R. as cited in Lax, D.A., and Sebenius, J.K. (July/August 2004). "How No-deal Options Can Drive Great Deals: When Actions Away from the Table Eclipse Face-to-Face Negotiation." *Ivey Business Journal.* Published by Ivey Management Services, a division of the Richard Ivey school of Business, posted on the internet: www.ivey businessjournal.com. Accessed February 22, 2011. <http://wwwold.iveybusinessjournal.com/view_article.asp?intArticle_ID=496>

[52] Fein, E. and Schneider, S. (1995). *The Rules: Time tested Secrets for Capturing the Heart of Mr. Right.* New York, NY: Warner Books Inc.

53 Ibid, p. 8.

54 Ibid, p. 66.

55 Walster, E., Walster, G.W., Piliavin, J., and Schmidt, L. (1973). "Playing Hard to Get: Understanding and Elusive Phenomenon." *Journal of Personality and Social Psychology, 26*, 113-121.

56 Some suggest a higher rate of divorce than 50%. For example, Martin and Bumpass estimate that "about 2/3 of all first marriages are likely to disrupt." Also, divorce rates for subsequent marriages are consistently higher than for first marriages. Source: Martin, T.C. and Bumpass, L.L. (1989). "Recent Trends in Marital Disruption," *Demography, 26*, p. 49.

57 Dr. Phil Show, aired on Thursday, March 19, 2008.

58 Bramlett, M.D., and Mosher, W.D. (2001). "First Marriage Dissolution, Divorce, and Remarriage: United States." (Advance data from vital and health statistics, no. 323). Hyattsville, Maryland: National Center for Health Statistics. (Figure 1).

Cherlin, A. (1979). "Work Life and Marital Dissolution." In *Divorce and Separation: Context, Causes, and Consequences.* Eds. G. Levinger and O. Moles. New York, NY: Basic Books, pp. 151-166.

59 Conger, R.D., Rueter, M.A. and Elder, G.H. (1999). "Couple Resilience to Economic Pressure." *Journal of Personality and Social Psychology, 76*, 54-71.

Liker, J.K., and Elder, G.H. (1983). "Economic Hardship and Marital Relations in the 1930s." *American Sociological Review, 48*, 343-359.

60 Karney, B.R., Story, L.B., and Bradbury, T.N. (2005). "Marriages in Context: Interactions Between Chronic and Acute Stress Among Newlyweds." In *Couples Coping with Stress: Emerging Perspectives on Dyadic Coping.* Eds. T. Revenson, K. Kayser, and G. Bodenmann. Washington, DC, US: American Psychological Association, pp. 13-32.

Karney, B. & Springer, S. (2004). "Should Promoting Marriage be the Next Stage of Welfare Reform?" In *Work-Family Challenges for Low-income Parents and Their Children*. Mahwah, NJ: Lawrence Erlbaum Associates.

Story, L.B., and Bradbury, T.N. (2002). "Understanding Marriages in Context" (draft under review posted in the public domain). Accessed February 17, 2011. <http://www.celf.ucla.edu/pdf/celf01-storybradbury.pdf>

61 Author unknown. "Edith Vanderbilt." Accessed February 20, 2011. <http://www.biltmore.com/our_story/stories/esv.asp>

62 Author unknown. "Cornelia's Garden Party." Accessed February 20, 2011. <http://www.biltmore.com/our_story/stories/cornelia_garden.asp>

63 "The Marriage Crunch." Newsweek Magazine article published June 2, 1986.

64 Driscoll, R., Davis, K.E., and Lipetz, M.E. (1972). "Parental Interference and Romantic Love: The Romeo and Juliet Effect." *Journal of Personality and Social Psychology, 24*, 1-10.

65 Van Epp, J. "PICK Program Overview." Accessed March 4, 2011. <http://www.lovethinks.com/PICK/PICK_Overview_>

(Permission to describe and illustrate the RAM model given to this writer directly by Dr. John Van Epp.)

66 Walt Disney version of *The Little Mermaid* (1989). New York, NY: Gallery Books, p. 33.

67 Van Epp, J. (2008). *How to Avoid Falling in Love with a Jerk: The Foolproof Way to Follow your Heart without Losing your Mind.* New York: McGraw-Hill.

68 Cloud, H. and Townsend, J. (1995). *Safe People: How to Find Relationships that are Good For You and Avoid Those That Aren't.* Grand Rapids, MI: Zondervan Press.

69 Ibid, p. 28.

70 Bernstein, A.J. (2001). *Emotional Vampires: Dealing with People who Drain you Dry*. New York: McGraw-Hill.

71 Ibid, pp. 130-131.

72 Twenge, J. (2007). Generation Me: Why Today's Young Americans Are More Confident, Assertive, Entitled—and More Miserable Than Ever Before. New York: Free Press.

73 Halpern, H.M. (1982) How to Break your Addiction to A Person. New York, NY: McGraw Hill, Inc.

74 Ibid., p. 102.

75 Sources: Goleman, D. (1995). Emotional Intelligence: Why it Can Matter more than IQ. New York, NY: Bantam Books.

Additional information accessed March 15, 2011. <http://www.businessballs.com/eq.htm>

76 Whiten, A. (1993). "Evolving a Theory of Mind: The Nature of Non-verbal Mentalism in Other Primates." In Understanding Other Minds: Perspectives From Autism, ed. S. Baron-Cohen, H. Tager-Flusberg, and D.J. Cohen. Oxford, England; Oxford University Press.

77 Williamson, Graham. "Theory of Mind." (posted January 12, 2011). Accessed February 20, 2011. <http://www.speech-therapy-information-and-resources.com/theory-of-mind.html>

78 Fein, E. and Schneider, S. (1995). The Rules: Time Tested Secrets for Capturing the Heart of Mr. Right. New York, NY: Warner Books, Inc., p. 66.

79 Sarton, M. (1975). Crucial Conversations. New York: W.W. Norton and Company, p. 112.

80 Gottman, J. (1994). Why Marriages Succeed or Fail...And How You Can Make Yours Last. New York: Fireside Books.

81 Paul, P. (2002). The Starter Marriage and the Future of Matrimony. New York: Villard Books, p. 100.

82 Koren, P., Carlton, K., and Shaw, D. (1980). "Marital Conflict: Relations Among Behaviors, Outcomes, and Distress. Journal of Consulting and Clinical Psychology, 48, 460-468.

83 Bradbury, T.N, and Fincham, F.D. (1990). "Attributions in Marriage: Review and Critique." *Psychological Bulletin, 107*, 3-33.

84 Eggerichs, E. (2004). Love and Respect: *The Love She Most Desires; The Respect He Desperately Needs*. Nashville, TN: Thomas Nelson, Inc.

85 Eggerichs, E. Accessed March 4, 2011. <www.loveandrespect.com>

86 Eggerichs, E. (2004). Love and Respect: *The Love She Most Desires; The Respect He Desperately Needs*. Nashville, TN: Thomas Nelson, Inc., p. 49.

87 Ibid, p. 37.

88 Ibid, p. 1.

89 Ibid, p. 6.

90 Ibid, p. 11.

91 Ibid, p. 53.

92 Ibid, p. 73.

93 Ibid, p. 182.

94 Ibid, p. 193.

95   Ibid, pp. 208-209.

96   Ibid, p. 207.

97   Ibid, p. 195.

98   Ibid, p. 221.

99   Ibid, p. 16.

100 Ibid, p. 63.

101 Ibid, p. 65.

102 Ibid, p. 68.

103 Ibid, p. 130.

104 U.S. Bureau of the Census. Table MS-2. Estimated Median Age at First Marriage, by Sex: 1890 to Present (Internet release date: September 15, 2004). Accessed March 8, 2011. http://www.census.gov/population/socdemo/hh-fam/tabMS-2.pdf

105 Crittenden, D. (1999). *What Our Mothers Didn't Tell Us: Why Happiness Eludes the Modern Woman*. New York, NY: Touchstone Press (a division of Simon & Schuster), p. 74.

106 Martin, T.C. and Bumpass, L.L. (1989). "Recent Trends in Marital Disruption," *Demography, 26*, 41.

107 Garrison, R.J., Anderson, V.E., and Reed, S.C. (1982). "Assortative Marriage." *Biodemography and Social Biology, 29*, 36-52.

Mascie-Taylor, C.G. and Vandenberg, S.G. (1988). "Assortative Mating for IQ and Personality Due to Propinquity and Personal Preference." *Behavior Genetics, 18*, 339-345.

Watson, D., Klohnen, E.C., Casillas, A., Nus Simms, E., Haig, J., and Berry, D.S. (2004). "Match makers and Deal Breakers: Analyses of

Assortative Mating in Newlywed Couples." *Journal of Personality, 72*, 1029-1068.

108 Neimeyer, G. J. (1984). "Cognitive Complexity and Marital Satisfaction." *Journal of Social and Clinical Psychology, 2*, 256-263.

109 Eggerichs, E. (2004). Love and Respect: *The Love She Most Desires; The Respect He Desperately Needs.* Nashville, TN: Thomas Nelson, Inc., p. 53.

110 Ibid, p. 221.

111 Ibid, p. 217.

112 Lerner, H. (1989). *The Dance of Intimacy.* New York: Harper and Row Publishers, p. 218.

113 Eggerichs, E. (2004). Love and Respect: *The Love She Most Desires; The Respect He Desperately Needs.* Nashville, TN: Thomas Nelson, Inc., p. 37.

114 Mulhern, D. (posted May 1, 2001). "How to be a Real Man." *Newsweek Magazine.* Accessed May 6, 2011. <http://www.thedaily beast. com/newsweek/2011/05/01/how-to-be-a-real-man.html>

115 "By the numbers: the State of Divorce," Time Magazine, Sept. 2000, p. 74.

116 Bradbury, T.N., Campbell, S.M., and Fincham, F.D. (1995). "Longitudinal and Behavioral Analysis of Masculinity and Femininity in Marriage." *Journal of Personality and Social Psychology, 68*, 328-341.

117 Bradbury, T. N., Campbell, S.M., and Fincham, F.D. (1995) "Longitudinal and Behavioral Analysis of Masculinity and Femininity in Marriage." *Journal of Personality and Social Psychology, 68*, pp. 328-342, who cite Antill, J. K. (1983). Sex Role Complementarity Versus Similarity in Married Couples. *Journal of Personality & Social Psychology, 45,* 145-155, p. 150.

[118] Bradbury, T. N., Campbell, S.M., and Fincham, F.D. "Longitudinal and Behavioral analysis of Masculinity and Femininity in Marriage," Journal of Personality and Social Psychology, 68, (1995), pp. 328-342 who cite Benter & Newcomb, 1978; Kurdek, 1991a, Kurdek, 1991b.

[119] Chapman, G. (1992) *The Five Languages of Love: How to Express Heartfelt Commitment to your Mate.* Chicago, IL: Northfield Publishing.

[120] Weiner Davis, M. (2003). *The Sex-Starved Marriage: A Couple's Guide to Boosting their Marriage Libido.* New York, NY: Simon and Schuster.

[121] Ibid, p. 4.

[122] Exercise modified from material gleaned from Chapman, G. (1992). *The Five Languages of Love: How to Express Heartfelt Commitment to your Mate.* Chicago, IL: Northfield Publishing.

[123] Eggerichs, E. (2004). Love and Respect: *The Love She Most Desires; The Respect He Desperately Needs.* Nashville, TN: Thomas Nelson, Inc., p. 193.

[124] Ibid, p. 203.

[125] Thoreau, H. (1854). Quote taken from "Solitude" within the book entitled *Walden, or Life in the Woods* as included in the *Norton Anthology of American Literature* (1994). Fourth Edition, Volume 1; New York: W.W. Norton and Company, p. 1789.

[126] Sarton, M. (1973). *Journal of a Solitude: The Intimate Diary of a Year in the Life of a Creative Woman.* Ontario, Canada: Penguin Books, p. 201.

[127] Ibid, p. 113.

[128] Anderson, J. (1999). *A Year by the Sea.* New York: Doubleday Press, a division of Random House, p. 49.

129 Proverbs 27:17, New International Version.

130 James, M. (1968). "Hooked on a Feeling." (Originally performed by B. J. Thomas.) From the album *On my Way*. [Recorded by Scepter Records].

131 Mumford and Sons (2009). "Sigh no More." From the album *Sigh no More*. [Produced by Markus Dravs, recorded in the UK: Eastcote Studio, released in the United States by the label Island, Glassnote.]

132 Trent, K., and South, S.J. (1989). "Structural Determinants of the Divorce Rate: A Cross-Sectional Analysis." *Journal of Marriage and the Family, 51*, 391-404.

133 Peskowitz, M. (2005). *The Truth Behind the Mommy Wars: Who Decides what makes a Good Mother?* Emeryville, CA: Seal Press, p. 41.

134 Fraser, J.A. (2001). *White Collar Sweatshop: The Deterioration of Work and its Rewards in Corporate America*. New York, NY: W.W. Norton & Company, p. 9.

135 Draut, T. (2005). *Strapped: Why America's 20- and 30-Somethings Can't Get Ahead*. New York: Anchor Books (A Division of Random House), p. 209.

136 Calhoun, J.B. (1962). "Population density and Social Pathology." *Scientific America, 206*: 139–148.

137 Milgram, S. (1974). *Obedience to Authority: An Experimental View*. New York: Harper Collins.

138 Florida, R. (2002). *The Rise of the Creative Class and how it's Transforming Work, Leisure, Community, and Everyday Life*. New York, NY: Basic Books, p. 115.

139 Allianz Life Insurance Company of North America. (2006). "The Allianz Women, Money and Power Study." Accessed February 24, 2011. <https://www.allianzlife.com/womenmoneypower/main3_5.html>

140 Clance, P. and Imes, S.A. (1978). "The Imposter Phenomenon in High Achieving Women: Dynamics and Therapeutic Intervention." *Psychotherapy: Theory, Research, and Practice, 15*, 241-247.

141 Hewlett, S.A. (2002). *Creating a Life: Professional Women and the Quest for Children.* New York: NY: Hyperion Books, p. 34.

142 Peskowitz, M. (2005). *The Truth Behind the Mommy Wars: Who Decides what makes a Good Mother?* Emeryville, CA: Seal Press, p. 16.

143 Brook, D. (2007). *The Trap: Selling Out to Stay Afloat in Winner-Take-All America.* New York: NY: Henry Holt and Company, 41-42.

144 Ibid, pp. 41-42.

145 Schnarch, D. (2009 reprint). *Passionate Marriage: Keeping Love and Intimacy Alive in Committed Relationships.* New York, NY: W.W. Norton and Company.

146 Schnarch, D. (2009). *Intimacy and Desire: Awaken the Passion in your Relationship.* New York, NY: Beaufort Books.

147 Weiner Davis, M. (2003). *The Sex-Starved Marriage: A Couple's Guide to Boosting their Marriage Libido.* New York, NY: Simon and Schuster.

148 Fisher, H. (2000). "Lust, Attraction, Attachment: Biology and Evolution of the Three Primary Emotion Systems for Mating, Reproduction, and Parenting." *Journal of Sex Education and Therapy, 25*, 96-104.

149 Schnarch, D. (2009). *Intimacy and Desire: Awaken the Passion in your Relationship.* New York, NY: Beaufort Books, p. 87.

150 Ibid, p. 47.

151 Glass, S. (2003) *Not Just Friends: Protect your Relationship from Infidelity and Heal the Trauma of Betrayal*. New York, NY: The Free Press, pp. 27-28.

152 Layton-Tholl, D. (1998). "Extramarital Affairs: The Link between Thought Suppression and Level of Arousal. Unpublished doctoral dissertation: Miami Institute of Psychology of the Caribbean Center for Advanced Studies as cited in Glass, S. (2003) *Not Just Friends: Protect your Relationship from Infidelity and Heal the Trauma of Betrayal*. New York, NY: The Free Press, p. 35.

153 Glass, S. (2003) *Not Just Friends: Protect your Relationship from Infidelity and Heal the Trauma of Betrayal*. New York, NY: The Free Press, p. 34.

154 Vaughan, P. (2003). *The Monogamy Myth: A Personal Handbook for Recovering from Affairs*. (3rd edition). New York, NY: Newmarket Press, p. 222-223.

155 Ibid, p. 115.

156 Sarton, M. (1973). *Journal of a Solitude: The Intimate Diary of a Year in the Life of a Creative Woman*. Ontario, Canada: Penguin Books, p. 70.

157 Tavris, C. and Aronson, E. (2007). *Mistakes Were Made (but not by me): Why we Justify Foolish Beliefs, Bad Decisions, and Hurtful Acts*. Orlando, FL: Harcourt Books.

158 Ibid, p. 6.

159 Hewlett, S.A. (2002). *Creating a Life: Professional Women and the Quest for Children*. New York, NY: Talk Miramax Books, p. 88.

160 "For pictures of some sinkholes, check out "Famous Sinkholes Around the World." Accessed May 12, 2011. <http://news.yahoo.com/photos/famous-sinkholes-1311358251-slideshow/#crsl=>

[161] Belsky, J., and Rovine, M. (1990). "Patterns of marital change across the transition to parenthood: Pregnancy to three years postpartum." *Journal of Marriage and the* Family, 52, 5-19.

Lawrence, E., Rothman, A.D., Cobb, R.J., Rothman, M.T., and Bradbury, T.N. (2008). "Marital Satisfaction Across the Transition to Parenthood." *Journal of Family Psychology*, 22, 41-50.

Waldron, H., and Routh, D.K. (1981). "The Effect of the First Child on the Marital Relationship." *Journal of Marriage and the Family*, 43, 785-788.

[162] <http://www.abraham-maslow.com/m_motivation/Hierarchy_of_Needs.asp> (Accessed 11-8-11).

[163] Burgess, E. W., & Wallin, P. (1953). *Engagement and Marriage*. Philadelphia, PA: J. B. Lippencott.

Salmela-Aro, K., Aunola, K., Saisto, T., Halmesmaki, E., and Nurmi, J-E. (2006). "Couples Share Similar Changes in Depressive Symptoms and Marital Satisfaction Anticipating the Birth of a Child." *Journal of Social and Personal Relationships*, 23, 781-803.

Wallace, P.M., and Gotlib, I.H. (1990). "Marital Adjustment During the Transition to Parenthood: Stability and Predictors of Change." *Journal of Marriage and the Family*, 52, 21-29.

[164] Cowan, C. P. & Cowan, P. A. (1992). *When Partners Become Parents: The Big Life Change for Couples*. New York, NY: Basic Books (a division of Harper Collins Publishers), p. x.

[165] Wallace, P.M., and Gotlib, I.H. (1990). "Marital Adjustment During the Transition to Parenthood: Stability and Predictors of Change." *Journal of Marriage and the Family*, 52, 21-29.

Wright, P. J., Henggeler, S. W., and Craig, L. (1986). "Problems in Paradise? A Longitudinal Examination of the Transition to Parenthood." *Journal of Applied Developmental Psychology*, 7, 277-291.

166 Teachman, J.D., Polonko, K.A., and Scanzoni, J. (1987). "Demography of the Family." In *Handbook of Marriage and the Family*. Eds. M.B. Sussman and S.K. Steinmetz. New York, NY: Plenum Press, pp. 3-36.

167 Lawrence, E., Rothman, A.D., Cobb, R.J., and Bradbury, T.N. (2010). "Marital Satisfaction Across the Transition to Parenthood: Three eras of Research." In *Strengthening Couple Relationships for Optimal Child Development: Lessons from Research and Intervention*. Eds. M.S. Schulz, M.K. Pruett, P.K. Kerig, and R.D. Parke. Washington, DC, US: American Psychological Association, pp. 97-114.

168 Belsky, J., Lang, M., and Huston, T.L. (1986). "Sex Typing and Division of Labor as Determinants of Marital Change Across the Transition to Parenthood." *Journal of Personality and Social Psychology, 50*, 517-522.

169 Hock, E., Schirtzinger, M.B., Lutz, W.J., and Widaman, K. (1995). "Maternal Depressive Symptomatology Over the Transition to Parenthood: Assessing the Influence of Marital Satisfaction and Marital Sex Role Traditionalism." *Journal of Family Psychology, 9*, 79-88.

170 Sarton, M. (1973). *Journal of a Solitude: The Intimate Diary of a Year in the Life of a Creative Woman*. Ontario, Canada: Penguin Books, p. 71.

171 Nelson, E.E., and Panksepp, J. (1998). "Brain substrates of Infant-Mother Attachment: Contributions of Opioids, Oxytocin, and Norepinephrine." *Neuroscience and Behavioral Reviews, 22*, 437-452.

172 Ferris, Craig F., Kulkarni, P., Sullivan, J.M., Harder, J.A., Messenger, T.L., and Febo, M. (2005). "Pup Suckling is More Rewarding than Cocaine: Evidence from Functional Magnetic Resonance Imaging and Three-dimensional Computational Analysis." *The Journal of Neuroscience, 25*, 149-156.

173 Marano, H.E. (2008). *A Nation of Wimps: The High Cost of Invasive Parenting*. New York, NY: Random House, Inc., p. 254.

[174] Lawrence, E., Rothman, A.D., Cobb, R.J., Rothman, M.T., and Bradbury, T.N. (2008). "Marital Satisfaction Across the Transition to Parenthood." *Journal of Family Psychology, 22*, 41-50.

[175] Hackel, L.S. and Ruble, D.N. (1992). "Changes in the Marital Relationship After the First Baby is Born: Predicting the Impact of Expectancy Disconfirmation." *Journal of Personality and Social Psychology, 62*, 944-957.

[176] Goldberg, A.E., and Perry-Jenkins, M. (2004). "Division of Labor and Working-Class Women's Well-Being Across the Transition to Parenthood." *Journal of Family Psychology, 18*, 225-236.

[177] Cowan, C. P., & Cowan, P. A. (1992). *When partners become parents.* New York: Basic Books.

[178] Johnson, S.M. (2002). *Emotionally Focused Couple Therapy with Trauma Survivors.* New York, NY: The Guilford Press.

[179] Ibid, p. 184.

[180] Dennis, C., and Ross, L. (2005). "Relationships among Infant Sleep Patterns, Maternal Fatigue, and Development of Depressive Symptomatology." *Birth, 32*, 187-193.

[181] Williamson A.M., and Feyer A.M. (2000). "Moderate Sleep Deprivation Produces Impairments in Cognitive and Motor Performance Equivalent to Legally Prescribed Levels of Alcohol Intoxication." *Occup Environ Med*, 57: 649–55.

[182] American Academy of Sleep Medicine. Internet-based article written on drowsy driving. Accessed March 2, 2011. <http://www.aasmnet.org/Resources/FactSheets/DrowsyDriving.pdf>

[183] Goes F.S., Zandi P.P., Miao K., et al. (2007). "Mood-incongruent Psychotic Features in Bipolar Disorder: Familial Aggregation and Suggestive Linkage to 2p11-q14 and 13q21-33." *American Journal of Psychiatry, 164*, 236–47.

Notes

184 Cowan, C. P. & Cowan, P. A. (1992). *When Partners Become Parents: The Big Life Change for Couples.* New York, NY: Basic Books (a division of Harper Collins Publishers), p. x.

185 Marano, H.E. (2008). *A Nation of Wimps: The High Cost of Invasive Parenting.* Random House, Inc., New York, NY, p. 44.

186 Brook, D. (2007). *The Trap: Selling out to Stay Afloat in Winner-Take-All America.* New York, NY, Henry Holt and Company, LLC., p. 10.

187 Johnson, S.M. (2008). *Hold me Tight: Seven Conversations for a Lifetime of Love.* New York: Little, Brown and Company, p. 21.

188 Brook, D. (2007). *The Trap: Selling out to Stay Afloat in Winner-Take-All America.* New York, NY, Henry Holt and Company, LLC., p. 11.

189 In Rathus, S.A., Nevid, J. S., and Fichner-Rathus, L. (2002). *Human Sexuality in a World of Diversity.* Fifth Edition, Boston, MA; Pearson Education Company, p. 293.

190 Cowan, C. and Cowan, P. (1992). *When Partners Become Parents.* New York: Basic Books, p. 102.

191 Ibid, p. 155.

192 Gilbert. D. (2005). *Stumbling on Happiness.* New York, NY: Vintage Books (a division of Random House, Inc.).

193 Killingsworth, M.A., and Gilbert, D.T. (2010). "A Wandering Mind is an Unhappy Mind." *Science, 330 (6006),* p. 932.

194 Burgess, E.W., and Wallin, P. (1953). *Engagement and Marriage.* Philadelphia, PA; Lippincott Press.

Glenn, N.D. (1998). "The Course of Marital Success and Failure in Five American 10-year Marriage Cohorts." *Journal of Marriage and the Family, 60,* 569-576.

Huston, T.L, McHale, S., and Crouter, A. (1986). "When the Honeymoon's Over: Changes in the Marriage Relationship Over the First Year." In *The Emerging Field of Personal Relationships*, eds. R. Gilmour and S. Duck. Hillsdale, NJ: Erlbaum, pp. 109-132.

[195] Umberson, D., Williams, K., Powers, D.A., Chen, M.D., and Campbell, A.M. (2005). "As Good as it Gets? A Life Course Perspective on Marital Quality." *Social Forces,* 84, 487-505.

[196] Adelmann, P.K., Chadwick, K., and Baerger, D.R. (1996). "Marital Quality of Black and White Adults Over the Life Course." *Journal of Social and Personal Relationships, 13,* 361-384.

Burgess, E. W., & Wallin, P. (1953). *Engagement and Marriage*. Philadelphia, PA: J. B. Lippencott.

Kapinus, C.A., and Johnson, M.P. (2003). "The Utility of the Family Life Cycle as a Theoretical and Empirical Tool: Commitment and Family Life-Cycle Stage." *Journal of Family Issues, 24,* 155-184.

Rollins, B.C., and Feldman, H. (1970). "Marital Satisfaction Over the Family Life Cycle." *Journal of Marriage and the Family, 32,* 20-28.

[197] Wallace, P.M., and Gotlib, I.H. (1990). "Marital Adjustment During the Transition to Parenthood: Stability and Predictors of Change." *Journal of Marriage and the Family, 52,* 21-29.

Wright, P. J., Henggeler, S. W., and Craig, L. (1986). "Problems in Paradise? A Longitudinal Examination of the Transition to Parenthood." *Journal of Applied Developmental Psychology, 7,* 277-291.

[198] Sparks, N. (2004). *The Notebook*. New York, NY: Warner Books, Inc.

[199] Abel, E.L. and Kruger, M.L. (2009). "The Widowhood Effect: A Comparison of Jews and Catholics." *Omega, 59,* 325-337.

Elwert, F., and Christakis, N.A. (2008). "The Effect of Widowhood on Mortality by the Causes of Death of Both Spouses." *American Journal of Public Health, 98,* 2092-2098.

Hart, C.L., Hole, D.J., Lawlor, D.A., Smith, G.D., and Lever, T.F. (2007). "Effect of Conjugal Bereavement on Mortality of the Bereaved Spouse in Participants of the Renfrew/Paisley Study." *Journal of Epidemiology and Community Health, 61*, 455-460.

Helsing, K.J., Comstock, G. W., and Szklo, M. (1982). "Causes of Death in a Widowed Population." *American Journal of Epidemiology, 116*, 524-532.

Parkes, C.M., Benjamin, B., and Fitzgerald, R.G. (1969). "Broken Heart: A Statistical Study of Increased Mortality Among Widowers." *British Journal of Medicine, 1*, 740-743.

Schaefer, C., Quesenberry, C.P, and Wi, S. (1995). "Mortality Following Conjugal Bereavement and the Effects of a Shared Environment." *American Journal of Epidemiology, 141*, 1142-1152.

[200] Kramer, P.D. (1997). *Should you Leave?* New York, NY: Penguin Books, p. 94.

[201] Knox, D.H. (1970). "Conceptions of Love at Three Developmental Levels." *The Family Coordinator, 2,* 151-157.

Munro, B., and Adams, G.R. (1978). "Love American Style: A Test of Role Structure Theory on Changes in Attitudes Toward Love." *Human Relations, 31*, 215-228.

[202] Carstensen, L.L., Gottman, J.M., and Levenson, R.W. (1995). "Emotional Behavior in Long-term Marriage." *Psychology and Aging, 10*, 140-149.

[203] Deutscher, I. (1964). "The Quality of Post Parental Life: Definitions of the Situation." *Journal of Marriage and the Family, 26*, 52-59, p. 55.

[204] Adelmann, P.K., Chadwick, K., and Baerger, D.R. (1996). "Marital Quality of Black and White Adults Over the Life Course." *Journal of Social and Personal Relationships, 13*, 361-384.

Anderson, S.A., Russell, C.S., and Schumm, W.R. (1983). "Perceived Marital Quality and Family Life-Cycle Categories: A Further Analysis." *Journal of Marriage and the Family, 45,* 127-139.

Burr, W.R. (1970). "Satisfaction with Various Aspects of Marriage Over the Life Course: A Random Middle Class Sample." *Journal of Marriage and the Family, 32,* 29-37.

Gorchoff, S.M., John, O.P., and Helson, R. (2008). "Contextualizing Change in Marital Satisfaction During Middle Age." *Psychological Science, 19,* 1194-1200.

Kapinus, C.A., and Johnson, M.P. (2003). "The Utility of the Family Life Cycle as a Theoretical and Empirical Tool: Commitment and Family Life-Cycle Stage." *Journal of Family Issues, 24,* 155-184.

Levenson, R.W., Carstensen, L.L., and Gottman, J.M. (1993). "Long-Term Marriage: Age, Gender, and Satisfaction." *Psychology and Aging, 2,* 301-313.

Orbuch, T.L., House, J.S., Mero, R.P., and Webster, P.S. (1996). "Marital Quality Over the Life Course." *Social Psychology Quarterly, 59,* 162-171.

Rollins, B.C., and Cannon, K.L. (1974). "Marital Satisfaction Over the Family Life Cycle: A Reevaluation." *Journal of Marriage and the Family, 36,* 271-282.

Rollins, B.C., and Feldman, H. (1970). "Marital Satisfaction Over the Family Life Cycle." *Journal of Marriage and the Family, 32,* 20-28.

White, L, and Edwards, J.N. (1990). "Emptying the Nest and Parental Well-Being: An Analysis of National Panel Data." *American Sociological Review, 55,* 235-242.

[205] U.S. National Center for Health Statistics (1978) as cited in Vaillant, C.O., and Vaillant, G.E. (1993). "Is the U-curve of Marital Satisfaction an Illusion? A 40-year study of Marriage." *Journal of Marriage and the Family, 55,* p. 236.

206 Menaghan, E. (1983). "Marital Stress and Family Transitions: A Panel Analysis." *Journal of Marriage and the Family, 45*, 371-386.

207 White, L, and Edwards, J.N. (1990). "Emptying the Nest and Parental Well-Being: An Analysis of National Panel Data." *American Sociological Review, 55*, 235-242, p. 235.

208 Gorchoff, S.M., John, O.P., and Helson, R. (2008). "Contextualizing Change in Marital Satisfaction During Middle Age." *Psychological Science, 19*, 1194-1200.

209 Johnson, D.R., Amoloza, T.O., and Booth, A. (1992). "Stability and Developmental Change in Marital Quality: A Three-Wave Panel Analysis." *Journal of Marriage and the Family, 54*, 582-594.

Vaillant, C.O., and Vaillant, G.E. (1993). "Is the U-curve of Marital Satisfaction an Illusion? A 40-year study of Marriage." *Journal of Marriage and the Family, 55*, p. 238.

210 Glenn, N. (1998). "The Course of Marital Success and Failure in Five American 10-Year Marriage Cohorts." *Journal of Marriage and the Family, 60*, 569-576.

Umberson, D., Williams, K., Powers, D.A., Chen, M.D., and Campbell, A.M. (2005). "As Good as it Gets? A Life Course Perspective on Marital Quality." *Social Forces, 84*, 493-511.

VanLaningham, J., Johnson, D.R., and Amato, P. (2001). "Marital Happiness, Marital Duration, and the U-shaped Curve: Evidence from a Five-Wave Panel Study." *Social Forces, 79*, 1313-1341.

211 Glenn, N. (1990). "Quantitative Research on Marital Quality in the 1980s: A Critical Review." *Journal of Marriage and the Family, 52*, 818-831, p. 823.

212 Glenn, N. (1998). "The Course of Marital Success and Failure in Five American 10-Year Marriage Cohorts." *Journal of Marriage and the Family, 60*, 569-576, p. 575.

[213] Vaillant, C.O., and Vaillant, G.E. (1993). "Is the U-curve of Marital Satisfaction an Illusion? A 40-year study of Marriage." *Journal of Marriage and the Family, 55*, p. 238.

[214] Karney, B.R. and Frye, N.E. (2002). "'But We've Been Getting Better Lately': Comparing Prospective and Retrospective Views of Relationship Development." *Journal of Personality and Social Psychology, 82*, 222-238.

[215] DeMichele, P.E., Gansneder, B., and Solomon, G.B. (1998). "Success and Failure Attributions of Wrestlers: Further Evidence of the Self-serving Bias." *Journal of Sport Behavior, 21*, 242-255.

[216] Yehudah, Y.B. (2002). "Self-serving Attributions in Teachers' Explanations of Students' Performance in a National Oral Essay Competition." *Social Behavior and Personality, 30*, 411-416.

[217] Vaillant, C.O., & Vaillant, G.E. (1993). "Is the U-curve of Marital Satisfaction an Illusion? A 40-year study of Marriage." *Journal of Marriage and the Family, 55*, p. 235.

[218] Ibid, p. 231.

Shauna Howarth Springer, Ph.D., earned her undergraduate degree in English Literature from Harvard University and her doctoral degree in Counseling Psychology from the University of Florida. She is currently a Staff Psychologist in the Veterans Health Care System of Northern California, where she treats a variety of mental health concerns and runs a couples clinic to help Veterans reconnect with their spouses following combat deployments. She has particular expertise in marital counseling, stressor effects on marriage, trauma recovery, and women's issues. She has also worked in a successful private practice, three University counseling centers, and a clinic specialized in the treatment of OCD and other anxiety disorders.

She has co-authored several publications in professional journals and books. Her research has been presented at multiple conferences and she was awarded the McLaughlin Dissertation Research Fellowship for her meta-analysis of stressor effects on marriage in an aggregated sample of over 164,000 married individuals.

While she does not believe in the idea of meeting one's "soul mate," she met her wonderful husband, Utaka Springer, 15 years ago, and has been very happily married for the past 10 years.

CPSIA information can be obtained at www.ICGtesting.com
Printed in the USA
LVOW011026130213
319923LV00009B/37/P